FAST &
FLASHY

BRUT

GLORIA FERRER
BRUT

D1534458

FAST & FLASHY

Hors d'Oeuvres

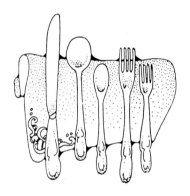

MICHELE BRADEN

ACROPOLIS BOOKS LTD.

WASHINGTON, D.C.

ACROPOLIS BOOKS LTD.
Alphons J. Hackl, Publisher
Colortone Building, 2400 17th St., N.W.
Washington, D.C. 20009

Printed in the United States of America by
COLORTONE PRESS
Creative Graphics, Inc.
Washington, D.C. 20009

Attention: Schools and Corporations
ACROPOLIS books are available at quantity discounts with bulk
purchase for educational, business, or sales promotional use. For
information, please write to: SPECIAL SALES DEPARTMENT,
ACROPOLIS BOOKS LTD., 2400 17th St., N.W.,
Washington, D.C. 20009.

**Are there Acropolis books you want but cannot find in your
local stores?**
You can get any Acropolis book title in print. Simply send title and
retail price. Be sure to add postage and handling: $2.25 for orders
up to $15.00; $3.00 for orders from $15.01 to $30.00; $3.75 for
orders from $30.01 to $100.00; $4.50 for orders over $100.00.
District of Columbia residents add applicable sales tax. Enclose
check or money order only, no cash please, to:

ACROPOLIS BOOKS LTD.
2400 17th St., N.W.
WASHINGTON, D.C. 20009

Library of Congress Cataloging-in-Publication Data

Braden, Michele.
  Fast & flashy hors d'oeuvres.

  Includes index.
  1. Cookery (Appetizers) I. Title. II. Title: Fast
and flashy hors d'oeuvres.
TX740.B645 1988   641.8'12   87-19608
ISBN 0-87491-884-7

Fast & Flashy Hors d'Oeuvres was designed by Pamela Moore, Art
Director and Kathleen K. Cunningham, Graphic Artist/Designer.
Beth Judy, Artist.
Edited by Kathleen Hughes.
Photography by Christopher Saul Photography, San Francisco, CA.
Food Styling by Michele Braden.
Wines provided by Dry Creek Vineyard Wines & Frexinet Sonoma
Caves.
Serving Pieces and Tablecloths provided by Home Express, CA
and Las Vegas.
Flowers provided by Designs by Celeste, O'Malley's Flowers,
Sacramento, CA.

DEDICATION

This book would not have been possible without the love, support, encouragement and vision that my husband, Alan gave me. My parents, daughter and brother instilled me with a special sense of self and strength that was not only invaluable, but also necessary. And finally in memory of my grandmother, Anne Levy.

Thank you!

ACKNOWLEDGMENTS

I sincerely thank and will always be grateful for the talents and efforts of:

Dry Creek Vineyard Wines and David S. Stare (winemaster)
For his wonderful wines.

Gloria Ferrer, Frexinet Sonoma Caves
For their fabulous sparkling wines.

Christopher Saul Photography—San Francisco, CA
It was a joy to work with such an artist!

Home Express—California and Las Vegas
For the use of their beautiful serving pieces and tablecloths.

Thomas Steiner
For his expertise and assistance in writing about wines.

Pamela Schubert
For being a great friend. She came to my rescue during the photography sessions. I was recuperating from back surgery at home, in a hospital bed, and her help was a life saver!

Designs by Celeste, O'Malley's Flowers—Sacramento, CA
For her beautiful floral designs.

Flo Braker, *The Simple Art of Perfect Baking,* William Morrow
For generously allowing me to use her pastry recipe.

Linda Wall
For her conscientious word processing.

TABLE OF CONTENTS

INTRODUCTION

*H*ave you ever found yourself still slaving over the entrée while your spouse passes the onion dip and crackers to your guests in the other room? What you had planned as a festive occasion, where acquaintances become friends, has turned into a strained and tepid affair, underscored by so-called appetizers that scream, "Who cares?"

Set the stage right from the beginning. You wouldn't think of starting off your evening by offering glasses of jug wine, while saving the good stuff for the main course. Make every occasion memorable with *Fast & Flashy Hors d'Oeuvres. FAST & FLASHY* entertainers are not locked away, playing the role of kitchen martyr while their guests enjoy themselves (or nervously nibble on crackers). *FAST & FLASHY* cooks enjoy their guests and their starring role, center stage.

The message of this book is that you *CAN* cook it all—from elegant hors d'oeuvres to fabulous desserts—without quitting your job, taking a second mortgage, or sending your family out for fast food the entire week before. *FAST & FLASHY* is an attitude and a lifestyle. It's fearless and flamboyant; a survival kit for today's busy person who also wants to be an innovative cook and a fabulous entertainer.

Hors d'oeuvres are a versatile food category, representing pure luxury and indulgence as well as the opportunity for a tremendous variety of stimulating tastes. Almost any dish can be made into an hors d'oeuvre simply by miniaturizing it. It is becoming increasingly common to create an entire menu of hors d'oeuvres. On the other hand, you'll find that many of these recipes can be turned into entrées. For example, CAVIAR SAUCE is divine over pasta, COLD MADEIRA BLEU CHEESE SAUCE is fantastic with roast beef, on salads, poached vegetables, or in baked potatoes. Most of the chafing dish items (Chapter 3) can be served over rice or pasta. Imagine pasta with a CRAB AND BRIE FONDUE sauce or ITALIAN VEAL, MOZ-ZARELLA & ANCHOVY BALLS on a bed of rice topped with FAST & FLASHY MARINARA or GARLIC ANCHOVY SAUCE.

Fast & Flashy Hors d'Oeuvres is a compilation of time-saving techniques and creative combinations I've developed over fourteen years as a cooking instructor, spirited epicurean, and radio and television chef. After each recipe you'll find:

Fast hints telling you how far in advance it can be prepared without sacrificing a fresh-made taste,

Flashy hints suggesting delicious accompaniments, and

Fabulous hints offering variations and creative alternatives to further tempt your palate.

These are merely suggested beginnings for you to create your own variations, because one of the secrets of *FAST & FLASHY* cooking is to trust your own taste. Never follow a recipe blindly, as if it were inspired divinely. Think, smell, and taste. Get involved with the recipes and have fun with the entire cooking process. Refuse to be a culinary clone—remember, you are an artist, not a technician.

For years, I have been preaching to my students the importance of smelling and tasting when cooking. Smelling helps determine the freshness and strength of ingredients, as well as how the cooking is progressing. Tasting is the only way to accurately monitor flavors and check the seasonings in a dish. The amount required to taste can be as little as a fraction of a teaspoon, so don't worry about calories or spoiling your appetite.

Don't confuse *FAST & FLASHY* with fast and tacky. There is no need to resort to prepared convenience foods or inferior ingredients in order to save time. By using only the freshest, most fragrant ingredients, you will have tastier results and more aesthetic food that captures the feeling of the season.

The only essential tool for the *FAST & FLASHY* cook is a food processor. This magical machine will save vast amounts of time and eliminate a great deal of mess. I have two and often they are both in use. The majority of the recipes in this book call for a food processor, but traditional tools may be substituted. If you should find an unfamiliar term or technique, please refer to the Helpful Terms section.

For a more thorough exploration of techniques, I recommend *Joy of Cooking* by Irma S. Rombauer and Marian Rombauer Becker, all or any of Julia Childs' books, and *The Art of Food Processor Cooking* by Jane Salzfass Freiman.

Enjoy and explore,
Michele Braden

THE FAST & FLASHY SHELF

*F*AST & FLASHY cooks and fabulous entertainers generally have the following items on hand. Don't panic and purchase everything at once. Collect these items gradually as you need them. As far as the financial investment, a great deal depends on your shopping skills. Do not go to the most chic grocery store. Instead, hunt around discount and import stores and take advantage of sales. The Fast & Flashy Shelf will enable you to create kitchen magic at a moment's notice.

ASSORTED DRIED HERBS AND SPICES:

basil
cardamom
chili powder
cumin (ground)
curry powder
dill weed
fennel seeds
fines herbes
green peppercorns
Hungarian sweet paprika
marjoram

mint leaves
oregano
rosemary
Szechuan peppercorns
tarragon
thyme
white pepper
whole red chiles
whole bay leaves
whole black peppercorns

ASSORTED OILS:

olive oil (extra virgin and
   regular)
sesame oil

peanut oil
grapeseed oil
avocado oil

ASSORTED OLIVES:

Spanish olives
black olives
Greek or Italian olives

ASSORTED NUTS AND SEEDS:

(store in the freezer, to prevent them from turning rancid)

pecans
almonds
sesame seeds
pistachios

pumpkin seeds (hulled)
sunflower seeds (shelled)
walnuts

BEANS:

great northern beans (dried)
garbanzo beans (canned or dried)
black beans (dried)

MARINATED OR PICKLED ITEMS:

capers
marinated artichoke hearts (in jars)

pickled ginger (in jars)
pickled mango (in jars)

RICE:

short grain
long grain
sweet rice

SAUCES:

barbecue sauce, Chinese-style
   (canned or in jar)
plum sauce, Chinese-style
   (canned or in jar)

hoisin sauce (canned or in jar)
Worcestershire sauce
soy sauce

STAPLES:

cornmeal (yellow)
baking soda
baking powder

flour (all purpose)
unflavored gelatin

VINEGARS:

balsamic vinegar
Chinese rice vinegar
cider vinegar
sherry wine vinegar

tarragon vinegar
white wine vinegar
red wine vinegar

WINES FOR COOKING:

dry vermouth
Madeira
Marsala

Merlot
port
sherry

MISCELLANEOUS:

anchovies (tinned or paste)
coarse ground mustard
Dijon-style mustard
fresh garlic
fresh onions
imported Greek pepperoncini

shiitake mushrooms (dried)
sun-dried tomatoes
tomato paste
tomatoes (canned or boxed)
tuna (canned)
whole green chiles (canned)

*Many of these items are explained in the Helpful Terms section, near the end of this volume.

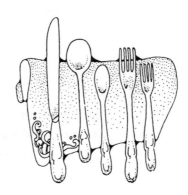

CHAPTER ONE

DUNKS

*L*et's begin with the fastest category of hors d'oeuvres. You'll notice I've avoided the word dip, as it brings to mind ready-made tubs of artificially-flavored gunk. It's unfortunate that the proliferation of quickie-mart versions have tainted the reputation of the entire category, because the real thing is not only delicious, but also extremely versatile and easy to prepare. In this chapter you'll find an international array of recipes suitable for every occasion, from backyard barbecues to champagne suppers. You'll also find that many of these recipes double as salad dressings or entree sauces.

COLD CREAM-STYLE SAUCES AND DUNKS

FAST & FLASHY cold cream-style sauces and dunks are safe, easy territory for even the most timid cook. These simple mixtures are based on mayonnaise or sour cream and seasonings. To reduce your intake of fats, substitute low-fat yogurt for the sour cream and/or mayonnaise. Remember: when serving one of these cold sauces or dunks for a more formal occasion, cold shrimp are elegant, chips are not.

COLD LEMON TARRAGON SAUCE

A delicate dunk to introduce an elegant meal.

(yields about 2 cups)

1 cup mayonnaise, homemade
   or purchased
1 cup sour cream
zest of 2 lemons, finely grated
1 tsp. Dijon-style mustard

¼ tsp. dried tarragon
1 tbsp. shallots, minced
salt, white pepper, and
   lemon juice to taste

Combine the ingredients. Taste and adjust the seasonings.

Fast: Can prepare up to 1 week in advance and refrigerate.
Flashy: With raw or cold blanched vegetables, especially cold, cooked asparagus.
Fabulous: With cooked seafood, poultry, veal, or pork, as an entree sauce.

COLD CAPER SAUCE

(yields about 2¼ cups)

¼ cup capers
2¼ cups olive oil
¼ cup mayonnaise or sour cream
¼ cup white wine vinegar or
   cider vinegar

¼ cup lemon juice
1 tsp. dried dill weed
2-4 cloves of garlic
salt and white pepper to taste

Combine all ingredients in a food processor fitted with the metal blade or a blender. Taste and adjust the seasonings.

Fast: Can prepare up to 1 week in advance and refrigerate.
Flashy: with raw or cold blanched vegetables, seafood, or pumpernickel squares.
Fabulous: As an entree sauce on poached salmon.

DILL CREAM SAUCE

(yields about 2 cups)

Another refreshing prelude to a rich meal.

¼ cup fresh dill weed or
   2 tbsp. dried
1½ tbsp. red wine vinegar
1 large egg yolk
1 hard-boiled egg yolk
1 tsp. sugar

1 tsp. Dijon-style mustard
2 tbsp. sour cream
¼ cup heavy cream, whipped
3 tbsp. oil
salt and white pepper to taste

1. Combine all ingredients, except for the heavy cream in a food processor fitted with the metal blade.
2. Just before serving, fold in the whipped cream.

Fast: Can prepare up to 1 week in advance and refrigerate.
Flashy: With hot or cold pieces of cooked seafood, poultry, or lamb.
Fabulous: On seafood and fish, as an entree sauce, or on baby red potatoes or in baked potatoes.

CURRY SAUCE

(yields about 2¼ cups)

A bit of Indian mystique.

½ cup mayonnaise
½ cup sour cream
1 ½ tsp. curry powder, or to taste

¼ tsp. ginger, ground, or to taste
4 tbsp. cilantro, minced, or to taste
lemon juice to taste

Combine all ingredients. Taste and adjust the seasonings.

Fast: Can prepare up to 1 week in advance and refrigerate.
Flashy: Dunk PITA CHIPS, raw cauliflower, or seafood.
Fabulous: As an entree sauce, with lamb or on a seafood salad.

DIJON SAUCE

(yields about 1 cup)

So simple, but so good!

1 cup mayonnaise
1 tbsp. Dijon-style mustard, or more to taste

Combine all ingredients. Taste and adjust the seasonings.

Fast: Can prepare up to 1 week in advance and refrigerate.
Flashy: With cooked sausages, chicken, or any vegetable.
Fabulous: Replace mustard with soy sauce to create a soy dunk. Add minced green onions or minced parsley to either sauce.

PICKLED MANGO SAUCE

(yields about 1½ cups)

This will work your entire palate—sweet, tart, salty, spicy—and delicious.

1 cup yogurt or sour cream
¼-½ cup pickled mango (depending on how zesty you want it)

1. Combine all ingredients in a food processor fitted with the metal blade or in a blender.
2. Taste and add more pickled mango if bland. If it is too zesty, add more yogurt or sour cream.

Fast: Can prepare up to 1 week in advance and refrigerate.
Flashy: With raw or blanched vegetables, BARBECUED PORK AND RED CABBAGE POTSTICKERS, CURRIED CARROT POTSTICKERS or CHINESE SKEWERED BITES.
Fabulous: To dress a spinach, pasta, rice, or potato salad.

CHINESE PAPAYA SAUCE

(yields about 2 cups)

A tropical flavor that's right at home during summer, and a welcome visitor during gloomy winter months.

½ cup papaya, minced
1 cup soy sauce
¼ cup rice vinegar
2 tbsp. sesame oil

1 tsp. garlic, minced
1 tbsp. ginger root, minced
2-4 green onions, minced

Combine all ingredients. Taste and adjust the seasonings.

Fast: Can prepare up to 1 week in advance and refrigerate.
Flashy: With SCALLOP AND SHRIMP BALLS, SESAME FRIED MUSH-ROOMS, DOUBLE FRIED CHICKEN WINGS, CHINESE CABBAGE SUI MAI WITH PORK AND SHRIMP.
Fabulous: Tossed into pasta or spinach salad, or to season cooked vegetables.

PLUM MAYONNAISE

Simple, with a hint of the Orient.

(yields about 1 cup)

1 cup mayonnaise, homemade or purchased
2 tbsp. plum sauce, or to taste

Combine and enjoy!

Fast: Can prepare up to 1 week in advance and refrigerate.
Flashy: With cooked or raw vegetables, fried wonton wrappers, cold sea-food, barbecued pork or chicken.
Fabulous: Create an Oriental delight by combining this sauce with tuna, minced green onion, and cilantro. Toss into a rice or pasta salad.

COLD MADEIRA BLEU CHEESE SAUCE

Wicked on chicken wings.

(yields about 2½ cups)

4 oz. bleu cheese, or more to taste
¼ cup Madeira
1 cup mayonnaise, homemade or
 purchased
1 cup sour cream
2 cloves garlic

2 shallots
zest of 2 lemons, finely grated
salt and white pepper to taste
dash of cayenne pepper and
 Worcestershire sauce

1. Combine all ingredients, except for the lemon zest, in a food processor fitted with the metal blade.
2. Add the zest and process briefly, taking care not to destroy the texture. Taste and adjust the seasonings.

Fast: Can prepare up to 3 days in advance and refrigerate.
Flashy: With vegetables, cooked beef, seafood, or chicken wings.
Fabulous: Fill hollowed-out baby red potatoes, cherry tomatoes, or mushroom caps. Use as an entree sauce with grilled steaks or roasted beef. Serve with Dry Creek Vineyard Chardonnay.

REMOULADE SAUCE

(yields about 1½ cups)

1 cup mayonnaise, homemade
 or purchased
1 tbsp. Dijon-style mustard,
 or to taste
1 tsp. lemon juice
1 clove garlic, peeled
1 tbsp. capers

2 tbsp. parsley, minced, or
 more to taste
1 hard-boiled egg (optional)
1 tsp. dried dill weed, or to taste
1 tbsp. green onions, minced
white pepper and cayenne
 to taste

Combine all ingredients in a food processor fitted with the metal blade or in a blender. Taste and adjust the seasonings.

Fast: Can prepare up to 4 days in advance and refrigerate.
Flashy: With hot or cold sautéed scallops, shrimp, bite-size pieces of chicken or crab legs.
Fabulous: As a dunk for lightly cooked green beans, asparagus, or broccoli. With a can of tuna, salmon, or clams mixed in.

COLD CUCUMBER SAUCE

(yields about 3 cups)

A refreshing choice during a heat wave.

1 cucumber, peeled, seeded, and minced	2 tbsp. fresh dill weed or ½ tsp. dried
½ pt. sour cream or yogurt	2 tbsp. sesame seeds, toasted
1 tbsp. capers	salt, white pepper, and
¼-½ cup green onions, minced	lemon juice to taste

1. Combine all ingredients in a food processor fitted with the metal blade. Taste and adjust the seasonings.
2. Chill for at least 30 minutes before serving.

Fast: Can prepare up to 3 days in advance and refrigerate.
Flashy: With PITA CHIPS, BAGEL CHIPS, or pumpernickel squares.
Fabulous: As an entree sauce for seafood or to dress a potato salad.

ZUCCHINI SAUCE

(yields about 4 cups)

Terrific solution for that age-old problem of zucchini glut!

2 cups zucchini, minced
 and blanched
8 oz. cream cheese
¼ cup Parmesan cheese,
 grated
¼ cup green onion, minced

1 tsp. garlic, minced
1 cup fresh basil leaves
¼ cup parsley, minced
¼ cup blanched almonds,
 chopped
salt and white pepper to taste

Combine all ingredients in a food processor fitted with the metal blade.
Taste and adjust the seasonings.

Fast: Can prepare up to 3 days in advance and refrigerate.
Flashy: With thinly sliced baguettes, crackers, or vegetables.
Fabulous: As an entree sauce on sautéed chicken breasts or fish.

COLD ITALIAN SPINACH SAUCE

Tremendously versatile; a lifesaver for last-minute guests.

(yields about 2½ cups)

10 oz. spinach (frozen),
 thawed and well drained
½ cup sour cream or
 mayonnaise
1 cup yogurt
¼ cup sesame seeds, toasted

¼ cup Parmesan cheese, grated
1 tsp. garlic, minced
½ tsp. dried dill weed, optional
salt, white pepper and lemon
 juice and freshly grated
 nutmeg to taste

1. Combine all ingredients in a food processor fitted with the metal blade.
Taste and adjust the seasonings.
2. Chill for at least 30 minutes before serving.

Fast: Can prepare up to 2 days in advance and refrigerate.
Flashy: With vegetables, BAGEL CHIPS, or PITA CHIPS.
Fabulous: To dress a pasta or rice salad, or to stuff baked potatoes.

COLD PAPAYA CREAM SAUCE

A great choice for summer entertaining.

(yields about 3 cups)

2 cups papaya, peeled, seeded,
   and minced
1 cup sour cream
1 tbsp. lime juice
¼ tsp. salt

1 tsp. sugar
1 tbsp. Dijon-style mustard,
   or more to taste
2 cloves garlic, puréed,
   or more to taste
White pepper to taste

Combine all ingredients. Taste and adjust the seasonings.

Fast: Can prepare up to 2 days in advance and refrigerate.
Flashy: Dunk barbecued or broiled pieces of pork, seafood, or lamb.
Fabulous: As a sandwich spread on pita, pumpernickel, or sourdough
bread.

COLD BACON & TOMATO SAUCE

Here's one for all you BLT fans!

(yields about 3 cups)

10 slices bacon, cooked until crisp
3 tomatoes, peeled and seeded
1 cup mayonnaise, homemade or
  purchased

1 tbsp. Dijon-style mustard
¼ cup green onions, minced
¼ cup parsley, minced
dash of hot pepper sauce

1. Drain the bacon and cool to room temperature.
2. Combine ingredients in a food processor fitted with the metal blade, taking care to preserve the texture. Taste and adjust the seasonings.

Fast: Can prepare up to 2 days in advance and refrigerate.
Flashy: With chips, crackers, or melbas.
Fabulous: Add chopped avocado or stuff in baked potatoes.

CAVIAR SAUCE

Divine decadence in minutes.

(yields about 1½ cups)

3 oz. caviar
1 cup sour cream
2 to 3 hard-boiled eggs, chopped

zest of 1 lemon, finely grated
2-4 green onions, minced
lemon juice to taste

Combine all ingredients. Taste and adjust the seasonings.

Fast: Can prepare up to 3 days in advance and refrigerate.
Flashy: With cold boiled baby new potatoes, pumpernickel squares, or BAGEL CHIPS.
Fabulous: To dress a pasta salad, or to toss into hot pasta and serve as an appetizer course.

HORSERADISH SAUCE

(yields about 1¼ cups)

1 cup sour cream	salt, white pepper, and
3 tbsp. prepared horseradish, or more to taste	lemon juice to taste

Combine all ingredients. Taste and adjust the seasonings.

Fast: Can prepare up to 5 days in advance and refrigerate.
Flashy: With meatballs, shrimp, fried or boiled potatoes.
Fabulous: As an accompaniment to roast beef, ham, or turkey entrees.

COLD SEAFOOD SAUCE

Light and elegant.

(yields about 3 cups)

8 oz. seafood, cooked (crabmeat, shrimp or lobster)	1 tsp. Dijon-style mustard, or to taste
8 oz. cream cheese	¼ cup each parsley and
½ cup sour cream	green onion, minced
¼ cup mayonnaise	salt, white pepper, and
½ tsp. dried dill weed	lemon juice to taste

Combine all ingredients. Taste and adjust the seasonings.

Fast: Can prepare up to 2 days in advance and refrigerate.
Flashy: With breads, crackers, celery, endive or romaine leaves, or peapods.
Fabulous: With any seafood or fish, ranging from tuna to lobster, or as a dressing for cold pasta or rice salad. Fill crepes, omelets, or pita bread, or top English muffins.

COLD SMOKED SALMON SAUCE

The Rolls-Royce of dunks.

(yields about 3 cups)

8 oz. smoked salmon
8 oz. cream cheese
½ cup sour cream
¼ cup mayonnaise
½ tsp. dried dill weed

¼ cup each parsley and
   green onion, minced
salt, white pepper, and
   lemon juice to taste

Combine the ingredients. Taste and adjust the seasonings.

Fast: Can prepare for up to 2 days in advance and refrigerate.
Flashy: With BAGEL CHIPS, pumpernickel squares, or thinly sliced cucumber.
Fabulous: As a dressing for pasta or rice salads. As a filling for crepes or omelets.

TAPENADE SAUCE

Italian tuna-olive sauce.

(yields about 3 cups)

7½ oz. tuna
20 black olives, pitted
2-4 tbsp. green onions, minced
1 6-ounce jar marinated
   artichoke hearts, drained
   and minced
1 tsp. green peppercorns*

1 cup olive oil
3 tbsp. capers
3 cloves garlic
6 tbsp. lime juice, or to taste
½ tsp. freshly ground black
   pepper
2-3 tbsp. brandy
½ cup parsley, chopped

1. Combine everything, except the olive oil and artichoke hearts, in a food processor fitted with the metal blade.

2. While the machine is running, slowly add the oil and process until sauce reaches the consistency of mayonnaise.

3. Mix in the artichoke hearts, taking care to preserve the texture. Taste and adjust the seasonings.

Fast: Can prepare up to 3 days in advance and refrigerate.
Flashy: With raw or cold blanched vegetables, melbas, BAGEL CHIPS, GARLIC CROUTON ROUNDS, or PITA CHIPS.
Fabulous: With shrimp, crab, or cooked fish instead of tuna.

___

*See Helpful Terms for information about green peppercorns

WALNUT PESTO SAUCE

A real Italian treat for summer, full of gusto!

(yields about 5 cups)

1 8-ounce can pitted black olives, drained	1 cup sour cream
1 cup walnuts, toasted	2 cloves garlic, or more to taste
2 cups fresh basil leaves, packed	½ cup parsley
½-1 cup olive oil	½ cup Parmesan cheese, grated
	salt and white pepper to taste

Combine all ingredients in a food processor fitted with the metal blade. Process until the desired texture is reached. Taste and adjust the seasonings.

Fast: Can prepare up to 4 days in advance and refrigerate, or freeze for up to 3 months.
Flashy: Dunk melbas, PITA CHIPS, GARLIC CROUTON ROUNDS or BAGEL CHIPS.
Fabulous: With fish, seafood, or poultry. For a basic pesto, simply eliminate the olives and sour cream. Add it to mayonnaise to create a pesto mayonnaise sauce and serve with artichokes.

ITALIAN-STYLE TARTAR SAUCE

(yields about 1½ cups)

3 hard-boiled egg yolks, mashed
1 cup mayonnaise, homemade
   or purchased
1 tsp. Dijon-style mustard
1 tsp. capers

2 tbsp. parsley, minced
1 tsp. pickled onion, minced
2 tbsp. pitted black olives,
   minced, or to taste
salt and white pepper to taste

Combine all ingredients. Taste and adjust the seasonings.

Fast: Can prepare up to 3 days in advance and refrigerate.
Flashy: Dip seafood, bite-size cooked pieces of poultry, fried calamari, cooked or raw vegetables, or GARLIC CROUTON ROUNDS.

VINAIGRETTES

I'm always amazed when I see people buying bottled salad dressings. Not only is it easy to prepare your own, the homemade version is fresh and fragrant. Why not spend your money instead on high-quality oils, vinegars, herbs, and mustards? Vinaigrettes can be used for everything from salad dressings, to marinades, to sauces.

TARRAGON CAPER VINAIGRETTE

(yields about 2¼ cups)

½ cup tarragon vinegar
¼ cup capers
1¼ cups grape seed oil,
   or your favorite oil

¼ cup lemon juice
salt, white pepper, and fresh
   or dried tarragon to taste

1. Combine all ingredients in a food processor fitted with the metal blade or in a blender. Taste and adjust the seasonings.
2. Store in the refrigerator in a tightly covered jar. Stir or shake before using.

Fast: Can prepare up to 2 weeks in advance and refrigerate.
Flashy: Dunk raw vegetables or cooked seafood.
Fabulous: Use to marinate mushrooms, bite-size pieces of chicken, or pork for kebabs to barbecue or broil.

BALSAMIC VINAIGRETTE

(yields about 1½ cups)

⅓ cup balsamic vinegar
2 tbsp. cider vinegar
1 cup olive oil
1-2 cloves garlic

1 tsp. Dijon-style mustard
1 tsp. salt
white pepper to taste

Combine all ingredients in a food processor with the metal blade or in a blender. Taste and adjust the seasonings.

Fast: Can prepare up to 3 weeks in advance and refrigerate.
Fabulous: To season JULIENNED CARROTS WITH WALNUTS.

CAESAR SAUCE

If anchovies worry you, relax—they act as subtle seasoning, not a pronounced flavor.

(yields about 1¾ cups)

1 cup olive oil
1 egg
1 tsp. Dijon-style mustard,
    or more to taste
1 tsp. garlic, minced, or
    more to taste

4-8 anchovy filets
1 tsp. Worcestershire sauce
½ cup Parmesan cheese, grated
lemon or lime juice to taste
salt and freshly ground,
    coarse black pepper to taste

Combine all ingredients in a food processor fitted with the metal blade or in a blender. Taste and adjust the seasonings.

Fast: Can prepare up to 2 days in advance and refrigerate.
Flashy: Dunk romaine, endive, or artichoke leaves, asparagus, broccoli, cauliflower, melba toast, or French bread.
Fabulous: Served with Gloria Ferrer Brut Sparkling Wine.

MEXICAN-STYLE SAUCES AND DUNKS

Fabulous flavors and safe territory for those in need of strengthening their culinary confidence. These sauces and dunks make great summertime choices as they require little if any cooking and have a relaxed, casual feel to them.

PUMPKIN SEED CHILE SAUCE

(yields about 2½ cups)

1 cup raw, hulled pumpkin
  or squash seeds
2-6 whole green chiles,
  seeded and deveined (canned)
2 tbsp. cilantro, minced
4 tbsp. green onion, minced

2 tomatoes, skinned and chopped
2 cups sour cream or more,
  depending on consistency
  desired
1 clove garlic, minced
salt, white pepper, and cumin to
  taste

1. Toast the seeds in a heavy frying pan until lightly browned. Cool.
2. Combine all ingredients in a food processor fitted with the metal blade. Process briefly, taking care to preserve the texture. Taste and adjust the seasonings.

Fast: Can prepare up to 3 days in advance and refrigerate.
Flashy: With tortilla chips.
Fabulous: Substitute almonds, walnuts, or sunflower seeds for pumpkin seeds. Use as a sauce for poultry or pork.

UNCOOKED SALSA

Great low-calorie choice.

(yields about 2 cups)

3 ripe tomatoes, cut up
½ cup onions, finely chopped
½ cup cilantro, chopped
2 whole green chiles, seeded
   and deveined (canned)

2 tbsp. olive oil
1-2 cloves garlic, minced
salt, white pepper, lemon
   juice, and sugar to taste

Combine all ingredients in a food processor fitted with the metal blade or in a blender. Taste and adjust the seasonings.

Fast: Can prepare up to 2 weeks in advance and refrigerate, or freeze for up to 1 year.
Flashy: With GREEN CHILE WON TON CUPS or tortilla chips, pork, poultry, seafood, or fish.
Fabulous: To season sauces, dressings, dunks, and marinades.

MEXICAN TOMATO SAUCE

An intriguing sauce with a mild, yet complex flavor.

(yields about 3 cups)

1 cup tomatoes, peeled
   and chopped
½ cup onions, chopped
2 cloves garlic, minced
1 can chicken broth,
   homemade or canned
1 tbsp. vinegar

4 tbsp. cilantro, minced
1 tbsp. olive oil
2 tbsp. tomato paste
1 tsp. sugar
½ tsp. salt
1 tbsp. flour
1-2 tbsp. water

1. Dissolve flour in water.
2. Sauté the onions and garlic in oil until tender.

3. Add the remaining ingredients, except for the flour and water. Simmer until the tomatoes disintegrate.
4. Purée in a blender or a food processor fitted with the metal blade.
5. Return the sauce to burner and bring to a boil. Stir in the flour and cook, stirring, until thickened.

Fast: Can prepare up to 1 week in advance and refrigerate, or freeze for up to 6 months.
Flashy: Dunk tortilla chips, ALBONDIGAS, cooked pieces of seafood, pork, or poultry.
Fabulous: Over pasta, rice, or chicken dishes.

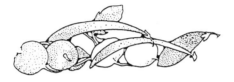

YUCATAN SAUCE

(yields about 2½ cups)

1 tomato, skinned and chopped	¼-1 Bermuda onion, minced
2 bell peppers, preferably red	6-8 green onions, minced
½ bunch cilantro, chopped	1 tbsp. vinegar
1 cup tomato juice	6 oz. beer

1. Place all the ingredients in a food processor fitted with the metal blade or in a blender and process.
2. Combine in a saucepan and warm gently; do not boil. Taste and adjust seasonings.

Fast: Can prepare up to 1 week in advance and refrigerate, or freeze for up to 6 months.
Flashy: Dunk tortilla chips, ALBONDIGAS, cooked pieces of seafood, pork, or poultry.
Fabulous: On pasta, rice, or chicken dishes.

GUACAMOLE

This summer favorite is cholesterol-free.

(yields about 1½ cups)

2 large avocados
several whole green chiles,
   seeded and deveined (canned)
1 clove garlic, or more to taste

2 tbsp. cilantro, minced
1 tbsp. cumin
salt, pepper, and lemon
   juice to taste

Combine all ingredients in a food processor fitted with the metal blade or in a blender. Taste and adjust the seasonings.

Fast: Can prepare up to 3 days in advance and refrigerate, or freeze for up to 6 months.
Flashy: With seafood or pork.
Fabulous: To dress rice or black bean salads or use as a sauce for poultry, pork, seafood, or fish.

AVOCADO DIPPING SAUCE

A creamy variation of guacamole.

(yields about 2½ cups)

2 ripe avocados
2-6 green onions, minced
1 tbsp. cumin
½-1 cup salsa, homemade
   or purchased

1 bunch cilantro, chopped
½ cup sour cream
2 cloves garlic
salt, white pepper, and
   lime juice to taste

Combine all ingredients in a food processor fitted with the metal blade or in a blender. Taste and adjust the seasonings.

Fast: Can prepare up to 3 days in advance and refrigerate.
Flashy: With GREEN CHILE WON TON CUPS or tortilla chips.
Fabulous: To dress pasta, rice, or black bean salads or use as sauce for poultry, pork, seafood, or fish.

MEXICAN CREAM SAUCE

If this is your first encounter with tomatillos, you'll be delighted with their tangy lemon-like flavor.

(yields about 2¼ cups)

6 tomatillos, husked and
    quartered
5 whole green chiles, seeded
    and deveined (canned)
½ avocado, peeled
¾ cup sour cream

¼ cup heavy cream
2 cloves garlic
¼ cup cilantro, or
    more to taste
salt, white pepper, cumin,
    and lemon juice to taste

Combine all the ingredients and purée in a food processor fitted with the metal blade or in a blender. Taste and adjust the seasonings.

Fast: Can prepare up to 2 days in advance and refrigerate.
Flashy: With tortilla chips, cold pork, seafood, fish, or chicken.
Fabulous: To dress a rice salad.

ITALIAN-STYLE SAUCES AND DUNKS

It's hard to believe that something so good and versatile could be so easy to prepare. These sauces become even more valuable when you realize that they can be turned into soups, by simply adding some broth.

FAST & FLASHY MARINARA

(yields about 2 cups)

Here's my version of a sauce I discovered at Modesto Lanzone's in San Francisco. The waiter served it to someone nearby and the aroma compelled me to order it.

1 lb. tomatoes, peeled, seeded, and puréed
1 bunch parsley, minced
1 onion, minced
2-6 tsp. garlic, puréed

2 tbsp. olive oil
¼ cup Madeira
salt, white pepper, and freshly grated nutmeg to taste

1. Sauté the garlic and onion in olive oil until tender.
2. Add the tomatoes and wine and bring to a simmer. Reduce the heat, and add the seasonings and parsley.
3. Simmer for 30 minutes or until the flavors develop to your taste.

Fast: Can prepare up to 4 days in advance and refrigerate.
Flashy: With FRIED CAMEMBERT, sliced Italian sausages, chicken wings, or GARLIC CROUTON ROUNDS.
Fabulous: Sauce everything from pasta to veal. Vary with touches of rosemary, basil, oregano, fennel, or marjoram.

CREAMED TOMATO SAUCE

An alternative with a French flair.

(yields about 2 cups)

1 2 lb., 3 oz. can Italian peeled tomatoes, drained and puréed	2-5 sprigs parsley, whole or minced
¼ cup sherry or Madeira	¼-½ tsp. dried thyme
½ cup heavy cream	1 bay leaf
1 tbsp. shallots, minced	salt and white pepper to taste

1. Combine all ingredients, except the cream, in a saucepan and bring to a boil.
2. Cook until the mixture thickens. Stir in the heavy cream and continue cooking until the sauce coats the back of a spoon. Taste and adjust the seasonings.
3. Strain to remove the bay leaf, parsley, and tomato seeds.

Fast: Can prepare up to 4 days in advance and refrigerate, or freeze for up to 6 months.
Flashy: With ITALIAN SAUSAGE AND MUSHROOM CALZETTE, ARTICHOKE HEART AND GOAT CHEESE CALZETTE, or LEEK AND GOAT CHEESE CALZETTE.
Fabulous: With touches of rosemary, basil, oregano, fennel, or marjoram.

TOMATO SAUSAGE SAUCE

An intensely aromatic, robust sauce.

(yields about 2½ cups)

1 lb. tomatoes, puréed
2 Italian sweet sausages,
  casings removed
2 onions, minced
6 cloves garlic, minced

¼ cup dry white or red wine
1 bunch parsley, minced
1 bay leaf
salt and white pepper to taste

1. Put the sausage, garlic and onions in a skillet. Break the sausage up and brown the mixture over low heat. Pour out excess fat.
2. Add the remaining ingredients and bring to a boil. Reduce heat and simmer for 15-30 minutes. Taste and adjust the seasonings.

Fast: Can prepare up to 4 days in advance and refrigerate, or freeze for up to 6 months.
Flashy: In a chafing dish or fondue pot with meatballs. Dunk fried zucchini, eggplant, or GARLIC CROUTON ROUNDS.
Fabulous: On pasta or scallopini of chicken, turkey, or veal.

CHINESE-STYLE DIPPING SAUCES

The mysterious East offers non-cooks yet another opportunity to build their culinary confidence in a playful way, while providing an unlimited repertoire of intriguing sauces.

Fast: Can prepare up to 3 months in advance, store in jars, and refrigerate.
Flashy: Mix and match with any Fast & Flashy Oriental-style hors d'oeuvre.
Fabulous: Use to season sauces, vegetables, soups, marinades, and stir-fry dishes.
Follow these Fast & Flashy hints for all of the following sauces.

SESAME-FLAVORED SAUCE

1 tbsp. sesame oil
¼ cup soy sauce

Combine all ingredients in a small bowl. Taste and adjust the seasonings.

SOY-MUSTARD DUNK

4 parts soy sauce
2 parts Dijon-style or hot mustard

Combine all ingredients in a food processor fitted with the metal blade or in a blender. Taste and adjust the seasonings.

CHILI-VINEGAR SAUCE

4 parts wine vinegar
1 part chili oil
4 parts oil (avocado, or peanut)

Combine all ingredients in a food processor fitted with the metal blade or in a blender. Taste and adjust the seasonings.

SOY-SHERRY DUNK

1 part sherry
1 part soy sauce

Mix ingredients together. Taste and adjust the seasonings.

COLD HOISIN WINE SAUCE

¾ cup hoisin sauce
⅓ cup Madeira or sherry
1 tbsp. sesame oil

2 tbsp. green onions, minced
1 tbsp. sesame seeds

Mix ingredients together. Taste and adjust the seasonings.

COLD SZECHUAN SAUCE

(yields about 2¾ cups)

1 cup rice vinegar
1 cup soy sauce
¼ cup sesame oil
4 tbsp. hoisin sauce
2 tbsp. plum sauce

¼ cup lime juice, or to taste
1 to 1½ tsp. Szechuan
    peppercorns
2 cloves garlic
white pepper to taste

Combine all ingredients in a food processor fitted with the metal blade or in a blender. Taste and adjust the seasonings.

CHINESE VINEGAR SAUCE

1 cup rice vinegar
4 tbsp. plum sauce
1 tbsp. sesame oil

4 tbsp. cilantro, minced
1 clove garlic
1-2 green onions, minced, optional

Combine all ingredients in a food processor fitted with the metal blade or in a blender. Taste and adjust the seasonings.

CHINESE CHUTNEY DIPPING SAUCE

(yields about 1½ cups)

4 tbsp. peach, plum, or
   mango chutney
1 cup rice vinegar
2 tbsp. soy sauce
1 tbsp. sesame oil

1-2 green onions, minced
1 clove garlic
4 tbsp. cilantro, minced,
   optional

Combine all ingredients in a food processor fitted with the metal blade or in a blender. Taste and adjust the seasonings.

HOT PEPPER OIL

For all you hot and spicy fanatics!

(yields about ¼ cup)

¼ cup dried red hot peppers
¼ cup peanut oil

1. Grind the peppers in a food processor fitted with the metal blade.
2. Heat the oil in a skillet or wok until it begins to smoke. Add peppers. Remove it from the heat and let stand for 30 minutes.
3. Strain the oil into a jar and store covered.

Fabulous: For an aromatic variation, add dried tangerine peel.

SWEET & SOUR-STYLE SAUCES

Too often this type of sauce gets translated into a sweet, overly thickened red glop. A good sweet and sour sauce should not be too sweet nor too sour, but an intriguing blend that involves your entire palate. Quick and easy to prepare, these sauces are welcomed at casual as well as elegant occasions.

Follow these *Fast, Flashy, & Fabulous* hints for all of the following sauces.

Fast: Can prepare up to 1 week in advance and refrigerate, or freeze forever, or up to 1 year, whichever comes first.
Flashy: With any fried Oriental hors d'oeuvre; barbecued pork, chicken, or lamb; or use as a marinade.
Fabulous: To season stir-fry dishes, or Chinese noodles.

FAST & FLASHY SWEET & SOUR SAUCE

(yields about 1 cup)

¼ cup catsup
¼ cup soy sauce
¼ cup white or brown sugar
¼ cup rice vinegar
2 tbsp. medium-dry sherry
   or port

1 tbsp. cornstarch
1 clove garlic
ginger root, about size of a
   quarter, minced
salt and white pepper
   to taste

1. Combine all ingredients in a food processor fitted with the metal blade and process until smooth.
2. Pour the mixture into a saucepan and heat slowly, stirring until thickened. Serve warm.

HOT SOUR SAUCE

(yields about 2½ cups)

½ green pepper, seeded
   and slivered
½ red pepper, seeded
   and slivered
2 dried red chili peppers
2 green onions, cut
   into 1″ lengths
2 tbsp. ginger root, slivered

4 tbsp. catsup
1 tbsp. soy sauce
4 tbsp. sugar
4 tbsp. vinegar
1 cup water
2 tbsp. cornstarch dissolved
   in 2 tbsp. sherry
salt to taste

1. Combine all ingredients, except for the cornstarch mixture, in a medium-sized saucepan, and bring to a boil.
2. Stir in the cornstarch mixture and cook for 1 minute, stirring continuously. Taste and adjust the seasonings.

PLUM MUSTARD SAUCE

(yields about ¾ cups)

¼ cup port
¼ cup rice vinegar
¼ cup plum sauce
1 tbsp. sesame oil

1 tbsp. cornstarch,
   dissolved in 1 tbsp. water
1 tbsp. sugar
1-2 tbsp. cilantro, minced
salt and white pepper to taste

1. Combine all ingredients, except for the cornstarch mixture, in a medium-sized saucepan and bring to a boil.
2. Add the cornstarch and cook for 1 minute, stirring continuously. Taste and adjust the seasonings.

HOISIN SWEET & SOUR SAUCE

(yields about 1 cup)

¼ cup hoisin sauce
¼ cup port
¼ cup rice vinegar
1 tbsp. sesame oil
2 tbsp. soy sauce
2 tbsp. sugar

1-3 tbsp. cilantro, minced
1 clove garlic, minced
ginger root, about size
 of a quarter, minced
1 tbsp. cornstarch, dissolved
 in 1 tbsp. water

1. Combine all ingredients, except the cornstarch mixture, in a medium-sized saucepan and bring to a boil.
2. Add cornstarch and cook for 1 minute, stirring continuously. Taste and adjust the seasonings.

SESAME RICE VINEGAR SAUCE

(yields about 1¼ cups)

1 tbsp. tahini (sesame paste)
2-3 cloves of garlic
1-2 tbsp. pickled ginger, minced

1 cup rice vinegar
2-4 tbsp. sesame oil

Combine all ingredients in a food processor fitted with the metal blade or in a blender. Taste and adjust the seasonings.

APRICOT & SESAME SAUCE

(yields about 1½ cups)

½ cup apricot preserves
¼ cup bourbon
1 tbsp. Dijon-style mustard
1 clove garlic, minced
ginger root, about size
   of a quarter, minced
¼ cup rice vinegar
¼ cup soy sauce

2 tbsp. sugar
1-3 tbsp. cilantro
1 tbsp. cornstarch, dissolved
   in 1 tbsp. water
1 tbsp. tahini (sesame paste)
1-2 tbsp. sesame seeds, toasted
pinch of Chinese five spice*
salt and pepper to taste

1. Combine all ingredients, except the cornstarch mixture in a medium-sized saucepan and bring to a boil.
2. Stir in the cornstarch mixture and cook for 1 minute, stirring continuously. Taste and adjust the seasonings.

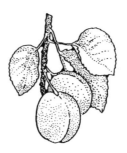

GINGERED ORANGE MUSTARD SAUCE

(yields about 1½ cups)

2 tbsp. pickled ginger
2 tbsp. orange marmalade
½ cup Dijon-style or
   Dusseldorf mustard

1 tbsp. brown sugar
¼ cup cider vinegar
½ cup avocado or peanut oil

Combine all ingredients in a food processor fitted with the metal blade or in a blender. Taste and adjust the seasonings.

*See Helpful Terms section for information about Chinese five spice

CHINESE LEMON SAUCE

A tangy alternative.

(yields about 2 cups)

3 tbsp. lemon juice, or to taste
zest of 1 lemon, finely grated
2 tsp. garlic, minced, or to taste
2 tbsp. ginger root, minced
1 tbsp. cornstarch dissolved
   in 1 tbsp. of sherry
2 tbsp. sesame seeds, toasted

1 cup chicken broth, homemade
   or canned
¼ cup sherry
⅓ plum sauce
1 tbsp. soy sauce
1 tsp. sugar
salt and white pepper to taste

1. Combine all ingredients, except for the cornstarch mixture, in a saucepan and bring to a boil.
2. Stir in the cornstarch mixture. Cook, stirring, until thickened. Taste and adjust the seasonings.

MERLOT GINGER SAUCE

A rich and intense flavor.

(yields about 2 cups)

1 cup Merlot wine
1 cup chicken broth,
   homemade or canned
2 tbsp. soy sauce
2 tbsp. butter
1 tbsp. cornstarch,
   dissolved in 1 tbsp. water

1 tbsp. ginger root,
   minced, or more to taste
1 tsp. garlic, puréed
2 green onions, minced
2 tbsp. brown sugar
salt and white pepper
   to taste

1. Melt the butter in a saucepan and briefly sauté the garlic, ginger, and green onions.

2. Add the remaining ingredients, except for the cornstarch mixture. Bring to a boil and cook over moderate heat until the flavors develop to your liking, for 5 to 15 minutes.

3. Return the sauce to a boil and stir in the cornstarch mixture. Cook, stirring, for 30 seconds. Taste and adjust the seasonings.

Further *Fabulous:* Strain the sauce before serving. Dunk CHINESE SAUSAGE POTSTICKERS, CRISPY COCKTAIL RIBS or DOUBLE-FRIED CHICKEN WINGS.

CILANTRO CUMIN SAUCE

(yields about 3 cups)

½ cup cilantro, minced	1 tbsp. Dijon-style mustard
¼ cup parsley, minced	½ tsp. cumin, or to taste
½-1 carrot, minced	2 cups chicken or lamb broth,
1 onion, minced	reduced to 1 cup
1 tsp. garlic, minced	½ cup dry white wine,
1 tbsp. butter	reduced to ¼ cup
2 tbsp. flour	salt and white pepper to taste

1. Melt butter in saucepan and slowly brown the carrots and onions.
2. Whisk in the garlic, mustard, and flour. Cook over low heat for 1 minute.
3. Add the remaining ingredients and stir until the mixture comes to a boil. Reduce heat and simmer until the sauce thickens and the flavors develop.
4. Taste and adjust the seasonings. Strain.

Fast: Can prepare up to 2 days in advance and refrigerate, or freeze for up to 3 months.
Flashy: Garnish with a sprinkling of minced cilantro.
Fabulous: With chicken, lamb, or pork.

SATE SAUCE

A variation of an Indonesian classic.

(yields about 3 cups)

¼ cup lemon juice
¾ cup sherry
¼ cup soy sauce, or more to taste
¼ cup plum sauce
½ cup cilantro
1 cup chicken broth,
   homemade or canned
1 cup peanuts, ground,
   or peanut butter

4 Brazil nuts
4 shallots
2-4 cloves garlic
4 whole green chiles,
   seeded and deveined (canned)
4 tbsp. peanut oil
salt, white pepper, and sugar
   to taste

1. Purée the shallots, garlic, chiles, nuts, and cilantro in a food processor fitted with the metal blade.
2. Heat the oil in a saucepan and fry the mixture.
3. Add remaining ingredients and cook until thickened. If the sauce is too thick, add more chicken broth.

Fast: Can prepare up to 1 week in advance and refrigerate.
Flashy: With bite-size pieces of barbecued chicken or pork.
Fabulous: As a marinade for chicken or pork.

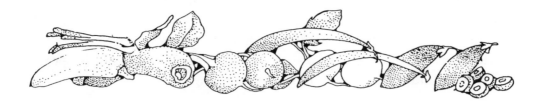

JAPANESE-STYLE DIPPING SAUCE

A teriyaki-style sauce.

(yields about 1½ cups)

1 cup Madeira or sherry
¼ cup soy sauce
¼ cup honey
2 tbsp. sesame seeds, toasted

¼ tsp. ginger, powdered, or
   1 tbsp. fresh ginger root, minced
1 tsp. garlic, minced
4 green onions, minced
2 tbsp. sesame oil

1. Combine all ingredients in a saucepan over medium heat.
2. Stir until the honey melts and the flavors develop. Serve hot or at room temperature.

Fast: Can prepare up to 3 months in advance, place in jars, and refrigerate.
Fabulous: As a marinade or dipping sauce for DOUBLE-FRIED CHICKEN WINGS, bite-size pieces of beef or pork.

Elegant Hors d'Oeuvres with Gloria Ferrer Royal Cuveé Sparkling Wine. (1) Carrot Croustades and Leek Croustades (2) Chevre and Lox Torta (3) Mushroom and Canadian Bacon Tartlets (4) Caviar Mousse with Bagel Chips (5) Beaten Biscuits with Seafood Filling.

above:
Cold Scallops Vinaigrette with
Dry Creek Vineyard Fumé Blanc.

Cold Madeira Bleu Cheese Sauce
with Dry Creek Vineyard
Chardonnay.

Christopher Saul Photography

Pearl Chutney Balls with Sesame
Rice Vinegar Sauce and Chinese
Chutney Dipping Sauce served
with Gloria Ferrer Brut
Sparkling Wine.

Dunks
56

CHAPTER TWO

COVER-UPS—MARINATED and PICKLED ITEMS

Cover-ups, just one of the strange chapter names, consists of vegetables and a few seafood items that have been pickled or marinated, allowing you to capture the essence of the season and preserve it for future enjoyment. Remember to prepare these recipes several days in advance to allow the flavors to develop. You'll be delighted by how inexpensive most of these items are to prepare, especially when you see how costly they are at your favorite deli. Many of these recipes have the additional benefit of being low in calories and fat, and are great for gifts.

Pickled and marinated items are just as appropriate for casual picnics as they are for gala cocktail parties. They provide flavor contrast and balance to menus. One of my favorite winter combinations is a pate served with PICKLED ONIONS. In the summer, ROASTED, MARINATED PEPPERS served with feta or chevre on PITA CHIPS or French bread make a wonderful hors d'oeuvre. Dress up your next hamburger barbecue with MIDDLE-EASTERN YOGURT EGGPLANT SAUCE or MIDDLE-EASTERN VEGETABLE RELISH. Those hamburgers will be transformed into an exotic treat!

SPICED MUSHROOMS

(yields about 6 to 8 servings)

1½ lb. button mushrooms, washed, and patted dry with paper towels
⅓ cup olive oil
1 cup dry white wine
¼ cup red wine vinegar
2 cloves garlic, minced

⅓ cup parsley, minced
8 green onions, minced
2 bay leaves
1 tsp. fenugreek
1 tsp. dried oregano
6 peppercorns
2 tsp. salt

1. Combine the mushrooms, olive oil, garlic, and green onions in a stainless steel or enameled skilled. Sauté for 3 minutes.
2. Add the remaining ingredients and simmer for 5 minutes.
3. Transfer the mixture to a ceramic bowl or glass jar. Cool and chill, covered for at least 4 hours.

Fast: Can prepare up to 2 weeks in advance and refrigerate.
Fabulous: Substitute different herbs and vegetables.

PICKLED ONIONS

(yields about 4 cups)

4 cups (about 1½ lb.) tiny white boiling onions, peeled, washed, and dried
¼ cup salt
3 cups malt or cider vinegar
¼ cup plus 2 tbsp. brown sugar

2 bay leaves
2 tsp. mustard seed
1 dried red pepper
1 tsp. black peppercorns
ginger root, size of a quarter, minced
several sprigs cilantro

1. Place onions in a large bowl and stir in the salt. Let stand covered, at room temperature, overnight to mellow them.
2. Rinse onions under cold water and drain.

3. Combine the remaining ingredients in a saucepan and boil for 5 minutes. Add onions and boil for 4 to 5 minutes. Onions should be crisp.
4. Refrigerate for 1 week before serving.

Fast: Can prepare up to 6 months in advance and refrigerate.
Flashy: With pates, cheeses, or cheese fondues.

PICKLED CAULIFLOWER

An old family recipe I got from my Aunt Fanny that always gets rave reviews.

(yields about 7 pints)

2 heads cauliflower (about 2 lb.)	¼ cup salt
1 small dried red pepper, or more to taste	1½ cups white vinegar, or to taste
	1 bay leaf
3 cloves garlic, peeled, or more	water

1. Cut the cauliflower into small flowerets.
2. To make brine, mix salt and vinegar with enough water so that it is not too salty or too sour.
3. Place the cauliflower in plastic or glass jars and cover with the brine. Add a piece of bay leaf, a piece of the red pepper, and a clove of garlic to each container.
4. Cover the containers and leave at room temperature for at least 3 days or until the flavors develop.

Fast: Can prepare up to 1 month in advance and refrigerate.
Flashy: With DIJON SAUCE and CURRY SAUCE.
Fabulous: With fresh or dry herbs, such as rosemary or fennel added to the brine. Substitute turnips, celery, green beans, carrots, or jicama for the cauliflower.

PICKLED MUSHROOMS

(yields about 3 cups)

1 lb. small to medium-sized mushrooms, washed (reserve stems for another use)
1 cup white wine vinegar
½ cup water
½-1 cup olive oil
2-4 cloves garlic, whole or minced
1 carrot, sliced thinly

2-4 green onions, cut into 1" pieces
several sprigs parsley, minced or whole
dried marjoram, rosemary, and oregano to taste
5 peppercorns
½ bay leaf
1½ tsp. salt

1. Combine all ingredients, except for the mushrooms, in a saucepan and bring to a boil. Reduce heat and simmer for 5 minutes.
2. Add mushrooms and simmer for 5 to 10 minutes. Taste and adjust the seasonings.
3. Cool. Pour in a jar and refrigerate, covered, for several days to allow mushrooms to absorb the flavors.

Fast: Can prepare up to 2 weeks in advance and refrigerate.
Fabulous: With celery, artichoke hearts, carrots, green beans, zucchini, and peppers instead of mushrooms. Substitute different herbs as well.

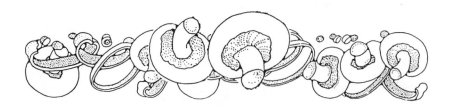

MUSTARD PICKLES

An exotic pickle with an East Indian flavor.

(yields about 2½ pints)

1 small cauliflower, cut into
small flowerets
3 small zucchini or yellow
squash, cut into ¾" cubes
1 small cucumber, pared,
halved, seeded, and cut
into ¾" cubes
½ cup shallots, peeled and
halved

¼ cup flour
½ cup brown sugar, or more
to taste
1 tbsp. dry mustard
1 tbsp. salt, or more to taste
3-4 cloves garlic, minced
½-1 tsp. ground ginger
1½ tsp. tumeric.
2-3 cups apple cider vinegar

1. Toss the cauliflower in a glass bowl with 1½ tsp. salt.
2. Toss the zucchini, cucumber, and shallots with the remaining salt in another glass bowl. Let stand overnight.
3. Make a paste of the sugar, flour, ginger, dry mustard, tumeric, and 2 tablespoons of vinegar.
4. Heat the remaining vinegar in a saucepan and bring it to a boil with the garlic. Slowly stir in the paste.
5. Drain the vegetables and stir them into the sauce.
6. Simmer for 5 minutes. Cool and place in glass jars and refrigerate for at least a week.

Fast: Can prepare up to 1 month in advance and refrigerate.
Fabulous: With pasta or rice salads. Serve as a relish with curry dinners.

CHERRY TOMATOES BON APPETIT

Colorful and refreshing.

(yields about 1 pint)

1 pt. (2 cups) cherry tomatoes
1 tbsp. fresh dill weed,
   finely chopped, or 1½ tsp.
   dried dill weed
2 green onions, minced

2 tbsp. parsley, minced
6 tbsp. olive oil
salt and freshly ground
   black pepper to taste

1. Place tomatoes in a lettuce basket or strainer and set in a deep bowl. Pour boiling water over them and let stand for about 30 seconds. Immediately plunge tomatoes in ice water; drain. Remove and discard the skins.
2. Place the tomatoes in a bowl with the remaining ingredients and toss gently.
3. Cover and allow them to marinate for at least 1 hour at room temperature. Serve with toothpicks.

Fast: Can prepare up to 3 days in advance and refrigerate.
Flashy: Add to an antipasto platter or serve with pates.
Fabulous: With toasted sesame seeds, anchovies, different herbs, capers, or grated Parmesan cheese.

EGGPLANT & CELERY ANTIPASTO

(yields about 4 pints)

2½ lb. eggplant, washed
   and stemmed
tender inner stalks from one
   bunch of celery, washed, dried,
   and cut in 1″ lengths
½ cup olives, Greek or Italian
1 onion, sliced thinly
½ cup parsley, minced

3 cloves garlic, minced
2 tbsp. capers
2-4 tsp. brown sugar
1¼ cups red wine vinegar
½ cup chicken broth,
   homemade or canned
3 oz. tomato paste
olive oil
salt and pepper to taste

1. Dice the eggplant with the peel left on. Sprinkle with salt and place in a colander for 1 hour. Rinse and dry with paper towels.
2. Sauté the eggplant in several tbsp. of olive oil until brown and tender. Remove it from the pan and set aside.
3. Sauté the celery and onion in a few tbsp. olive oil until just barely softened.
4. Return eggplant to the pan and add all remaining ingredients. Simmer until the flavors are pleasing. Serve hot, cold, or at room temperature.

Fast: Can prepare up to 1 week in advance and refrigerate, or freeze for up to 6 months.
Flashy: With crackers or thinly sliced French bread.
Fabulous: Substitute fennel bulbs for celery, zucchini for eggplant, and add mushrooms and carrots. Season with fennel seeds, marjoram, oregano, and basil.

ROASTED, MARINATED PEPPERS

(yields about 2 cups)

6-8 large bell peppers, red
  or green, sliced in half,
  seeded and deveined
4 tbsp. parsley, minced

2-4 cloves garlic, minced
8 tbsp. olive oil
salt, white pepper, and lemon
  juice to taste

1. Place the peppers on a cookie sheet and bake (cut side down) at 350°
until completely blackened, about one hour.
2. Remove and peel when cool enough to handle.
3. Slice into thin strips.
4. Toss the peppers with oil and season with the remaining ingredients.
Allow the mixture to marinate for at least 1 hour.

Fast: Can prepare up to 5 days in advance and refrigerate, or freeze for up to
6 months.
Flashy: Chop peppers up and serve in CROUSTADES or on an antipasto
platter with French bread. Mince and add to dunks or fondues.
Fabulous: As a relish or seasoning ingredient. Season with fresh basil, rosemary, dill, or oregano.

JULIENNED CARROTS WITH WALNUTS

(yields about 3 cups)

1 lb. carrots, peeled and
  julienned or shredded
½ cup walnuts, chopped
½ cup parsley, minced
¼ cup green onions, minced

½ cup BALSAMIC VINAIGRETTE
  (see recipe)
freshly ground black pepper,
  and lemon juice to taste

1. Combine all the ingredients. Toss and let sit for at least 4 hours.
2. Pour off excess juices before serving.

Fast: Can prepare up to 1 week in advance and refrigerate.
Flashy: With HUMMUS, to fill CROUSTADES, or as part of an antipasto platter.
Fabulous: With zucchini, celery root, white radish, or Jerusalem artichokes, instead of carrots. Toss into a pasta, spinach, or rice salad.

MIDDLE-EASTERN VEGETABLE RELISH

(yields about 3 cups)

1 large tomato, peeled and
　　chopped
1 cucumber, peeled, seeded
　　and chopped
2-4 green onions, minced
¼ cup cilantro, minced

¼ cup parsley, minced
1 tsp. garlic, minced
1 cup sour cream or yogurt
salt, white pepper, and
　　lemon juice to taste

Combine all ingredients and refrigerate for at least 1 hour or overnight. Taste and adjust the seasonings.

Fast: Can prepare up to 5 days in advance and refrigerate.
Flashy: Dunk PITA CHIPS or GARLIC CROUTON ROUNDS.
Fabulous: Toss into pasta, bulghur, or rice, and serve cold.

EGGPLANT CAVIAR

My version of peasant caviar.

(yields about 4 cups)

2 large eggplants
2-4 red peppers, roasted,
  peeled, seeded, and minced
1 cup parsley, minced
2 cloves garlic, or more to taste

¼ cup sesame seeds, toasted
olive oil, several tbsp. to taste
½ cup feta cheese, crumbled
salt, freshly ground black pepper,
  and lemon juice to taste

1. Place eggplant on a cookie sheet and pierce with a fork in several places to allow the steam to escape. Bake at 400° until tender, for about 40 minutes. Remove and set aside until cool enough to handle.
2. Scoop out the meat of the eggplant and combine with the remaining ingredients in a food processor fitted with the metal blade; chop coarsely. Taste and adjust the seasonings.

Fast: Can prepare up to 5 days in advance and refrigerate, or freeze up to 3 months.
Flashy: With assorted crackers, melbas or PITA CHIPS.
Fabulous: Season with oregano and serve as a cold sauce with roast lamb.

MIDDLE-EASTERN YOGURT EGGPLANT SAUCE

(yields about 1½ cups)

1 cup eggplant, minced
1 tsp. salt
1 tbsp. olive oil
1 cup yogurt
2 green onions, minced

¼ cup parsley, minced
1 clove garlic, minced
½ tsp. cumin
2 tbsp. sesame seeds, toasted
salt and white pepper to taste

1. Place the eggplant in a colander with 1 tsp. salt and let drain for 30 minutes. Rinse and dry.

2. Heat oil in skillet and sauté eggplant until tender.
3. Transfer the eggplant to a bowl and add the remaining ingredients. Refrigerate until cool. Taste and adjust seasonings.

Fast: Can prepare up to 5 days in advance and refrigerate.
Flashy: Dunk meatballs, PITA CHIPS, or EASTERN-STYLE GARBANZO BALLS.
Fabulous: With minced, marinated artichoke hearts or ROASTED MARINATED PEPPERS mixed in.

FETA SALSA

A happy cross-cultural marriage.

(yields about 5 cups)

1 lb. feta cheese, crumbled	juice of 1 lime
1 cup olive oil	1 tbsp. dried oregano
6 green onions, minced	2 tsp. dried or 2-3 tbsp.
½ cup parsley, minced	fresh dill weed
3-4 tomatoes, skinned and puréed	white and freshly ground
½ pt. Greek or Italian olives, pitted and coarsely chopped	black pepper to taste

1. Combine all ingredients in a food processor fitted with a metal blade or in a blender. Taste and adjust the seasonings.
2. Chill at least 30 minutes before serving.

Fast: Can prepare up to 2 days in advance and refrigerate.
Flashy: With PITA CHIPS.
Fabulous: To dress pasta salad or to accompany lamb or chicken as an entree sauce.

COLD SCALLOPS VINAIGRETTE

(serves 4 to 8)

A taste surprise!

1 lb. baby scallops, washed
1 clove garlic, minced, or
    more to taste
2 tbsp. parsley, minced
3-6 green onions, cut into
    ½" lengths

2 tbsp. sun-dried tomatoes,
    minced
2 tbsp. sesame oil
chevre or mozzarella, optional
1 cup olive oil
salt, white pepper, and
    lime juice to taste

1. Bring all the ingredients, except for the scallops and cheese, to a boil in a non-corrosive saucepan.
2. Add the scallops; cook until just opaque. Pour the entire contents into a bowl and cool to room temperature.
3. If desired, cut cheese into cubes and place in the bowl. Coat well with the marinade.
4. Cover the bowl and chill for 12 hours, or overnight, before serving.

Fast: Can prepare up to 2 days in advance and refrigerate.
Flashy: With thinly sliced baguettes and toothpicks.
Fabulous: With shrimp, monkfish, shark, or swordfish cut into bite-size pieces instead of the scallops. Served with Dry Creek Vineyard Fumé Blanc.

MARINATED SHRIMP

(serves 4 to 8)

1½ lb. shrimp, cooked,
   shelled, and cleaned (any
   size, fresh or frozen)
¼ cup parsley, minced
¼ cup green onions, minced

2 tbsp. capers, or more to taste
¼ cup sesame seeds, toasted
lemon juice to taste
½ cup TARRAGON CAPER
   VINAIGRETTE (see recipe)

Combine all ingredients and marinate in the refrigerator for at least 4 hours. Taste and adjust the seasonings.

Fast: Can prepare up to 2 days in advance and refrigerate.
Flashy: In CROUSTADES or with toothpicks.
Fabulous: Substitute crab, mussels, or scallops for the shrimp. Served with Dry Creek Vineyard Fumé Blanc.

CHAPTER THREE

TOPS

We aren't talking blouses here, but we are talking marvelous mixtures that are designed to be spread on or served in . . . hence the title, TOPS.

When time is a critical factor, you will find a bounty of items that can be whipped together at a moment's notice, and for even greater convenience, prepared in advance and frozen.

As for versatility, most of these recipes can be transformed into entrees by being tossed into freshly cooked pasta; served over rice, barley, or couscous; or used to fill crepes or pasta shells.

Many of these recipes for spreads, fillings, and chafing dish items can be mixed and matched with the recipes for croustades, melbas, and pastry bases in Chapter 5. For example, CREAMED FETA served with BAGEL CHIPS, CAULIFLOWER MORNAY served on BEATEN BISCUITS, or POTTED BLACK BEANS served in TORTILLA CUPS.

SPREADS

Even though this word has a less than glamorous image, these items are exciting to eat. This category offers you the exceptional convenience of using little dribs and drabs of ingredients, common or exotic, and turning them into something delicious in a matter of minutes. As an example, when I once found myself faced with drop-in guest panic, I created POTTED CAMEBERT. My refrigerator contained butter, leftover pieces of camembert, and a couple of shallots. Since then, it has become one of my favorites. Necessity is the mother of invention!

POTTED BLACK BEANS

A delicious source of vitamins, minerals, and fiber.

(yields about 2½ cups)

½ lb. black turtle beans
1 cup walnuts, chopped
1 tbsp. olive oil
1 small onion, minced
2-4 whole green chiles, seeded, deveined, and chopped (canned)
1 tbsp. chili powder
1 tbsp. cumin
1 bunch cilantro, minced
¼-½ cup green onions, minced
2 cloves garlic, minced
3 cups chicken broth, homemade or canned
½ cup sherry
1 bay leaf
salt to taste

1. Wash the beans and soak them overnight; drain.
2. In the oil sauté the onion and garlic in a pot until soft. Add the bay leaf, broth, sherry, and beans. Bring to a boil. Simmer for 45 minutes or until the beans are tender.
3. Drain the beans and place in a food processor fitted with the metal blade. Add the chiles, seasonings, cilantro, green onions, and walnuts. Process until a pleasing consistency is reached. Taste and adjust the seasonings.
4. Place in casserole and heat in a 350° oven until hot.

Fast: Can prepare up to 2 days in advance and refrigerate, or freeze for up to 3 months.

Flashy: Serve with chips or in TORTILLA CUPS. Serve cold with GUACAMOLE.

Fabulous: When combined with generous amounts of sour cream and grated cheese (Jack, cheddar, or mozzarella). Use as warm dipping sauce to accompany CHILE SQUARES. Served with Dry Creek Vineyard Zinfandel.

HUMMUS

A bit of Middle-Eastern exotica that can be served whenever you would serve guacamole.

(yields about 2½ cups)

2 cups chickpeas, cooked or
    canned and drained
½ cup olive oil
¼-½ cup tahini (sesame
    paste)

⅓ cup lemon juice or to taste
2 cloves garlic
¼ cup parsley, minced
¼ cup cilantro, minced
salt and white pepper to taste

Process all the ingredients in a blender or food processor fitted with the metal blade until smooth. Taste and adjust the seasonings.

Fast: Can prepare up to 2 days in advance and refrigerate, or freeze for up to 6 months.

Flashy: Garnish with parsley or cilantro and serve with PITA CHIPS.

Fabulous: Substitute walnuts for the tahini. Served with Dry Creek Vineyard Fumé Blanc.

WHITE BEAN PATÉ WITH HAM & JACK CHEESE

(yields about 5 cups)

2 cups cooked white beans
1 cup ham, minced
1 cup Jack cheese, grated
1 cup cottage or ricotta cheese
4 oz. cream cheese
1 tsp. Dijon-style mustard

2-4 green onions, minced
½ cup walnuts, chopped
½ cup stuffed green olives,
 minced
salt, white pepper, and fresh
 or dried rosemary to taste

1. Purée the cheeses, beans, mustards and seasonings in a food processor fitted with the metal blade.
2. Add the remaining ingredients and process, using care not to destroy their texture. Taste and adjust the seasonings.

Fast: Can prepare up to 2 days in advance and refrigerate, or freeze for up to 3 months.
Flashy: Spread on crackers or breads.
Fabulous: Fill CROUSTADES, cherry tomatoes, raw mushrooms, peapods, or celery.

POTTED PORK DEGAN

Rustic in feeling, great for picnics, holiday gatherings, and gifts.

(yields about 6 cups)

3 lb. boneless pork roast
3-4 parsley sprigs
1 onion, coarsely chopped
1 carrot, coarsely chopped
2 cups white wine
water to cover the ingredients

1 lb. butter or cream cheese,
 at room temperature
salt, black peppercorns,
 garlic cloves, thyme, rosemary,
 bay leaves to taste

1. Place all ingredients in a large pot and bring to boil. Boil for 5 minutes.
2. Reduce heat to low and simmer until tender, about 2 hours.

3. Cool to room temperature and chill overnight. Skim off the fat and shred meat by hand or in a food processor fitted with the metal blade.

4. Combine the shreds with butter or cream cheese in the food processor fitted with the metal blade or by hand. Taste and adjust the seasonings.

5. Pack the mixture into crocks, jars, or small serving containers.

Fast: Can prepare up to 3 days in advance and refrigerate, or freeze for up to 6 months.

Flashy: Serve at room temperature with mustards, gherkins, PICKLED ONIONS, and thinly sliced French bread.

Fabulous: Add any or all of following ingredients to the pork mixture, in amounts to taste: minced cilantro; minced green onions; minced, browned onions; lemon or orange zest; caraway seeds; dill weed; minced, roasted red or green peppers, green chiles, capers, thyme, green peppercorns, or your favorite seasoning. Served with Dry Creek Vineyard Cabernet Sauvignon.

POTTED HAM & CHEESE

(yields about 3 cups)

¾ lb. cooked ham, minced	1 tsp. dried dill weed
1 cup sharp cheddar cheese, grated	¾ cup mayonnaise, homemade or
4 tbsp. green onions, minced	purchased
2 tbsp. capers	2 tbsp. sherry
1 tsp. Dijon-style mustard,	white pepper and freshly
or more to taste	grated nutmeg to taste

1. Combine all ingredients in a food processor fitted with the metal blade. Process until a pleasing consistency is reached. Taste and adjust the seasonings.

2. Pack the mixture into a crock or mold. Chill for several hours.

Fast: Can prepare up to 2 days in advance and refrigerate, or freeze for up to 3 months.

Flashy: Serve with thinly sliced breads or crackers.

POTTED REUBEN

If you like Reuben sandwiches, you'll love this.

(yields about 7 cups)

¾ lb. corned beef, minced
1 cup sauerkraut, drained
2 cups onions, minced
2 tbsp. butter
¾ cup mayonnaise, homemade
   or purchased
4 oz. cream cheese
1 cup Swiss cheese, grated

2 tbsp. Dijon-style mustard
1 tsp. caraway seeds, or more
   to taste
½ cup parsley, minced, or
   more to taste
1 tsp. dried dill weed
white pepper to taste

1. Brown the onions in butter.
2. Combine all the ingredients in a food processor fitted with the metal blade. Process until smooth. Taste and adjust the seasonings.
3. Pack the mixture into small crocks or serving containers. Chill for several hours.

Fast: Can prepare up to 2 days in advance and refrigerate, or freeze for up to 3 months.
Flashy: Serve with assorted breads, crackers, and melbas.
Fabulous: In CROUSTADES made with rye bread, or with small pieces of rye bread.

PICKLED HERRING PATÉ

This recipe converts herring-haters every time.

(yields about 1½ cups)

6 oz. pickled herring, drained
8 oz. cream cheese

3 tbsp. fresh dill weed
zest of 1 lemon, finely grated

1. Blend all ingredients in a food processor fitted with the metal blade. Process until smooth.
2. Pack the mixture into crocks or small soufflé dishes and refrigerate until firm.

Fast: Can prepare up to 4 days in advance and refrigerate.
Flashy: Garnish the top with dill weed and serve with pumpernickel squares or BAGEL CHIPS.

TUNA & ARTICHOKE PATÉ

Tuna need not be boring.

(yields about 2 cups)

7 oz. tuna	½ cup parsley, minced
½ cup marinated artichoke hearts, chopped	3 tbsp. capers
	1 stick unsalted butter
4 anchovy filets	2 tbsp. brandy
½ cup green onions, minced	juice of 1 lemon
	white pepper to taste

1. Purée all ingredients in a food processor fitted with the metal blade. Process until a pleasing consistency is reached. Taste and adjust the seasonings.
2. Chill for at least 30 minutes.

Fast: Can prepare up to 3 days in advance and refrigerate.
Flashy: Spread on assorted crackers, melbas, or breads. Fill CROUSTADES.
Fabulous: Stuff into raw mushrooms, cherry tomato halves, or peapods. Substitute watercress for the parsley and crab or salmon for the tuna.

SARDINE SPREAD

(yields about 1½ cups)

1 can (3¾ oz.) sardines
8 oz. cream cheese
4 green onions, minced, or
   more to taste

1 bunch parsley, minced
zest of 1 lemon, finely grated
salt, white pepper, and
   lemon juice to taste

Combine all the ingredients in a food processor fitted with the metal blade. Process until a pleasing consistency is reached. Taste and adjust the seasonings.

Fast: Can prepare up to 2 days in advance and refrigerate.
Flashy: Serve in cherry tomatoes or CROUSTADES or with melbas, crackers, or BAGEL CHIPS.
Fabulous: Substitute smoked trout, smoked salmon, kippered cod, cooked salmon, cooked shrimp, or crabmeat for sardines.

CRAB & EGG SPREAD

(yields about 4 cups)

10 oz. crab or imitation crab
4 hard-boiled eggs
½ cup mayonnaise, homemade
   or purchased
½ cup sour cream
¼ cup Parmesan cheese,
   grated

1 red pepper, roasted,
   skinned, and seeded
1 tbsp. Dijon-style mustard
¼ cup fresh or 1½ tbsp.
   dried dill weed
1 shallot, minced
lemon juice to taste

1. Combine all ingredients in a food processor fitted with the metal blade, using care not to destroy the texture. Taste and adjust the seasonings.
2. Pack the mixture into a crock or serving bowl. Chill for at least 30 minutes.

Fast: Can prepare up to 1 day in advance and refrigerate.
Flashy: Serve cold with assorted crackers, breads, or raw vegetables.
Fabulous: Stuff raw mushrooms, cherry tomatoes, or CROUSTADES. For a firmer spread, substitute cream cheese for the mayonnaise.

CURRIED EGG SPREAD

(yields about 6 cups)

8 hard-boiled eggs
2 pears, cored and chopped
⅓ cup cilantro, minced,
   or more to taste
⅓ cup parsley, minced,
   or more to taste
¾-1 cup mayonnaise
⅓ cup sour cream

2 tbsp. Dijon-style mustard,
   or to taste
3 tbsp. mango chutney (optional)
4-8 green onions, minced
1 8 oz. can of water chestnuts,
   minced
½ cup peanuts, chopped
1½ tsp. curry powder, or to taste
salt and white pepper to taste

1. Combine all ingredients, except the peanuts and water chestnuts in a food processor fitted with the metal blade.
2. Process in the remaining ingredients, taking care not to destroy the texture. Taste and adjust the seasonings.
3. Chill for at least 30 minutes.

Fast: Can prepare up to 2 days in advance and refrigerate.
Flashy: With crackers or as a cold filling for CROUSTADES or TARTLETS, or to stuff raw mushrooms, cucumber cups, or cherry tomatoes.
Fabulous: Season with a dash of cardamon. Substitute apples or any other fruit for the pears.

CELERY ROOT PATÉ

(yields about 2 cups)

1 celery root, peeled and
  grated
3 tbsp. sesame seeds, toasted,
  or more to taste
½ cup mayonnaise, homemade
  or purchased

1 tbsp. coarse-grained or
  Dijon-style mustard
3-6 green onions, minced
lemon juice and or apple
  cider vinegar to taste
salt and white pepper
  to taste

1. Combine all ingredients. Taste and adjust the seasonings.
2. Chill for at least 30 minutes.

Fast: Can prepare up to 4 days in advance and refrigerate.
Flashy: With pumpernickel squares or PITA CHIPS.
Fabulous: Stuff CROUSTADES or raw mushrooms.

ROASTED GARLIC DECADENCE

Guaranteed to keep vampires away.

(yields about 1½ cups)

3 heads garlic
2-4 tbsp. cream sherry
8 oz. chevre (or 4 oz. chevre
  and 4 oz. unsalted butter)

olive oil
salt and white pepper
  to taste

1. Cut ⅓ of the garlic off from top of bulb to expose all of the cloves.
2. Place the bulbs on baking dish and coat with oil to prevent burning.
Bake at 250° until the cloves are soft and buttery.
3. Squeeze the garlic cloves out of their wrappers and into a food processor
fitted with the metal blade.
4. Combine garlic with the remaining ingredients in the food processor.

5. Process until smooth and creamy. Taste and adjust the seasonings.
6. Chill for at least 1 hour.

Fast: Can prepare up to 5 days in advance and refrigerate, or freeze for up to 6 months.
Flashy: Serve with assorted crackers and breads.
Fabulous: Add roasted and chopped pecans or almonds. Serve with grilled poultry and meats, kebabs, raw or cooked vegetables. Add cream and/or chicken broth to create a marvelous sauce. Plain as Roasted Garlic. Serve with Dry Creek Vineyard Zinfandel.

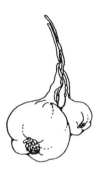

SEASONED BUTTERS

Seasoned butter mixtures create instant taste sensations. Top barbecued steak, chicken breast filets, or fish with a dollop of seasoned butter rather than a more complex sauce.

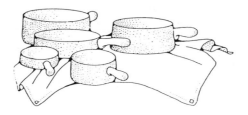

PROSCIUTTO BUTTER

(yields about 1½ cups)

¼ lb. prosciutto, chopped
  (or smoked ham)
½ lb. butter
4 oz. cream cheese

¼ cup shallots, minced,
  or to taste
2 tbsp. Madeira
white pepper to taste

1. Combine all ingredients in a food processor fitted with the metal blade. Taste and adjust the seasonings.
2. Chill until firm before serving.

Fast: Can prepare up to 5 days in advance and refrigerate, or freeze for up to 6 months.
Flashy: With melbas, BAGEL CHIPS, pumpernickel squares, or French bread.
Fabulous: For Salmon Butter, substitute smoked salmon for the prosciutto and season with dill weed and minced green onion. For Hearts of Palm or Artichoke Butter, substitute drained hearts of palm or drained marinated artichoke hearts for the prosciutto. For Shiitake Mushroom Butter, substitute rehydrated shiitake mushrooms for the prosciutto. For Roasted Garlic Butter, substitute 1-2 heads of roasted garlic for the prosciutto.

CREAMED FETA

(yields about 1 cup)

4 oz. feta cheese
4 oz. unsalted butter,
    at room temperature

½-1 shallot
white pepper to taste

1. Combine all ingredients in a food processor fitted with the metal blade and process until smooth.
2. Pack in a crook or serving bowl and chill, until firm, about 1 hour.

Fast: Can prepare up to 5 days in advance and refrigerate, or freeze for up to 3 months.
Flashy: Serve with PITA CHIPS, BAGEL CHIPS, thinly sliced baguettes, or crackers.
Fabulous: With rosemary, cilantro, oregano, or dill. Use to stuff mushrooms, peapods, Belgium endive, cherry tomatoes, or celery.

POTTED CAMEMBERT

(yields about 1½ cups)

½ lb. Camembert cheese
¼ lb. unsalted butter
1-2 tbsp. brandy or bourbon

½-1 shallot
white pepper to taste

1. Combine all ingredients in a food processor fitted with the metal blade and process until smooth. Taste and adjust the seasonings.
2. Pack in a crook or serving bowl and chill until firm, about 1 hour.

Fast: Can prepare up to 5 days in advance and refrigerate, or freeze for up to 6 months.
Flashy: Serve with PITA CHIPS, BAGEL CHIPS, thinly sliced baguettes, or crackers.
Fabulous: Toss into hot pasta or place dollop on grilled steak. Substitute brie for the Camembert.

BRIE DECADENCE

A truly special combination of flavors.

(serves 2 to 4)

8 oz. brie cheese, cut up
4-8 green onions, minced
1 lb. tomatoes, peeled, seeded,
  chopped, and drained

½ cup walnuts, chopped
½ cup WALNUT PESTO SAUCE
  (see recipe), or frozen

1. Place the brie in an au gratin dish or small oven-proof casserole and top
with all the remaining ingredients.
2. Heat in a 350° oven until cheese just begins to soften.

Fast: Can assemble up to 4 days in advance and refrigerate.
Flashy: Serve with thinly sliced baguettes.
Fabulous: Cut brie into ½" pieces. Place a piece of cheese and a bit of all the
ingredients on 1" squares of uncooked puff pastry. Place the squares on a
cookie sheet and bake at 425° until puffed. Can prepare ahead and refrigerate for a day or freeze for up to 1 month on cookie sheets.

MADEIRA CHEESE

(yields about 2¾ cups)

½ cup bleu cheese, crumbled
1½ cups sharp cheddar,
  grated
5 tbsp. Madeira

1 clove garlic, minced
3 green onions, minced
½ cup butter
white pepper to taste

1. Combine the cheeses, butter, white pepper, garlic, and Madeira in a food
processor fitted with the metal blade.
2. Mix in the green onions. Pack into a container and refrigerate for at least
24 hours before serving.

Fast: Can prepare up to 1 week in advance and refrigerate, or freeze for up to 3 months.
Flashy: Excellent with pumpernickel squares or melbas.

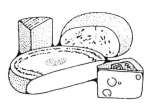

BLEU CHEESE WITH MADEIRA

(yields about 1½ cups)

½ lb. (8oz.) bleu cheese
  or Gorgonzola, room
  temperature
½ cup (1 stick) unsalted
  butter, room temperature

2 tbsp. Madeira
salt and white pepper
  to taste
Green grapes or sliced
  nectarines for garnish

1. Cream the first 4 ingredients in a food processor fitted with the metal blade.
2. Pack the cheese mixture into an oiled mold. Refrigerate until firm, about 4 hours.

Fast: Can prepare up to 1 week in advance and refrigerate, or freeze for up to 3 months.
Flashy: To serve, invert the mold onto a platter. Garnish with grapes and/or sliced nectarines in the summer. Serve with crackers, French bread, and apple slices.
Fabulous: Add nuts and/or herbs.

GORGONZOLA WITH WALNUTS

Abbondanza!

(yields about ¾ cup)

2 oz. Gorgonzola cheese	¼ cup butter
½ cup walnuts, toasted and chopped	1 tbsp. shallots, minced
	1-2 tbsp. brandy
2 tbsp. sour cream	white pepper to taste

1. Process all ingredients, except the walnuts, in a food processor fitted with the metal blade, until smooth.
2. Add the nuts and process, using care not to destroy the texture.

Fast: Can prepare up to 4 days in advance and refrigerate, or freeze for up to 3 months.
Flashy: Spread on BEATEN BISCUITS or in CROUSTADES.
Fabulous: In cherry tomatoes.

PEPPERONCINI CHEESE

Simple but zesty and versatile.

(yields about 1 cup)

8 oz. cream cheese
¾-1 cup imported pepperoncini, stemmed (mild Greek peppers)
¼ cup Parmesan cheese, grated

1. Process all ingredients in a food processor fitted with the metal blade.
2. Pack into a container and refrigerate for at least 1 hour before serving.

Fast: Can prepare up to 1 week in advance and refrigerate, or freeze for up to 3 months.
Flashy: Serve with assorted breads and/or crackers.

Fabulous: Substitute marinated artichoke hearts or imported or domestic olives for the pepperoncini. Stuff peapods or cherry tomatoes. Spread on thinly sliced baguettes or pumpernickel squares and bake in 350° oven until hot.

FILLINGS

This section will provide you with a filling for every possible occasion. When time permits, use these items in combination with the Wraps in Chapter 5. For a simpler, but still delicious, presentation, serve with an assortment of crackers and breads. For example, the CRAB & CHEESE FILLING is wonderful in CROUSTADES, TARTLETS, Flo Braker's Magic Puff Pastry, or PHYLLO CUPS. The MEXICAN ALMOND PORK is a natural filling for TORTILLA CUPS, and is also delicious in WON TON CUPS.

BASIC CHEESE MIXTURES

(yields about 4 cups)

1 8-oz. pkg. cream cheese
3 cups sharp cheddar cheese, grated
4 tbsp. Madeira

2 tsp. Dijon-style mustard
1-3 cloves garlic
salt, white pepper, and sweet Hungarian paprika to taste

1. Combine all ingredients in a food processor fitted with the metal blade. Taste and adjust the seasonings.
2. Chill for at least 1 hour before serving to allow the flavors to develop.

Fast: Can prepare up to 1 week in advance and refrigerate, or freeze for up to 3 months.
Flashy: Serve with assorted crackers and thinly sliced baguettes. Use as a filling for mushrooms, puffs, crepes, CROUSTADES, lavosh (cracker bread), or pita bread. For a wonderful sauce, add some of the cheese mixture to a white sauce or to chicken broth.
Fabulous: Try any of these variations:
  Plummed Cheddar Spread: Add Chinese plum sauce, to taste.
  Apricot Cheddar Spread: Add 6 oz. dried apricots and ¼ cup toasted sesame seeds.
  Almond Cheddar Spread: Add 1 cup chopped, toasted almonds to the basic spread.

Dilled Almond Cheddar Spread: Add 1 tsp. dried dill weed or more to the Almond Cheddar Spread.
Salami & Cheddar Spread: Add 1 cup minced Italian salami and ½ cup minced green onions to the basic spread.

CRAB & CHEESE FILLING

(yields about 4 cups)

12 oz. crabmet, fresh, frozen, or imitation
1-2 cups Swiss, Gruyère, cheddar, or Jack cheese, grated
11 oz. cream cheese
1½ tbsp. sherry
1 tbsp. Dijon-style mustard

½ cup green onions, minced
6 tbsp. parsley, minced
1 tbsp. capers, drained
½ tsp. Worcestershire sauce
½ tsp. prepared horseradish
salt, white pepper, and lemon juice to taste

1. Combine the cream cheese, cheese, and sherry in a food processor fitted with the metal blade until creamed.
2. Add all the remaining ingredients. Taste and adjust the seasonings.
3. Fill CROUSTADES, TARTLETS, PHYLLO CUPS, or Flo Braker's Magic Puff Pastry. Place on a cookie sheet and bake at 350° until golden and set, about 15 minutes. Top each tartlet with more cheese before baking if desired.

Fast: Can prepare the filling up to 1 day in advance and refrigerate or freeze for up to 3 months. Tartlets or CROUSTADES can be filled up to 3 hours in advance and left at room temperature. Can also be completely assembled and flash frozen for up to 3 months.
Fabulous: As a hot dunk. As a sauce, thin the filling with cream, broth, or white wine. Serve over fish, chicken breasts, broccoli, asparagus, or pasta. Substitute tuna for the crab for a less expensive alternative.

SPINACH & HAM FILLING

(yields about 3 cups)

10 oz. frozen chopped spinach,
    thawed and drained
¼-½ cup ham, chopped
1-2 tsp. garlic, minced
4 tbsp. parsley, minced
6 tbsp. onion, minced
2 tbsp. butter
2 tbsp. flour

½ cup heavy cream
3 tbsp. brandy
½-1 tsp. Dijon-style mustard
¼ cup Swiss cheese, grated
¼ cup Parmesan cheese, grated
white pepper and freshly
    grated nutmeg to taste

1. Melt the butter in a saucepan. Add garlic and onions and sauté until tender.
2. Whisk in the flour and cook for 1 minute. Remove the pan from the burner and whisk in the heavy cream and brandy. Return to the burner and cook until thickened.
3. Over medium heat, stir in the Swiss cheese, spinach, ham, mustard, parsley, nutmeg and white pepper. Reduce the heat to low, and stir until flavors develop and the cheese melts (about 10 minutes).
4. Taste and adjust the seasonings. Fill CROUSTADES, Flo Braker's Magic Puff Pastry, or TARTLETS. Top with Parmesan cheese and place under a hot broiler for a few minutes.

Fast: Can prepare the filling up to 2 days in advance and refrigerate or freeze for up to 3 months. Tartlets or CROUSTADES can be filled up to 3 hours in advance and left at room temperature. They can also be assembled completely and flash frozen for up to 3 months. Do *not* thaw before using!
Flashy: For a faster version, spread the mixture on thinly sliced baguettes or pumpernickel squares.
Fabulous: Substitute chard, broccoli, bok choy, or asparagus for the spinach.

ONION & HAM TARTLET FILLING

(yields about 6 cups)

A rich and heavenly winter recipe that works as well at an après ski party as at a Christmas gala.

6 large onions (about 2 lb.),
   minced
½ lb. smoked him, minced
2-4 gloves garlic, minced
¼ cup parsley, minced
4 tbsp. butter
2 tbsp. flour
2 tsp. Dijon-style mustard
1 cup heavy cream

1 cup Jack cheese, cut up
   into small pieces or grated
4 large eggs, beaten
½ cup sherry
2 tbsp. brandy
½ tsp. dried thyme leaves
salt, white pepper, and
   freshly grated nutmeg
   to taste

1. Melt the butter in a large skillet and slowly cook the onions, garlic, and ham until tender.

2. Stir in the flour and mustard and cook for 1 minute.

3. Add the sherry and brandy and cook until they are absorbed.

4. Stir in the cream, parsley, Jack cheese, thyme leaves, salt, white pepper, and nutmeg. Simmer until the flavors develop and the mixture is nicely thickened, for about 5 minutes. Taste and adjust the seasonings.

5. Cool the mixture and stir in the eggs.

6. Fill CROUSTADES, TARTLETS, PHYLLO CUPS, or Flo Braker's Magic Puff Pastry. Place on a cookie sheet and bake at 350° until golden and set, about 15 minutes. Top each one with more cheese before baking, if desired.

Fast: Can prepare the filling up to 2 days in advance and refrigerate, or freeze for up to 3 months. Tartlets or CROUSTADES can be filled up to 3 hours in advance and left at room temperature. Can also be assembled completely and flash frozen for up to 3 months.

Flashy: For a faster version, use thinly sliced baguettes or pumpernickel squares to spread the mixture on.

MEXICAN CRAB & CHEESE

(yields about 2½ cups)

1 cup crabmeat (fresh, frozen, or imitation)
4 green onions, minced
¼-½ cup cilantro, minced
½ cup sour cream or more, to taste

1 cup Jack cheese, grated
salt, pepper, chili powder, cumin, and lemon or lime juice to taste

1. Combine all the ingredients in mixing bowl.
2. Fill TORTILLA CUPS or CROUSTADES. Place on a cookie sheet and bake at 425° until the cheese melts, about 8 to 10 minutes.

Fast: Can prepare the filling up to 2 days in advance and refrigerate, or freeze for up to 3 months. TORTILLA CUPS or CROUSTADES can be filled up to 3 hours in advance and left at room temperature. Can also be completely assembled and flash frozen for up to 3 months.
Flashy: For a faster version, spread the mixture on tortilla chips.

CHILE CHEESE

(yields about 4½ cups)

⅔ cup whole green chiles, seeded, deveined, and chopped (canned)
2 cups Jack cheese, grated
1 tsp. dried oregano
½ cup green onions, minced
½ cup pitted black olives, chopped

1 cup refried beans, purchased or homemade
½ cup sour cream
1 tbsp. cumin
6 tbsp. cilantro, minced
2 cloves garlic, minced

1. Combine all ingredients in a mixing bowl. Taste and adjust the seasonings.
2. Fill CROUSTADES, TARTLETS, TORTILLA CUPS, or Flo Braker's Magic Puff Pastry. Place on a cookie sheet and bake at 350° until hot, about 10 minutes.

Fast: Can prepare filling up to 2 days in advance and refrigerate or freeze for up to 3 months. TORTILLA CUPS, Flo Braker's Magic Puff Pastry, or CROUSTADES can be filled up to 3 hours in advance and left at room temperature. Can also be assembled completely and flash frozen for up to 3 months.
Flashy: For a faster version, spread the mixture on tortilla chips.

CURRIED OLIVE & CHEESE

Keep olives on hand and you will be able to whip this up at a moment's notice.

(yields about 3 cups)

1½ cups pitted black olives, minced	½-1 cup parsley, minced
½ cup mayonnaise, homemade or purchased	4 tbsp. green onions, minced, or more to taste
1 cup sharp cheddar cheese, grated	¼-½ tsp. curry powder, or to taste

Mix all ingredients together. Taste and adjust the seasonings.

Fast: Can prepare up to 4 days in advance and refrigerate.
Flashy: Stuff mushrooms or top GARLIC CROUTON ROUNDS, fill Flo Braker's Magic Puff Pastry, TARTLETS or CROUSTADES. Place under a hot broiler until bubbly. For a faster version, spread the mixture on thinly sliced baguettes or pumpernickel squares.
Fabulous: For a Southwestern variation, substitute cilantro for the parsley and cumin for the curry powder.

MEXICAN ALMOND PORK

(yields 2½ cups)

1 cup pork, cooked and minced
½ cup almonds, toasted and
   chopped
1 red onion, minced
1 tsp. garlic, puréed
7 oz. whole green chiles,
   seeded, and deveined (canned)

1 tomato, peeled, seeded,
   and chopped
1½ tbsp. olive oil
¼-½ cup cilantro, minced
salt, white pepper and
   cumin to taste

1. Heat oil in skillet and sauté the onion until tender.
2. Add garlic, cilantro, chiles, pork, tomato, and seasonings. Cook until the flavors develop and stir in the almonds.
3. Fill TORTILLA CUPS, place on a cookie sheet and bake at 350° until hot, about 10 minutes.

Fast: Can prepare the filling up to 2 days in advance and refrigerate, or freeze for up to 3 months. TORTILLA CUPS can be filled up to 3 hours in advance and left at room temperature. Can also be assembled completely and frozen for up to 3 months.

Fabulous: Add sour cream, green onions, chopped olives, and/or grated Jack cheese. Serve on English muffins or rice, in crepes, enchiladas, tacos, pita bread, or mushrooms. Also as a filling for WON TON CUPS.

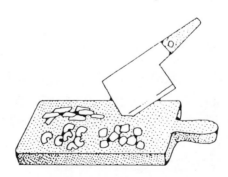

DOUBLE MUSHROOM FILLING

Nirvana for devout mushroom lovers.

(yields about 3 cups)

1 oz. shiitake mushrooms,
   rehydrated, stemmed,
   and chopped
1 lb. mushrooms, minced
¼ cup shallots, minced,
   or more to taste
¼ cup parsley, minced
1 cup heavy cream

½ cup Madeira
2 tbsp. butter
1 tbsp. oil
1 tbsp. cornstarch dissolved
   in 1 tbsp. water (optional)
salt, white pepper, dried
   thyme, and freshly ground
   nutmeg to taste

1. Melt the butter with oil in a skillet and sauté the shallots until tender.
2. Add the mushrooms and sauté until the liquid from the mushrooms evaporates.
3. Add Madeira, parsley, and seasonings. Cook until the liquid reduces by half.
4. Stir in the cream and cook until thickened. Season to taste.
5. Use to fill PHYLLO CUPS, PHYLLO TRIANGLES, CROUSTADES, Flo Braker's Magic Puff Pastry, or TARTLETS. Place on a cookie sheet and bake at 350° until hot, about 10 minutes. If filling PHYLLO TRIANGLES, thicken with the dissolved cornstarch.

Fast: Can prepare the filling up to 2 days in advance and refrigerate, or freeze for up to 3 months. PHYLLO CUPS, PHYLLO TRIANGLES, CROUSTADES, Flo Braker's Magic Puff Pastry or TARTLETS can be filled up to 3 hours in advance and left at room temperature. Can also be assembled completely and flash frozen for up to 3 months.
Fabulous: Add minced seafood, prosciutto, poultry, or veal. Remember, if you are adding the dissolved cornstarch to thicken the mixture, have it boiling before stirring the cornstarch in. Stir it in slowly and add only as much as needed. Delicious served in a chafing dish for large groups. A wonderful sauce for veal, pork, poultry, or pasta.

CAULIFLOWER MORNAY

Well received at winter cocktail parties and as the prelude to formal dinners.

(yields about 1¾ cups)

8 oz. (about 1 cup) fresh
   cauliflower, minced
3 oz. Swiss cheese, grated
½ cup Mornay Sauce
   (recipe follows)

salt, white pepper, and
   freshly grated nutmeg, to taste
BEATEN BISCUITS (see
   recipe)

1. Blanch the cauliflower until just tender.
2. Combine the Mornay Sauce and cauliflower in a bowl. Spread on BEATEN BISCUITS and top with grated cheese.
3. Brown under a hot broiler and serve hot. (May be kept warm in a low oven.)

Mornay Sauce:

(yields about ½ cup)

1 tbsp. butter
1 tbsp. flour
1 shallot, minced
1 tbsp. Dijon-style mustard,
   or more to taste
½ cup hot milk, less 3 tbsp.

3 tbsp. sherry
4 tbsp. Parmesan or Gruyère
   cheese, grated, or more
   to taste
salt, white pepper, and freshly
   grated nutmeg, to taste

1. Melt the butter in a saucepan over low heat and sauté the shallot until soft.
2. Blend in the mustard and flour and cook over low heat for 2 minutes without browning.
3. Slowly stir in the milk and sherry. Whisk while bringing the mixture to a boil. Season and simmer while whisking, until thickened.

4. Reduce the heat to medium. Stir in cheese and cook until melted over low heat.

Fast: Can prepare the filling up to 2 days in advance and refrigerate, or freeze for up to 3 months. Flo Braker's Magic Puff Pastry or CROUSTADES can be filled up to 3 hours in advance and left at room temperature. Can also be assembled completely and flash frozen for up to 3 months.

Flashy: For a faster version, spread the mixture on thinly sliced baguettes or pumpernickel squares.

Fabulous: Substitute broccoli, hearts of palm, spinach, mushrooms, eggplant, etc., for the cauliflower. Excellent on BEATEN BISCUITS, and in CROUSTADES or Flo Braker's Magic Puff Pastry. Top with a bit of caviar for a touch of decadence!

CRAB FILLING

(yields about 2½ cups)

6½ oz. crab meat, frozen, fresh or imitation	¼ cup cream cheese, at room temperature
¼-½ cup pitted black olives, minced	¼-½ cup Jack cheese, grated
2-4 tbsp. green onion, minced	2-4 tbsp. capers
½ cup mayonnaise, homemade or purchased	4 tbsp. parsley, minced
	2 tbsp. fresh dill weed
	salt and white pepper to taste

1. Blend all ingredients together in a food processor fitted with the metal blade. Taste and adjust the seasonings.
2. Fill CROUSTADES, WON TON CUPS, Flo Braker's Magic Puff Pastry or TARTLETS and bake at 350° for 8 to 10 minutes or until puffy and golden.

Fast: Can prepare the filling up to 1 day in advance and refrigerate.

Fabulous: Stuff in raw mushrooms or spread on small, thin pieces of sourdough bread. Bake in 350° oven 8 to 10 minutes, until puffy and golden. Serve warm. Substitute cooked chicken, shrimp, or tuna for the crab.

SPRING MORNAY FILLING

Prepare and freeze large batches during the asparagus season.

(yields about 2½ cups)

½ cup asparagus tips,
  chopped and blanched
1 tsp. garlic, minced
1 6 oz. jar marinated
  artichoke hearts, drained
3 hard-boiled eggs,
  peeled and quartered

3 oz. sharp cheddar cheese,
  grated
¼ cup Mornay Sauce
  (see recipe)
3 tbsp. capers
salt and white pepper
  to taste

1. Combine the eggs, garlic, artichoke hearts, and capers in a food processor fitted with the metal blade; chop coarsely.
2. Transfer the above mixture to a bowl along with the Mornay Sauce, asparagus, garlic, seasonings and cheese. Mix well.
3. Spread on BEATEN BISCUITS or place in CROUSTADES or PHYLLO CUPS and brown under the broiler, **or** heat in a 350° oven.

Fast: Can prepare the filling up to 2 days in advance and refrigerate, or freeze for up to 3 months. PHYLLO CUPS, BEATEN BISCUITS, or CROUSTADES can be filled up to 3 hours in advance and left at room temperature. Can also be assembled completely and flash frozen for up to 3 months.

Flashy: For a faster version, spread the mixture on thinly sliced baguettes or pumpernickel squares.

Fabulous: In crepes or on English muffins for brunches or luncheons and on pasta or rice for dinners. Add crab to the filling. Can also use as a filling for WON TON CUPS.

MEDITERRANEAN CHICKEN

(yields approximately 1½ cups)

1 cooked chicken breast or
   1 cup leftover chicken meat
1 shallot, minced
4-8 tbsp. fresh basil, minced
¼ lb. unsalted butter,
   cut into 8 pieces
2 cloves garlic, minced

6 tbsp. parsley, minced
8 tbsp. mushrooms, minced
8 tbsp. water chestnuts, minced
3 tbsp. olive oil
4 tbsp. prosciutto, minced
2 tbsp. brandy, or more to taste
salt and white pepper to taste

1. Sauté the mushrooms, garlic, and shallot in olive oil until the liquid released from the mushrooms is evaporated. Season with salt and pepper.
2. Combine the chicken and butter in a food processor fitted with the metal blade and process until smooth.
3. Add the remaining ingredients and combine, using care not to destroy the texture. Taste and adjust the seasonings.
4. Top BEATEN BISCUITS or fill CROUSTADES and serve cold.

Fast: Can prepare up to 3 days in advance and refrigerate.
Flashy: For a faster version, serve on thinly sliced baguettes, pumpernickel squares, or crackers.
Fabulous: Substitute walnuts for the water chestnuts. Use to stuff cherry tomatoes, raw mushroom caps, or peapods. Substitute leftover turkey for the chicken.

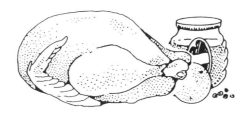

CHAFING DISH ITEMS

The mere reference to a chafing dish brings to mind refined images of days gone by. Many cooks also think stuffy or complicated when they see chafing dish recipes. Neither word need apply. Serving hot hors d'oeuvres in this manner is very practical for large groups and even smaller gatherings. It allows you to keep food warm without constantly running back and forth to kitchen.

There are many beautiful chafing dishes available for purchase, but if your budget demands more creativity and less expense, relax! You can use an inexpensive fondue pot or flame-proof casseroles with sterno, or your barbecue for casual outdoor entertaining. If you are having a large party, I recommend renting a chafing dish. It will not only look wonderful on your table, but it also will hold enough food to accommodate everyone.

Anything that you want to serve hot and that won't crush or crumble, you can put in a chafing dish. Obviously, hot filled pastry items are out, unless you only put one layer in. Sauced items are ideal.

MUSHROOMS IN MADEIRA BLEU CHEESE SAUCE

Sheer bliss!

(yields about 8 servings)

Sauce:

¾ cup Madeira
2 tbsp. shallots, minced
1 cup heavy cream
½ cup beef broth,
   homemade or canned
½ stick butter

2-6 oz. bleu cheese,
   crumbled
1-2 tbsp. Dijon-style mustard
salt, white pepper, dried
   thyme and freshly grated
   nutmeg to taste

1. Boil the Madeira and shallots in a saucepan until liquid reduces to 2 tbsp.
2. Add the cream and broth. Reduce it to 1 cup.
3. Meanwhile, combine the cheese, mustard, and butter in a food processor fitted with the metal blade. Whisk a tbsp. at a time of this mixture into the sauce, until the consistency and flavor is pleasing. You may not wish to use all of it.
4. Simmer for a few minutes.

Mushroom Mixture:

1 lb. mushrooms, washed	3 tbsp. parsley, minced
3-4 shiitake mushrooms, rehydrated, stemmed, and thinly sliced	2 tbsp. butter
	2 tbsp. olive oil
	salt and white pepper
1 tsp. garlic, puréed	to taste

1. Melt butter with the olive oil in a skillet.
2. Add remaining ingredients and sauté until cooked.

Assembly:
1. Place the sauce in a fondue pot, chafing dish or burner-proof casserole.
2. Add the mushroom mixture. Serve with toothpicks and French bread.

Fast: Can prepare any or all elements up to 4 days in advance and refrigerate, or freeze for up to 3 months. Reheat in a 350° oven.
Fabulous: Substitute 1 lb. of scallops or uncooked shrimp for the mushrooms. Serve the cheese and butter mixture as a spread for French bread, pumpernickel squares, or crackers. Use it to season cooked vegetables.

MUSHROOM ESCARGOT

Mushrooms prepared with an escargot-style butter.

(yields about 4 to 8 servings)

1 lb. mushrooms, washed
½-1 cup parsley, minced
4 cloves garlic, minced,
   or more to taste
½ lb. unsalted butter

2 tbsp. brandy
juice of 1 lemon and the
   zest, finely grated
salt and white pepper
   to taste

1. Melt butter in a large skillet and sauté the garlic and parsley with the mushrooms over medium high heat.
2. Season with lemon juice and zest, brandy, salt, and white pepper. Sauté until the mushrooms are just cooked. Taste and adjust the seasonings.

Fast: Can prepare up to 2 days in advance and refrigerate. It's best to slightly undercook it and finish cooking before serving.
flashy: Serve with croutons, French bread, or GARLIC CROUTON ROUNDS.
Fabulous: As a side dish with roast beef, pork, veal, or poultry.

MUSHROOMS MICHELE

The Ultimate!

(yields about 8 servings)

1 lb. fresh mushrooms, washed
⅔ cup ham, minced
4 tbsp. butter
2 tbsp. olive oil
2 cloves garlic, minced
6 tbsp. parsley, minced
1-3 tbsp. shallots, minced
½ tsp. dried thyme leaves

1 tbsp. Dijon-style mustard,
   or to taste
1 cup beef broth, homemade
   or canned
¼ cup bourbon
3 tbsp. heavy cream
salt and white pepper
   to taste

1. Melt butter with the olive oil in large, heavy skillet.
2. Add the garlic and brown the mushrooms in several batches. Transfer to a bowl.
3. Add the ham, shallots, and bourbon to the skillet. Cook until the bourbon is reduced to a glaze.
4. Add the remaining ingredients and cook until the liquid is reduced to a nice thickness and the flavors are developed, about 5 to 10 minutes. Taste and adjust the seasonings.
5. Return mushroom mixture to the sauce and cook over low heat until fully cooked. Transfer to a chafing dish or casserole.

Fast: Can prepare up to 2 days in advance and refrigerate, or freeze for up to 3 months.
Flashy: Serve with toothpicks. Dunk GARLIC CROUTON ROUNDS or sliced baguettes into the sauce.
Fabulous: As a vegetable dish for dinner.

BAGNA CAUDA

One more Italian garlic and anchovy sauce.

(yields about 1½ cups)

1 cup butter	4-6 anchovy filets
4 tbsp. olive oil	¼ cup parsley, minced
4 cloves garlic, minced	zest of 1 lemon, finely grated

1. Heat butter and oil together in a skillet.
2. Add the remaining ingredients and cook over low heat until the anchovies dissolve.

Fast: Can prepare up to 3 days in advance and refrigerate, or freeze for up to 3 months.
Flashy: Serve with raw or cooked vegetables and French bread.
Fabulous: As a dunk for cooked artichoke leaves.

MUSHROOMS, HEARTS OF PALM, & SHRIMP IN A TARRAGON CREAM SAUCE

Absolutely elegant!

(yields about 8 servings)

1 lb. shrimp, raw, medium-sized, and cleaned
½-1 lb. mushrooms, washed (small to medium-sized)
1 can (7-8 oz.) hearts of palm, cut into ¾" lengths
¼ cup shallots, minced
5 tbsp. butter
2 tbsp. parsley, minced
1 tsp. dried tarragon

⅓-½ cup sun-dried tomatoes, minced
¾ cup dry white wine
⅔ cup clam juice, bottled
1⅓ cup heavy cream
1 tbsp. cornstarch
1 tbsp. broth, white wine, or water
lemon or lime juice and zest, finely grated, to taste
salt and white pepper to taste

1. Melt 2 tbsp. of butter in a heavy skillet and sauté the mushrooms. Season with salt, white pepper, and minced shallots. When cooked, remove to an ovenproof dish and keep warm.

2. Add 3 tbsp. of butter and the shrimp. Sauté briefly until the shrimp are almost fully cooked. Remove them to the dish with the mushrooms.

3. Add the sun-dried tomatoes, tarragon, wine, lemon or lime juice, zest, and clam juice. Bring to boil and reduce by one-third.

4. Add the cream and reduce by half. Taste and adjust the seasonings.

5. Dissolve the cornstarch in broth, white wine, or water.

6. Bring the sauce to a boil and slowly stir in the cornstarch mixture, until the proper consistency is reached. (This will stabilize the sauce and prevent it from separating.)

7. Add the hearts of palm, shrimp, and mushrooms to the sauce. Simmer until the shrimp are fully cooked, being careful not to overcook them.

8. Transfer this to an oven-proof serving dish or chafing dish and serve with toothpicks or on small hors d'oeuvre plates with forks.

Fast: Can prepare the sauce up to 3 days in advance and refrigerate, or freeze for up to 3 months. Or prepare the complete dish up to 1 day in advance, bring to room temperature, and warm in a 350° oven.

Fabulous: Cut ingredients into smaller pieces and fill Flo Braker's Magic Puff Pastry, TARTLETS, or CROUSTADES.

GARLIC ANCHOVY SAUCE

Beware, all vampires!

(yields about 1½ cups)

2 cloves garlic, minced, or more to taste

2 anchovy filets, rinsed and mashed, or more to taste

1 tbsp. shallots, minced

2 tbsp. butter

2 tbsp. flour

1 cup chicken broth, homemade or canned

¼ cup dry vermouth

1 tbsp. fresh basil, puréed, or 1 tsp. dried

1 tbsp. parsley, minced

salt, white pepper, and lemon juice to taste

1. Melt butter in a saucepan and sauté garlic and shallots briefly; do not brown.
2. Stir in the flour and cook over low heat for a minute more, without browning.
3. Remove the pan from the burner and stir in the broth and vermouth. Return to the burner and cook until thickened, while stirring.
4. Stir in the remaining ingredients. Taste and adjust the seasonings. Simmer for about 5 minutes.

Fast: Can prepare up to 4 days in advance and refrigerate, or freeze for up to 3 months.

Flashy: Dunk FRIED CAMEMBERT. Serve in chafing dish and dunk seafood, bite-size pieces of poultry, veal, or mushrooms.

Fabulous: Over pork, poultry, beef, or veal as an entrée sauce.

PORK & MUSHROOMS MERLOT

A robust cold-weather dish.

1 lb. pork, cut into ½" cubes
½-1 lb. mushrooms, washed
2 cups beef broth, homemade
   or canned
⅔ cup plus 1 tbsp. Merlot
   wine
4 tbsp. butter
2 tbsp. olive oil
1 tbsp. Dijon-style mustard
2 large shallots, minced

1 tsp. dried rosemary,
   crushed, or more to taste
½ tsp. dried thyme leaves,
   crushed
2 tbsp. parsley, minced
2 tbsp. flour
1-2 cloves garlic, minced
1 tbsp. cornstarch
¼-½ cup cup heavy cream,
   optional

Pork marinade (optional):

2 tbsp. olive oil
⅓ cups Merlot wine
2 cloves garlic, minced
2 tbsp. parsley, minced

1-2 tbsp. dried rosemary,
   crushed
½-1 tsp. dried thyme
2 green onions, minced
1 egg

1. For added flavor, marinate the pork. Combine all the marinade ingredients with the pork cubes. Allow them to sit at room temperature for up to 2 hours, or refrigerate for up to 48 hours.

2. Remove the pork from the marinade and coat with the flour, using as much as necessary.

3. In a skillet or wok, melt butter with olive oil and brown the pork in batches. Do not fully cook! Add more butter and oil as needed. Remove the browned pork and set aside.

4. Add mushrooms to the skillet and quickly brown them in 2 tbsp. of butter.

5. Add the beef broth, ⅔ cup of Merlot wine, parsley, mustard, shallots,

garlic, and herbs. Bring this to a boil and cook, stirring, until the flavors develop fully.

6. Dissolve the cornstarch in 1 tbsp. of Merlot.

7. Slowly stir this mixture into the boiling sauce. Stir in the cream, if desired.

8. Return the pork to the sauce. Cook over low heat until the pork is barely pink. Taste and adjust the seasonings.

Fast: Can prepare up to 2 days in advance through step 7 and refrigerate, or freeze for up to 3 months.

Fabulous: Substitute different varieties of mushrooms. Serve over rice or pasta as an entree.

CRISPY COCKTAIL RIBS

Make plenty—they will disappear like popcorn!

2½ lb. spareribs (have butcher cut them into 2″ lengths)
cornstarch
salt and pepper to taste

1. Preheat the oven to 425°.

2. Wash and trim the ribs. Blot off excess moisture with paper towels.

3. Place the ribs in large bowl and season them with salt and pepper. Then coat them lightly with cornstarch and shake off excess.

4. Place the ribs on a cookie sheet and bake in a 425° oven for about 20 minutes, or until fully cooked and crisp.

Fast: Can prepare through step 3 up to 1 hour before serving and leave at room temperature.

Flashy: Serve with any combination of Oriental sauces in Chapter 1, especially the Sweet & Sour-style sauces.

Fabulous: Marinate the ribs up to 2 days ahead with your sauce of choice for added flavor. Delicious deep-fat fried!

CHINESE SKEWERED BITES

Let your guests get into the act by cooking their own while having cocktails outside.

(serves 4 to 6)

Marinade:

1 cup dry red wine

½ cup soy sauce

2 tbsp. plum sauce, or
more to taste

2 tbsp. sesame oil

1 tsp. garlic, puréed

½ cup green onions, minced

¼-½ tsp. dried thyme

2 tbsp. sesame seeds,
toasted

1 pkg. bamboo skewers,
soaked in water

Meat:

1 lb. pork, beef, chicken, or turkey, cut into bite-size pieces

1. Combine all the marinade ingredients and place in saucepan. Bring to boil; reduce the heat and simmer until the flavors develop. Cool.
2. Place the cut-up meat in bowl and pour the marinade over. Let this sit for 1 hour or refrigerate for up to 2 days.
3. Skewer the meat. While broiling or barbecuing the meat, boil the marinade for about 10 minutes, so it can be used as a sauce.
4. Place SKEWERED BITES in a chafing dish with the marinade and serve.

Fast: Can marinate up to 2 days in advance and refrigerate, or freeze for up to 1 month. The marinade can be prepared up to 3 months in advance and refrigerated.

Fabulous: Add chopped dried prunes or apricots to the marinade for a flavor surprise. Embellish the sauce made from the marinade by adding Dijon-style mustard and heavy cream at step 3.

RATATOUILLE NICOISE

Created for all those gardeners with more vegetables than ideas for what to do with them.

(yields about 8 to 12 servings)

3 cups onions, minced
2-3 tomatoes, peeled, seeded, and chopped
3-4 medium-sized zucchini, peeled and chopped
1 eggplant, peeled and chopped
3 red or green peppers, seeded and chopped
1 6-oz. jar marinated artichoke hearts, drained and minced
½ cup olive oil

3 cloves garlic, minced, or more to taste
1 bunch parsley, minced
½ cup Italian or Greek olives, minced
¼-½ cup Parmesan cheese, grated
1 cup mozzarella cheese, grated
¼ tsp. dried thyme
¼ tsp. dried rosemary, crumbled
1 bay leaf
salt and white pepper to taste

1. Sauté the onions and garlic in olive oil over low heat until softened.
2. Add all remaining ingredients, except for the cheeses. Simmer, covered, until the vegetables reach the desired degree of tenderness.
3. Stir in the cheeses. Taste and adjust the seasonings. Cook gently until the cheese melts.
4. Serve in a chafing dish with GARLIC CROUTON ROUNDS, PITA CHIPS, or thinly sliced bread.

Fast: Can prepare up to 4 days in advance and refrigerate, or freeze for up to 6 months.
Fabulous: Hot or cold over pasta, couscous, bulghur, or rice. Makes a wonderful crepe filling.

CHILEQUILES APPETIZERS

Fun and casual—perfectly suited for large groups.

1 3-lb. chicken
tortilla chips
10 oz. tomatillos, husked
  and minced
3 cloves garlic, minced
7 oz. green chiles, seeded,
  deveined, and minced (canned)
1 onion, quartered

2 tbsp. olive oil
1½ cups sharp cheddar
  cheese, grated
1½ cups sour cream
1 can pitted black olives, sliced
cilantro, minced, to taste
green onions, minced, to taste
½-1 tsp. cumin
salt and pepper to taste

1. Place the chicken in roasting pan. Rub it with oil, salt, and garlic. Put the quartered onion, salt, and cumin inside the chicken. Bake at 400° for 45 minutes to 1 hour.
2. Remove the chicken and cool; then shred it.
3. Combine the chicken with all the remaining ingredients. Taste and adjust the seasonings.
4. Place this mixture in an oven-proof casserole or chafing dish and bake at 350° until hot and bubbly, about 5 minutes. Serve in chafing dish with tortilla chips for dunking.

Fast: Can prepare up to 2 days in advance and refrigerate.
Fabulous: Add chili powder or salsa. Substitute pork for the chicken or use up your leftover turkey. Fill TORTILLA CUPS.

ALMOND MUSTARD DUNK

A creamy, crunchy delight.

2 tbsp. Dijon-style mustard
3 oz. blanched almonds,
  slivered and lightly toasted
  (about ⅔ cup)
2 tbsp. butter
¼-½ cup heavy cream

2 cups chicken broth,
  homemade or canned
6 tbsp. dry white wine
  or dry vermouth
2 tbsp. sherry
3 tbsp. shallots, minced
salt and white pepper to taste

1. Melt butter in a saucepan and sauté the shallots until tender.
2. Stir in the wine and reduce until it forms a glaze, for about 2 minutes.
3. Add the broth and reduce it by half.
4. Stir in all the remaining ingredients and bring to a boil. Taste and adjust the seasonings.

Fast: Can prepare up to 1 week in advance and refrigerate, or freeze for up to 6 months.
Flashy: Serve in a chafing dish and dunk cooked cauliflower, pork, or seafood.
Fabulous: With pork, poultry, beef, or veal for an entree sauce.

CHINESE BLACK BEAN DUNK

A pungent Oriental delicacy.

½ lb. pork, ground
2 tbsp. fermented black beans
2 tbsp. ginger root, minced,
  or to taste
2 cloves garlic, chopped,
  or to taste
2 tbsp. peanut oil
2 green onions, cut into
  1" lengths

1 egg, slightly beaten
2 tbsp. sherry
1 cup chicken broth,
  homemade or canned
1 tbsp. cornstarch
1 tbsp. broth, white
  wine, or water
white pepper to taste
pinch of sugar

1. Chop the ginger, garlic, and beans together in a food processor fitted with the metal blade.
2. Fry the pork in a wok; remove and, drain on paper towels.
3. Add 2 tbsp. oil to the wok and sauté the bean mixture, being careful not to burn it. Add the pork and broth and bring it to a boil.
4. Stir in the egg. Add the green onions.
5. Dissolve the cornstarch in the broth, white wine, or water and add it, along with the sherry, to the wok. Cook until thickened. Taste and adjust the seasonings.

Fast: Can prepare up to 3 days in advance and refrigerate, or freeze for up to 3 months.
Flashy: Serve in chafing dish as a dunk for small pieces of pork, chicken, shrimp or CRISPY COCKTAIL RIBS.

FRIJOLES CALIENTES

Hot and spicy bean dunk.

3 cups refried beans,
   homemade or purchased
2 cups Jack cheese, grated
½ pt. sour cream, or more
   to taste
1 bunch green onions, minced
3 cloves garlic, minced

1 bunch cilantro, minced
4-10 whole green chiles,
   seeded, deveined, and
   chopped (canned)
cumin, salt, and chili
   powder to taste

1. Combine all ingredients in an ovenproof casserole or chafing dish.
2. Bake at 350° until hot and bubbly.

Fast: Can prepare up to 1 day in advance and refrigerate, or freeze for up to 6 months.
Flashy: Serve with tortilla chips (homemade or purchased).

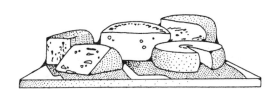

FONDUES

Just like certain songs, certain foods or groups of food create nostalgia. Fondues instantly take me back to my college days. I used them for hors d'oeuvres, entrees, and desserts. They always produced fun, casual parties. This section covers the hors d'oeuvre variety (many of which could be turned into entrees), but you haven't lived until you have tried a chocolate fondue served with fresh fruit for dipping. Fondues are the perfect cold weather hors d'oeuvre served in front of a roaring fire.

You will find that they are instant ice-breakers and create an atmosphere of warmth and intimacy; after all, you're sharing the same pot! As for their versatility—just by changing the kind of cheese, wine, or herbs used, you can create a new dish.

MADEIRA JACK FONDUE

(yields about 3 cups)

1 lb. Jack cheese, grated
3 tbsp. Madeira
2 cups dry white wine

1-2 cloves garlic, minced
1 tbsp. cornstarch
white pepper and freshly
grated nutmeg to taste

1. Toss the cornstarch and cheese together in a bowl.
2. Place the white wine in heavy saucepan along with the garlic. When the wine almost boils, reduce the heat and stir in the cheese. Stir constantly until the cheese melts, but do not boil.
3. Stir in Madeira and remaining seasonings.
4. When thickened, transfer to heavy, heat-proof casserole or fondue dish. Keep warm over an alcohol lamp or fondue warmer. Use 1" cubes of French bread for dunking.

Fast: Can prepare up to 3 days in advance and refrigerate or freeze for up to 3 months. Reheat in a double boiler before serving.
Flashy: Dunk rye, black, or sourdough bread cubes. Also dunk blanched vegetables, especially boiled baby potatoes or baby artichokes.

Fabulous: Use ½ Jack and ½ shallot Jack, Jack and/or cheddar and green chiles, or cheddar and browned onions.

SWISS HAM FONDUE

Have this ready and waiting for the gang when they come in from the slopes.

(yields about 3½ cups)

1 lb. Swiss, Gruyère, or
   Emmenthaler cheese, shredded
⅓ lb. ham, cut into
   bite-size pieces
⅓-⅔ cup dry white wine
⅔ cup heavy cream

1 tbsp. shallots, minced
1 tsp. Dijon-style mustard
1 tbsp. cornstarch
salt, white pepper, and
   freshly grated nutmeg to taste

1. Combine the cornstarch and cheese in bowl.
2. Bring the cream, shallots, mustard, and wine to a boil in a heavy saucepan.
3. Reduce the heat and slowly stir in the cheese. Add the ham and stir over medium-low heat until cheese mixture melts. Taste and adjust the seasonings.

Fast: Can prepare up to 3 days in advance and refrigerate, or freeze for up to 3 months.
Flashy: Dunk French bread cubes, blanched asparagus, cauliflower or broccoli flowerets, cooked artichoke leaves, or shrimp.
Fabulous: As a sauce for vegetable dishes, pasta, chicken, or veal.

CHILE CHEESE FONDUE

A Mexican twist to a classic Swiss dish.

(yields about 4 cups)

⅔ cup green chiles, seeded, deveined, and chopped (canned)
2 cups Jack cheese, grated
1 tbsp. cornstarch
1 cup heavy cream
⅓ cup dry sherry
1 tsp. dried oregano
½ cup green olives, minced
½ cup pitted black olives, minced
1 tbsp. cumin
6 tbsp. cilantro, minced
2 cloves garlic, minced
salt and white pepper to taste

1. Mix the cornstarch and cheese together in a bowl.
2. Combine all the ingredients, except for the cheese, in a saucepan. Bring to a boil.
3. Reduce the heat and slowly stir in the cheese. Taste and adjust the seasonings. Serve when the cheese has melted.

Fast: Can prepare up to 3 days in advance and refrigerate, or freeze for up to 3 months. Reheat in a double boiler before serving.
Flashy: Serve with warm tortillas or tortilla chips. Dunk boiled baby potatoes or zucchini.
Fabulous: Served with Dry Creek Vineyard Zinfandel.

FAST & FLASHY BAKED CHEESE

If you can slice cheese, you can prepare this.

(yields about 6 servings)

12-18 oz. cheese (cheddar or Jack)

1. Preheat the oven to 450°.
2. Slice cheese thinly. Place in 2 layers in shallow, oven-proof dish or cast iron skillet.

3. Bake until melted. Watch carefully.
4. Mix and match toppings of choice.

Toppings:

green chiles, seeded, deveined, and minced (canned)

cilantro, minced

green onions, minced

pitted black olives, sliced

almonds, toasted, and chopped

salsa

cooked baby shrimp

ham, minced

tomatoes, raw and minced

Fast: Can prepare the toppings up to 1 day in advance and refrigerate.
Flashy: Serve the toppings in separate bowls and let guests make their own. Serve with warm tortillas, tortilla chips, or TORTILLA CUPS. For summer barbecues, cook in skillet on the grill, instead of in the oven.
Fabulous: Substitute mozzarella for Jack or cheddar and serve with minced anchovies, pesto, walnuts sautéed in olive oil and garlic, roasted red or green peppers, marinated artichoke hearts, and minced, sun-dried tomatoes, for an Italian version.

HERB CREAM FONDUE

(yields about 3 cups)

2 cups Jack cheese, grated

½ cup chicken broth, homemade or canned

¼ cup dry white wine or dry vermouth

½ cup heavy cream

¼ cup butter

1 cup mushrooms, minced

¼ cup shallots, minced

1 tsp. garlic, minced

2 tsp. flour

¼ tsp. dried oregano

¼ tsp. dried basil

pinch of dried thyme

1 tbsp. capers

2 tbsp. parsley, minced

zest of 1 lemon, finely grated

salt, white pepper and lemon juice to taste

1. Melt the butter in a saucepan and sauté the mushrooms, shallots, and garlic over medium heat for 2 to 3 minutes, until the ingredients are soft.

2. Blend in the flour and stir in all of the remaining ingredients, except the cheese. Stir until the sauce thickens and the flavors develop. If it is too thick, thin with cream, wine, or chicken broth.

3. Reduce the heat, stir in cheese, and cook gently until the cheese melts.

Fast: Can prepare up to 3 days in advance and refrigerate, or freeze for up to 4 months.

Flashy Dunk cubes of French bread, cooked vegetables, or cooked seafood pieces.

Fabulous: As a sauce for grilled or poached fish or poultry.

SHRIMP & BOURSIN FONDUE

Quick, with a French accent!

(yields about 3 cups)

1 lb. bay shrimp, cooked	2 tbsp. flour
1 4-oz. container French-style spiced cheese	2 tbsp. butter
	1 tsp. shallots, minced
½ cup heavy cream	salt and white pepper
½ cup dry vermouth	to taste

1. Melt the butter in a saucepan and add the shallots. Sauté for a few minutes.

2. Remove the saucepan from the burner and whisk in the flour. Return it to the burner and cook for a minute.

3. Whisk in the vermouth.

4. Cook until thickened, whisking continuously.

5. Whisk in the cream, shrimp, and cheese. Cook until the cheese melts and the mixture is nicely thickened. Do not allow it to boil.

6. Taste and adjust the seasonings.

Fast: Can prepare up to 2 days in advance and refrigerate, or freeze for up to 4 months.
Flashy: Dunk sourdough bread cubes, BAGEL CHIPS, or PITA CHIPS.
Fabulous: As a sauce for pasta, fish, veal, or poultry. Substitute crabmeat or imitation crabmeat for the shrimp.

CRAB & BRIE FONDUE

Upscaled!

(yields about 5 cups)

8 oz. fresh or frozen crabmeat (imitation crab can be used)	2 tbsp. shallots, minced
	1 tsp. Dijon-style mustard
	1 tbsp. cornstarch
1 lb. brie cheese, rind removed and cut into small chunks	salt, white pepper, and freshly grated nutmeg to taste
2 cups dry white wine	

1. Mix the brie and cornstarch together in a bowl.
2. Bring the wine, mustard, and shallots to a boil in a saucepan. Allow it to boil for about 5 minutes.
3. Reduce the heat to medium high and slowly stir in the cheese and crab. Stir for about 5 minutes, until the flavors develop and the alcohol cooks away.
4. Taste and adjust the seasonings.

Fast: Can prepare up to 2 days in advance and refrigerate, or freeze for up to 3 months.
Flashy: Dunk sourdough bread cubes.
Fabulous: As a sauce over broccoli, asparagus, chicken breasts, or fish. Season with either ½ tsp. dried, crushed tarragon or 2-4 minced green chiles. Served with David S. Stare Estate Bottled Chardonnay.

PARMESAN BECHAMEL FONDUE

(yields about 3 cups)

½ cup Parmesan cheese,
  freshly grated
1½ cups milk
¼ cup dry white wine or
  dry vermouth
½ cup Madeira or sherry
2 tbsp. butter

3 tbsp. flour
5 sprigs parsley
1 tsp. shallots, minced
½-1 bay leaf
¼ tsp. dried thyme
salt, white pepper, and freshly
  grated nutmeg to taste

1. Melt the butter in a saucepan and sauté the shallots until tender. Whisk in the flour and cook over low heat for 1 minute.

2. Remove the saucepan from the burner and whisk in the milk. Return it to the burner and add the thyme, parsley, and bay leaf. Bring to a boil while whisking.

3. Add the wine and remaining ingredients. Simmer for 5 minutes or until the flavors develop.

4. Remove and discard parsley and bay leaf. Taste and adjust the seasonings.

Fast: Can prepare up to 3 days in advance and refrigerate, or freeze for up to 3 months.

Flashy: Dunk cooked vegetables, French bread cubes, seafood, or poultry.

Fabulous: Add clams or mussels, or mix with cooked spinach, eggplant, artichoke hearts, seafood, chicken, or ham and fill TARTLETS, Flo Braker's Magic Puff Pastry, CROUSTADES, crepes, or mushrooms.

CHAPTER FOUR

FORMS

*N*ot a design course, forms refers to interestingly seasoned mixtures that are formed. The items covered include: meatballs, patés and terrines, mousses, molds, tortas, puffs, fried hors d'oeuvres, frittatas, and flans. Most of these items are extremely well-suited to large events, while they range in character from sublimely elegant to warm, homey, and unpretentious.

MEATBALLS

Meatballs! There has to be a better way to refer to this sort of hors d'oeuvre. Not only is the name bad but the meatball has acquired a tarnished reputation. I imagine that's because of all those unimaginatively catered parties that included meatballs consisting mainly of fillers, floating in puddles of tasteless sauce. You know the sauce—catsup and heaven only knows what else. No wonder the meatball has become so disgraced. Several years ago, I did a live television spot in a viewer's kitchen where she prepared her favorite hors d'oeuvre, meatballs in a catsup, grape jelly, and dehydrated parsley sauce. Need I say more?

The following recipes will show you that meatballs have been given a bum rap. Give them a chance!

ALBONDIGAS

Mexican meatballs.

(yields about 20 meatballs)

Meatballs:

½ cup rice, cooked
1 lb. ground, lean pork
4 green onions, chopped
½ onion, chopped

½ cup cilantro, minced
3 tbsp. dried oregano
salt, cumin, and chili
powder to taste

1. Combine all ingredients and mix well.
2. Shape the mixture into small meatballs and brown them in a skillet or under the broiler.
3. Add meatballs to the sauce (recipe follows) and simmer for about 20 minutes.

Sauce:

2 tbsp. butter
1 carrot, chopped
1 onion, chopped
2 cloves garlic, chopped
2 cups tomatoes (canned)
salsa, to taste (homemade
   or canned)
¼ cup dry vermouth

2 cups chicken broth,
   homemade or canned
2 tbsp. cumin
4 tbsp. cilantro, chopped,
   or more to taste
juice of 1 lemon
chili powder and dried
   oregano to taste
salt and white pepper to taste

1. Sauté the onions and carrots in butter until tender.
2. Add the remaining ingredients. Bring to a boil and simmer for at least 30 minutes. Taste and adjust the seasonings.
3. When the sauce is cool, purée it in a blender or in a food processor fitted with the metal blade.

Fast: Can assemble, but do not simmer, up to 2 days in advance and refrigerate, or freeze for up to 4 months. Simmer before serving.
Fabulous: On rice or pasta as an entree, with 1 cup of sour cream added to the finished sauce.

ITALIAN VEAL, MOZZARELLA & ANCHOVY BALLS

(yields about 30 meatballs)

1½ lb. lean veal, ground
6 Italian tomatoes, canned, opened flat, seeded, and the juice drained
½ to 1 cup mozzarella cheese, grated
12 anchovy filets
1 piece sourdough bread, torn into pieces
3 tbsp. milk

½ cup parsley, minced
2 cloves garlic, or more to taste
1 egg
¾ cup fine cracker crumbs, spread on a dinner plate
olive oil
1 tsp. dried oregano, or more to taste
salt and white pepper to taste

1. Preheat the oven to 400°.
2. Soak the bread in the milk in a small bowl.
3. Put the meat in a food processor fitted with the metal blade and add the remaining ingredients, except for the cracker crumbs.
4. Shape the mixture into 1″ balls.
5. Roll the balls in cracker crumbs to coat them.
6. Place the balls on a greased cookie sheet and liberally drizzle olive oil over them. Bake at 400° until golden. Avoid overcooking; they should still be slightly pink inside.

Fast: Can prepare through step 5 up to a day in advance and refrigerate, or flash freeze for up to 3 months. It is not necessary to defrost before cooking.
Flashy: Serve alone or with any Italian-style dunk in Chapter 1.
Fabulous: Substitute beef or pork for the veal.

TURKEY HAM SPHERES

(yields about 60 meatballs)

1½ lb. turkey, ground
1½ lb. pork, ground
½ lb. ham, ground
1½ cups soft sourdough
  breadcrumbs
¾ cup heavy cream
1 onion, minced
2 tbsp. butter

6 tbsp. parsley, minced
2-4 cloves garlic, minced
1 tbsp. Dijon-style mustard,
  or more to taste
zest of 1 lemon, finely grated
flour for dusting
salt, white pepper, and
  dried thyme to taste

1. Combine all ingredients, except for the flour. Fry one tsp. of the mixture to check the seasonings.
2. Shape the mixture into small balls and coat with flour.
3. Place on a greased cookie sheet. Broil or bake at 400° until fully cooked.

Fast: Can prepare through step 2 up to 1 day in advance and refrigerate, or flash freeze for up to 3 months. Cook before serving.
Flashy: Dunk in COLD LEMON TARRAGON SAUCE, DILL CREAM SAUCE, or DIJON SAUCE.
Fabulous: Substitute leftover rice for the breadcrumbs.

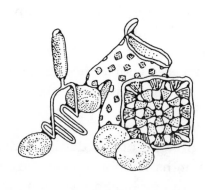

HAM MEATBALLS

(yields about 32 meatballs)

½ lb. smoked ham, finely ground

1 lb. fresh, lean pork, finely ground

1 cup sourdough breadcrumbs

3 tbsp. milk

2 tbsp. dried dill weed, or more to taste

½ tsp. caraway seeds

¼-½ cup green onions, minced

4 tbsp. parsley, minced

2 cloves garlic, minced

1 tbsp. Dijon-style mustard

2 tbsp. butter

1 egg, lightly beaten

2 tbsp. peanut oil

½ cup red wine

¼ cup brandy

salt, white pepper, and freshly ground nutmeg to taste

1. Preheat the oven to 400°.
2. Soak the crumbs in milk for 5 minutes.
3. Combine the ground meats with the soaked crumbs in a food processor fitted with the metal blade. Add all the seasonings and the egg. Mix well.
4. Form into 1" balls and chill for at least ½ hour.
5. Melt butter with the oil in a skillet over high heat. Add the meatballs to the skillet and toss them in the butter mixture until well coated.
6. Transfer the balls to a baking dish or jelly roll pan. Bake at 400° for about 10 minutes, or until well browned. Shake the pan periodically to rotate the meatballs.
7. Add the wine and brandy to the skillet. Reduce it by half and pour it over the balls. Cover tightly with foil, lower oven temperature to 350°, and bake for about 20 minutes. Serve in chafing dish with toothpicks.

Fast: Can prepare through step 6 up to 2 days in advance and refrigerate, or flash freeze for up to 3 months. Bring to room temperature before finishing.

Fabulous: Add 1 tsp. Dijon-style mustard and ¼ cup heavy cream to the sauce.

PEARL CHUTNEY BALLS

(yields about 36 meatballs)

1 lb. ground round	2-4 green onions, minced
½ lb. ground pork	4 tbsp. cilantro, minced
¼ cup soy sauce	¼ tsp. dried ginger,
⅔ cup mango chutney	or more to taste
2 tbsp. sherry	1 cup sweet rice*
1 egg	salt and white pepper to taste

1. Cover the rice with cold water to cover and soak for 4 hours. Drain.
2. Combine all the ingredients, except for the sweet rice, in a food processor fitted with the metal blade. Fry 1 tsp. of the mixture to check the seasonings.
3. Shape the mixture into 1″ balls and coat them with the drained rice.
4. Place the balls in a steamer and steam for 30 minutes.

Fast: Can prepare through step 3 up to 1 day in advance, or flash freeze for up to 3 months.
Flashy: Serve with any Chinese-style dunk from Chapter 1.
Fabulous: Served with Gloria Ferrer Brut Sparkling Wine.

*See Helpful Terms section for an explanation of sweet rice.

SKEWERED GROUND LAMB SAUSAGES

Let guests grill their own.

(yields about 30 sausages)

2 lb. ground lamb	1 tbsp. Dijon-style mustard
2 eggs	zest of 2 lemons, finely
2-4 cloves garlic	grated
1 large onion	freshly ground black pepper
¼ cup parsley, minced	to taste
¼ cup cilantro, minced	2 tsp. salt, or more to taste

fresh mint leaves, minced,
   to taste
2 tbsp. butter
1 tbsp. sweet Hungarian paprika

bamboo skewers, soaked in
   water, to prevent burning
Cold Yogurt Sauce (recipe
   follows)

1. Chop the onion and garlic in a food processor fitted with the metal blade.
2. Add all the remaining ingredients, except for the butter and paprika. Process until well combined.
3. Fry 1 tsp. of mixture to check the seasonings.
4. Shape the mixture into 1½" sausages. Let them stand at room temperature 1 hour or refrigerate overnight.
5. Skewer the sausages. Melt the butter with the paprika and brush on the sausages.
6. Broil or barbecue the sausages and serve with Yogurt Sauce.

Cold Yogurt Sauce:
2 cups yogurt
2 cloves garlic, peeled
2 tbsp. fresh mint, minced,
   or 1½ tsp. dried
2-4 green onions

¼ cup parsley, minced
¼-½ tsp. fenugreek
1 tsp. salt, or to taste
white pepper and lemon
   juice to taste

1. Process all ingredients in a food processor fitted with the metal blade.
2. Taste and adjust the seasonings.

Fast: Can prepare through step 5 up to 2 days in advance and refrigerate, or flash freeze for up to 3 months. Can prepare the sauce up to 4 days in advance and refrigerate.
Flashy: Serve with quartered pita breads surrounded by bowls of chopped fresh tomato, chopped imported olives, crumbled feta cheese, lemon wedges, minced green onions, fresh mint, and minced cilantro.
Fabulous: Substitute beef or pork for all or part of the lamb.

EASTERN-STYLE GARBANZO BALLS

Unusual, delicious and healthy!

(yields about 20 balls)

1½ cup garbanzo beans, cooked
1 cup bulghur
1 cup walnuts, toasted
1 onion
2-4 cloves garlic
1-2 carrots, peeled
½ cup cilantro, minced
½ cup green onions, minced
¼-½ cup parsley, minced

¼ cup plum sauce, or more to taste
¼ cup pickled ginger, minced, or more to taste
½ cup Chinese barbecued pork or cooked Chinese sausages, minced
1 egg, slightly beaten
peanut oil
cornmeal

1. Soak the bulghur in hot water for about 20 minutes, or until softened. Drain.
2. Mince the onion, garlic and carrots, in a food processor fitted with the metal blade. Transfer to a skillet and sauté in 2 tbsp. of oil. Cook until golden. Set aside.
3. Combine the egg, ginger, bulghur, green onions, plum sauce, cilantro, parsley, garbanzo beans, and walnuts in a food processor fitted with the metal blade, until well blended.
4. Process in the pork or sausage and the onion mixture, being careful not to destroy the texture. For added texture, add more nuts.
5. Place the mixture in the freezer until well-chilled, for about 30 minutes. Shape into small balls and roll in the cornmeal.
6. Can be oven or pan-fried. To oven-fry, coat with the oil and bake on a baking sheet at 425° for 10 minutes, or until crisp. To pan-fry, heat some oil in skillet and fry until crisp.

Fast: Can prepare through step 4 up to 1 day in advance and refrigerate, or assemble and flash freeze for up to 3 months.
Flashy: Serve with PLUM MAYONNAISE.

INDIAN-STYLE GROUND LAMB SAUSAGES

(yields about 20 sausages)

1 lb. ground lamb
1 cup onions, minced
¼ cup flour
¼ cup almonds, blanched
2 tbsp. pickled ginger,
   minced
2 tsp. curry powder, or to taste
¼ cup cilantro, minced

¼ cup parsley, minced
4 tbsp. lemon juice
2 tbsp. yogurt
zest of 1-2 oranges, finely grated
2 tsp. salt
freshly ground pepper to taste
bamboo skewers, soaked in
   water to prevent burning

1. Grind the almonds in a food processor fitted with the metal blade. Add the remaining ingredients and process well. Allow the mixture to sit for 30 minutes.

2. Form the mixture into sausage shapes and skewer.

3. Broil under a hot broiler or over white-hot coals until browned on the outside and slightly pink on the inside.

Fast: Can prepare through step 2 up to a day in advance and refrigerate, or flash freeze for up to 3 months.

Flashy: Dunk in CURRY SAUCE, PICKLED MANGO SAUCE, or CHINESE PAPAYA SAUCE.

Fabulous: Substitute pork or turkey for all or part of the lamb.

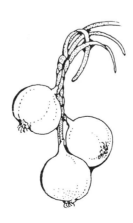

PECAN-CHICKEN BALLS

A great way to use up leftover chicken.

(yields about 24)

1 cup pecans, finely chopped
1 cup chicken, cooked and ground
8 oz. cream cheese or chevre

curry powder, salt, white
pepper, chutney, capers,
chopped green onions, minced
cilantro, mustard to taste
(any or all)

1. Combine all ingredients, except the pecans, in a food processor fitted with the metal blade. Taste and adjust the seasonings. Chill.
2. Form into balls and roll in pecans to coat them. Serve chilled.

Fast: Can prepare in up to 3 days advance and refrigerate.
Fabulous: Substitute minced green onions, cilantro, or coconut for the pecans. Substitute any leftovers, especially fish or pork, for the chicken.

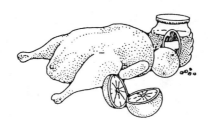

SKEWERED BARBECUED CHEESE

This isn't a meatball, but it just seemed to belong here!

(yields about 4 servings)

12-14 oz. Jack cheese, cut
   into 1 to 1½″ chunks
½ cup olive oil
2-4 cloves garlic, minced
1 12-14″ loaf sourdough
   bread, crusts removed,
   cut into 1″ cubes

¼ cup fresh basil, or
   herb of your choice, minced,
   or 1 tbsp. dried
mild pickled peppers
   to taste
bamboo skewers, soaked in
   water to prevent burning

1. Combine the garlic, olive oil, and herbs in a small bowl and let sit for at least 1 hour.
2. Skewer the bread, cheese, and peppers. String them close together, beginning and ending with bread.
3. Brush all the ingredients with the oil.
4. Broil or barbecue until the bread toasts and the cheese softens, about 1-2 minutes. Serve on cocktail plates.

Fast: Can prepare through step 3 up to 2 days in advance and refrigerate.
Fabulous: Substitute mozzarella, cheddar, or Gruyère for the Jack. Add slices of salami, Canadian bacon, or prosciutto to the skewers.

PATÉS AND TERRINES

Whether planning a picnic with panache or a more elegant cocktail party, a paté or a terrine will fit the occasion. They provide rich and interesting blends of flavor and texture. Too often, these two categories are intimidating. Relax, they are just simple mixtures, and can be viewed as glamorous meatloaves. Patés and terrines are convenient for the cook as they can be refrigerated for several days or prepared up to six months in advance and frozen. You can make huge quantities to serve an army or make them up in very small batches. You will be thrilled by the savings from preparing your own, rather than purchasing them.

Please allow me to put another fear to rest: Patés and terrines are not all made from liver. They can be made from vegetables, pork, veal, poultry, liver, or seafood.

The difference between a paté and terrine is fuzzy. Traditionally, a terrine is cooked in an earthenware mold (from *terre*, the French word for earth). It is loaf-shaped and consists of chopped or puréed meat, seafood, and/or vegetables bound with eggs, heavy cream, and/or fat and seasonings. It may also consist of some strips or chunks of ingredients to provide a contrast in texture.

Technically, patés are meant to be enclosed in pastry and baked. However, patés have come to stand for any well-seasoned, minced, or puréed mixture. It can either be baked or cooked by another means and may be molded or unmolded.

I have included a wide variety of recipes for patés and terrines, ranging from very simple spreads to more complex mixtures. None of the recipes are difficult or overly rich. Often, you'll see paté recipes calling for a great deal of fat. This produces fabulous results, but I cannot do that in good conscience. Feel free to splurge and increase the amount of fat on your own.

SAUSAGE & WHITE BEAN PATÉ WITH COLD TOMATO SAUCE

Created when I was featured in *Bon Appetit*.

(yields about 12 servings)

1 lb. sweet Italian sausage, casings removed
2 cups (16 oz.) dried white beans
1 ham hock
10 black peppercorns
1 medium onion, quartered
1 celery stalk
1 bay leaf
4 parsley sprigs
2 cloves garlic, peeled and smashed
1 tsp. salt
3 eggs, separated
⅔ cup fine dried breadcrumbs
½ cup Parmesan or Romano cheese, freshly grated

¼ cup heavy cream
¼ cup capers, drained
1-2 tsp. garlic, minced
1 1-lb. eggplant (approximately), peeled and coarsely grated
2 cups onion, minced
3 tbsp. fresh basil, minced, or 1 tsp. dried, crumbled
2 tsp. fresh lemon juice
1 lb. bacon, sliced
Parmesan cheese, grated (optional)
salt, white pepper, and freshly grated nutmeg to taste
Cold Tomato Sauce (recipe follows)

1. Rinse the beans and soak them in a large bowl of water overnight. Discard any beans that float to the surface.

2. Drain the beans and place them in a large saucepan with the ham hock, peppercorns, quartered onion, celery, bay leaf, parsley, smashed garlic, and 1 tsp. salt. Cover with water and simmer over low heat until the beans are tender, for about 30 minutes.

3. While the beans are cooking, place the eggplant in a colander, sprinkle with salt, and let drain for 30 minutes. Rinse eggplant lightly, and blot dry with paper towels. Set aside.

4. Drain the beans well. Transfer to a food processor fitted with the metal blade and purée in batches. Measure 3 cups of purée and pour it into a large bowl. Add the egg yolks, breadcrumbs, cheese, cream, capers, minced garlic, nutmeg, salt, and pepper to the bowl and blend thoroughly.

5. Beat the egg whites in a medium-sized bowl or in a food processor fitted with the metal blade, until they hold peaks. Mix ⅓ of the whites into the purée mixture, blending thoroughly. Gently fold in the remaining whites.

6. Sauté the sausage in a large skillet over medium heat until well-browned, breaking it up with a fork as it cooks. Remove the sausage from the skillet with a slotted spoon and drain on paper towels. Transfer to a food processor fitted with the metal blade and process until it is ground fine.

7. Discard all but 2 tbsp. of the fat from the skillet. Add the minced onion to the same skillet and cook until it is well browned. Stir in the eggplant and basil and cook for 3 minutes. Season with lemon juice, salt, and pepper. Remove from the heat and stir in the sausage.

8. Preheat the oven to 400°. Line a 1½ qt. terrine or soufflé dish with bacon slices, allowing them to hang over sides of the dish. Layer the bean purée on top of the bacon, then add a layer of the sausage mixture. Continue alternating mixtures until the dish is filled. Sprinkle with Parmesan cheese, if desired. Fold the bacon flaps over the top to enclose the paté completely. Cover tightly or wrap carefully in aluminum foil.

9. Set the terrine in large baking pan with boiling water that reaches halfway up the sides of the terrine. Bake until set, about 45 minutes. Remove the terrine from the water and cool to room temperature. Refrigerate overnight (the paté will be firm when completely chilled.)

10. To serve, remove the bacon from the paté and invert the paté onto a platter. Discard the bacon.

Cold Tomato Sauce:

4 cups fresh tomato purée,
  strained
¾ cup green onion, minced
½ cup parsley, minced

¼ cup fresh basil, minced,
  or 2 tsp. dried, crumbled
2-4 cloves garlic, minced
2 tsp. fresh lemon juice
salt and white pepper to taste

1. Combine all ingredients for the tomato sauce in a food processor fitted with the metal blade. Taste and adjust the seasonings. Refrigerate until ready to use, serve with the paté.

Fast: Can prepare up to 3 days in advance and refrigerate, or freeze for up to 3 months. Freeze the paté still wrapped in bacon to retain the maximum amount of moisture. Substitute canned beans when pressed for time.

Flashy: Serve with thinly sliced baguettes, crackers, or pumpernickel squares. Garnish the top of the paté with olives, fresh basil, lemon zest, and/or paprika. Surround with lemon slices. Serve with the COLD TOMATO SAUCE.

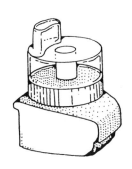

PATÉ DE CARNITAS

Mexican paté inspired by Peg Tomlinson.

(yields about 50 servings)

Carnitas:

3 lb. brisket or chuck roast
3 cans beer
4 cups catsup
6 large cloves garlic, smashed
1 bunch cilantro, chopped

2 large onions, chopped
6 whole green chiles, seeded,
  deveined, and chopped
  (canned)
½ tsp. salt

Other Ingredients:

2 cups tortilla chips
  (8 oz. bag), crushed
6 eggs
2 bunches cilantro, chopped
4 cups refried beans,
  canned or homemade
2 cups sour cream
1 cup green chiles, seeded,
  deveined, and shredded (canned)

1 onion, chopped
2 cups pitted black olives,
  chopped
1 tbsp. cumin, or to taste
1 tbsp. chili powder, or to taste
salt to taste
cheddar or Jack cheese,
  grated (as garnish)

1. Place the meat in a large Dutch oven or covered baking pan. Add the remaining ingredients for the carnitas. Cover, cook for 1 hour at 350°, then lower the temperature to 200° and cook for 6 hours.

2. Remove the meat from the oven. When cool enough to handle, take the meat out of the sauce and shred it.

3. Combine all the other ingredients with the meat and mix well. Place the mixture in 2 to 3 oiled loaf pans or terrines and set in a baking pan with hot water that reaches halfway up sides of the loaf pans. Cover with foil and bake at 400° for 1 hour. Remove and allow to cool.

4. Unmold onto a large platter. Frost the top and the sides with Guacamole Frosting (recipe follows). Sprinkle with grated cheddar and Jack cheese.

Guacamole Frosting:

6 avocados	juice of 2 lemons
2-3 cloves garlic, chopped	1 8-oz. pkg. cream cheese
8-12 oz. of SALSA (see recipe), homemade or purchased	1 tsp. cumin salt to taste

Combine all the ingredients together in a food processor fitted with the metal blade. Taste and adjust the seasonings.

Fast: Can prepare the paté and Guacamole up to 3 days in advance and re-frigerate, or freeze for up to 3 months.
Flashy: Garnish with minced green onions and surround the mold with chopped tomatoes. Serve cold with tortilla chips and/or tortillas.
Fabulous: Substitute black beans for the refried beans or omit beans entirely and use twice as many tortilla chips.

ITALIAN VEGETABLE TERRINE

Tastes best when prepared several days in advance.

(yields about 7 cups)

½ lb. eggplant, cut into ¼" slices
olive oil, as needed
1 cup sun-dried tomatoes or
  roasted red peppers, minced
1 9-oz. pkg. frozen artichoke
  hearts, thawed and chopped
2 eggs
1 lb. raw chicken or turkey meat
¾ cup heavy cream
1 cup ricotta cheese
2 cloves garlic

3 shallots, minced
2 large pepperoncini
  (imported Greek peppers),
  seeds removed if hot
¼ cup Parmesan cheese,
  grated, or more to taste
1 tbsp. Dijon-style mustard
green onions and parsley,
  minced to taste
salt, white pepper and freshly
  grated nutmeg to taste

1. Oil an 8 cup terrine or mold of your choice. Line the bottom with minced green onions and parsley.
2. Sprinkle the eggplant slices with salt and drain in colander for 30 minutes. Rinse lightly and blot dry with paper towels. Brush both sides of the eggplant slices with olive oil and place them on a cookie sheet. Bake at 400° for about 10 minutes or until just tender.
3. Meanwhile, combine the meat, eggs, mustard, cheeses, garlic, shallots, cream, pepperoncini, and seasoning in a food processor fitted with the metal blade.
4. Fry 1 tbsp. of the mixture. Taste and adjust the seasonings.
5. Place a layer of the processed filling in the terrine and top with several eggplant slices and then a layer of sun-dried tomatoes and artichoke hearts, alternating layers until all the vegetables and filling are used up, ending with a layer of green onions and parsley.
6. Cover tightly with parchment and top with foil. Pierce a small hole in the foil.
7. Place the mold in pan of hot water that reaches halfway up the side of the mold.

8. Bake at 300° for 1½ hours, or until a meat thermometer inserted in the middle registers 150°.

9. Cool to room temperature.

10. Refrigerate topped with a 2-lb. weight or 1 to 2 lb. cans.

11. When chilled, unmold and slice.

Fast: Can prepare up to 3 days in advance and refrigerate.

Flashy: Serve with thin slices of French bread and assorted mustards.

Fabulous: Substitute your favorite vegetables and/or add imported olives. Dust each vegetable layer with extra Parmesan cheese for added flavor.

ROLLED VEAL LOAF

(serves 4 to 8)

½ lb. ground veal
⅓ cup fresh breadcrumbs
⅓ cup parsley and/or
   fresh basil, minced
1-2 cloves garlic
1 large egg, beaten
2 oz. dry salami, thinly sliced
½ cup chicken broth,
   homemade or canned

1 cup dry white wine
½-1 tsp. Dijon-style mustard
⅓ cup green onions, minced
1 sprig parsley
1 bay leaf
dried thyme to taste
¼ cup Parmesan cheese,
   grated, or more to taste
salt and white pepper to taste

1. Combine the veal, 1 tbsp. of parsley, garlic, breadcrumbs, 1 tbsp. of egg, salt, and pepper in a food processor fitted with the metal blade. Place the mixture on a piece of wax paper or foil and cover it with second piece of paper or foil. Shape into a rectangle, and remove the top piece of paper.

2. Place the salami on top of the veal.

3. Combine the remaining parsley, mustard, egg, cheese, and green onion. Spread this over the veal and salami and leave a border of 1″.

4. Place the remaining salami on top in a row running down the center. Roll up jelly roll fashion. Pinch together the seams and chill for 1 hour.

5. Dust the meat with flour.

6. Heat oil over moderately high heat and brown the roll in a Dutch oven or large skillet. Add the broth, bay leaf, sprig of parsley, white wine and thyme and bring to a boil. Cook partially covered, over moderately low heat, for 30 minutes.

7. Remove the meat, cool, refrigerate overnight, and slice.

Fast: Can prepare up to 4 days in advance and refrigerate, or freeze for up to 3 months.

Flashy: Serve with thinly sliced baguettes and PESTO MAYONNAISE SAUCE, ROASTED RED PEPPER SAUCE, or any mayonnaise-based sauce from Chapter 1. Excellent served with watercress sprigs, cucumber slices, mustards, and gherkins.

Fabulous: With a variety of fresh herbs for seasoning.

BAKED SAUSAGE & NUT TERRINE

(yields about 2 cups)

2 tbsp. butter
¼ lb. Italian sausage
¼ lb. ham, minced
½ cup walnuts, coarsely
   chopped
¼ lb. frozen spinach, thawed
1 onion, minced

2 tsp. garlic, puréed
2 tbsp. butter
½ cup parsley, minced
1 egg
⅓ cup dry sourdough crumbs
1 lb. bacon, approximately
1 bay leaf

1. Preheat the oven to 350°.
2. Sauté the onions and garlic in butter until golden.
3. Press all the excess moisture out of the spinach. Combine with the onion-garlic mixture and purée in a food processor fitted with the metal blade.
4. Add remaining ingredients, except the bacon, walnuts, and bay leaf to the purée. Fry 1 tsp., to test the seasonings. Stir in the walnuts.
5. Line a 2 to 4 cup terrine with bacon strips, overlapping the strips slightly.
6. Fill the terrine with the mixture and place bay leaf on top.
7. Cover with the overlapping bacon strips.
8. Top with foil and a lid, or three layers of foil.
9. Place the terrine in pan of hot water that reaches halfway up the sides of the terrine and bake in preheated 350° oven for 1 hour.

Fast: Can prepare up to 4 days in advance and refrigerate, or freeze for up to 3 months.
Flashy: Serve with thinly sliced cucumbers, baguettes, gherkins, assorted mustards, and pumpernickel squares.
Fabulous: Substitute ground pork and liver for the sausage.

CHICKEN & HAM TERRINE

(serves 10 to 12)

2 3 lb. chickens, baked at 425°
2 cups chicken broth,
   homemade or canned
¼-½ lb. smoked ham, minced
1 tbsp. Dijon-style mustard,
   or more to taste
½ cup hot milk
6 eggs, beaten

1 tbsp. capers, or more to taste
½ cup parsley, minced
¼ lb. walnuts, coarsely chopped
½ cup green onions, minced
½ tsp. dried thyme
2 cups sourdough bread,
   cubed
salt and white pepper to taste

1. Preheat the oven to 350°.
2. Pour the milk over the bread cubes and allow them to absorb the liquid. Squeeze out the excess liquid from the bread.
3. When the chicken is cool enough to handle, remove the meat from the skin and bones and chop in a food processor fitted with the metal blade.
4. Add all ingredients to the food processor and mix well.
5. Pour the mixture into a buttered terrine or loaf pan(s). Set in a larger pan of boiling water that reaches halfway up the sides of the loaf pan(s) or terrine and bake for 1 hour at 350°.
6. Unmold and serve hot or cold.

Fast: Can prepare up to 4 days in advance and refrigerate, or freeze for up to 3 months.
Flashy: Serve with COLD TOMATO SAUCE (see recipe), or any mayonnaise-based sauce from Chapter 1.
Fabulous: Substitute leftover turkey for the chicken.

CHICKEN & VEAL PATÉ WITH SHIITAKE MUSHROOMS

(yields about 5 cups)

1½ lb. raw chicken breasts, skinned, boned, cut in chunks, and chilled
½ lb. ground veal
2 egg whites
2 cups heavy cream, cold
2 tbsp. Dijon-style mustard

1 oz. Shiitake mushrooms, rehydrated, stemmed, and minced
2 shallots, cut up
dried thyme to taste
salt, white pepper, and freshly grated nutmeg to taste
grape leaves or lemon slices

1. Preheat the oven to 350°.
2. Oil a 6 to 8 cup terrine, oval mold, or loaf pan and line the bottom with parchment.
3. Line the bottom and sides with grape leaves or lemon slices.
4. Process the veal, shallots, mustard, and chicken in a food processor fitted with the metal blade.
5. After the chicken is puréed, add egg whites, then the cream and seasonings.
6. Fry 1 tsp.; taste and adjust the seasonings.
7. Mix mushrooms into the chicken mixture and transfer to the prepared terrine.
8. Place in a pan of hot water that reaches halfway up the sides of the loaf pan and bake for 1 hour at 350°. Chill before serving.

Fast: Can prepare up to 3 days in advance and refrigerate, or freeze for up to 3 months.
Flashy: Serve with assorted mustards and thinly sliced breads.
Fabulous: Add ½-1 cup chopped pistachios to this paté when adding the mushrooms.

POACHED CHICKEN & PISTACHIO PATÉ

Another recipe created for *Bon Appetit*.

(serves 6-8)

Paté Mixture:

14 oz. chicken meat, uncooked
½ cup smoked ham, minced
¼ cup pistachios, shelled,
   or more to taste
1 medium-sized potato,
   boiled until tender
½ cup goat cheese (chevre
   or feta), or to taste
1 egg
1-2 cloves garlic

1 tsp. dried basil
10 imported green olives,
   minced, or to taste
3 tbsp. parsley, minced
¼ cup sun-dried tomatoes,
   or more to taste (optional)
salt and white pepper
   to taste
Herbed Raspberry Mayonaise
   (recipe follows)

1. Combine the potato (peeled or unpeeled), goat cheese, egg, garlic, chicken, parsley, basil, salt, and white pepper in a food processor fitted with the metal blade. Purée well.

2. Fry 1 tsp. of the mixture, taste, and adjust the seasonings.

3. Moisten a piece of cheesecloth and squeeze out the excess moisture. Lay it out flat and place the chicken mixture, flattened, on it.

4. In the center of the mixture add olives, ham, pistachios, and sun-dried tomatoes and roll it jelly roll fashion in cheesecloth. Shape the mixture into a log about 2½" in diameter. Wrap in a second layer of cheesecloth; twist the ends and place them under the log.

5. Place the log in saucepan or casserole and add all the ingredients for the Flavored Poaching Liquid (recipe follows) plus enough water to cover the log by 1".

6. Bring to a boil and reduce the heat to allow it to simmer gently for 45 minutes.

7. Remove paté and cool it to room temperature. Unwrap it and serve chilled or at room temperature.

Flavored Poaching Liquid:

1 cup dry white wine
   or dry vermouth
1 carrot, cut up

celery leaves plus 1 stalk, cut up
6 parsley stems
1 onion, chopped
salt and pepper to taste

Herbed Raspberry Mayonnaise (to serve with paté):

1 egg yolk
1 cup olive oil
2 tbsp. raspberry vinegar,
   or more to taste
2 tbsp. capers
½-1 shallot

½ tsp. anchovy paste, or to taste
dried basil, to taste,
   or fresh if you have it
2 tbsp. parsley, minced
½ tsp. each, salt and
   white pepper, or to taste

1. While the paté cooks, prepare the mayonnaise. Whip the egg yolk, salt, anchovy paste, basil, capers, parsley, and shallot in a food processor fitted with the metal blade until the yolk is pale yellow and the consistency resembles thick cream.

2. While the machine is running, add the oil very slowly and process until the mixture thickens.

3. Process in the vinegar. Taste and adjust the seasonings. Add more vinegar if you prefer a thinner mayonnaise.

Fast: Can prepare paté and mayonnaise up to 3 days in advance and refrigerate.

Flashy: Serve with Herbed Raspberry Mayonnaise, thinly sliced baguettes, and cucumber slices.

Fabulous: Substitute prosciutto or Italian salami for the smoked ham. Try raw turkey, tuna, shrimp, or salmon instead of the chicken.

PATÉ DE NICOLE

Named for my daughter, who wouldn't even consider tasting it.

(yields about 5 cups)

1½ lb. veal, ground
1½ lb. chicken liver, trimmed
sherry, for soaking the liver
½ cup parsley, chopped
2-4 cloves garlic
2 tbsp. flour
1 tbsp. salt

2 eggs
1 onion
¼ tsp. dried thyme
4 bay leaves
2 tsp. white pepper
1 tbsp. poultry seasoning
2 oz. brandy
1 lb. bacon, sliced

1. Preheat the oven to 350°.
2. Clean the liver and cut it into pieces. Cover it with sherry and soak for at least 1 hour at room temperature or overnight in the refrigerator. Drain, rinse, and blot with paper towels.
3. Grind the meat, liver, onion, garlic, and parsley in a food processor fitted with the metal blade.
4. Add all remaining ingredients, except the bay leaves and bacon, and process. Fry 1 tsp. of the mixture; taste and adjust the seasonings.
5. Line a 6 to 8 cup loaf pan or terrine with bacon and pack in the mixture. Place bay leaves on top and cover with the flaps of bacon.
6. Set the loaf pan on terrine in a pan of hot water that reaches halfway up sides of the terrine pan. Place in a 350° oven, covered, for 1 hour, 45 minutes.
7. Cool to room temperature; place a light weight on top and refrigerate.

Fast: Can prepare up to 4 days in advance and refrigerate, or freeze for up to 6 months.
Flashy: Remove and discard bacon. Serve with sprigs of watercress, gherkins, assorted mustards, and pumpernickel squares.

PATÉ SPREAD WITH FIGS & WALNUTS

An exotic paté with rich, contrasting textures and unusual flavors.

(yields about 4 cups)

1 lb. chicken livers, trimmed
    and soaked in milk for
    1 hour or overnight and
    refrigerated, then drained
8 oz. dried figs, cut up and
    soaked in Marsala or port for
    at least 1 hour
½ cup walnuts, toasted
½ lb. unsalted butter

1 onion, sliced
4 shallots, minced
¼ cup brandy
½ tsp. salt, or more to taste
½ tsp. poultry seasoning,
    or more to taste
1 tsp. lemon juice, or
    more to taste
white pepper to taste

1. In a skillet, melt 3 tbsp. of butter and sauté the onion and shallots until golden.

2. Add the figs and sauté until tender.

3. Add 3 tbsp. more of butter and the drained liver. Sauté over moderately high heat until the outsides of the livers are browned and insides are pink.

4. Add the brandy and flame or just cook until it evaporates.

5. Put the liver mixture in a bowl and place it in the freezer until chilled.

6. When chilled, place it in a food processor fitted with the metal blade. While the machine is running, add the remaining butter, cut into small pieces, along with the seasonings. Taste and adjust the seasonings.

7. Process in the walnuts, using care not to destroy their texture.

8. Pack in a crock or serving container of your choice.

Fast: Can prepare up to 3 days in advance and refrigerate, or freeze for up to 3 months.

Flashy: Serve with crackers and/or thinly sliced breads, thinly sliced cucumbers, and sprigs of watercress.

Fabulous: With prunes or tart green apple, peeled, instead of the figs. Served with Dry Creek Vineyard Zinfandel.

COUNTRY HERB PATÉ

Robust and hearty.

(yields about 4½ cups)

¾ lb. ground turkey, chicken, or veal
¾ lb. ground pork
¾ lb. chicken livers, trimmed and soaked in milk for 1 hour or overnight in the refrigerator
¼ lb. Italian sausage, hot or mild, with casings removed
2 eggs
⅓ cup dry red wine (Cabernet Sauvignon or Zinfandel)
2 tbsp. flour

½ cup heavy cream
zest of 1 lemon, finely grated
1 onion, minced and sautéed in 2 tbsp. butter
¼ cup parsley, minced
2 tbsp. Dijon-style mustard
1 tsp. fennel seeds
1 tbsp. dried basil
1 tbsp. *fines herbes*
2 tsp. salt, or more, to taste
white pepper and freshly grated nutmeg to taste
bay leaves
1 lb. bacon, sliced

1. Preheat the oven to 350°.
2. Process all the ingredients, except the cream, in a food processor fitted with the metal blade until well blended.
3. Add the cream and blend. Fry 1 tbsp. of the mixture. Taste and adjust the seasonings.
4. Line a 6 to 8 cup loaf pan, terrine or several smaller pans with bacon. Fill with the mixture and place 1 to 2 bay leaves on top, depending on the side of the paté. Fold the flaps of bacon over the top.
5. Cover tightly with foil and place the paté in a larger pan of boiling water that reaches halfway up the sides of the paté pan.
6. Bake at 350° for 1½ to 1¾ hours or until juices run clear when tested.
7. Cool to room temperature and place a can on top of the paté to weight it down. Refrigerate for at least 6 hours before serving.

Fast: Can prepare up to 3 days in advance and refrigerate, or freeze for up to 6 months.

Flashy: Remove and discard bacon. Serve on a large platter with sprigs of watercress, thinly sliced cucumbers, gherkins, assorted mustards, thinly sliced baguettes, and pumpernickel squares.

Fabulous: With all ground pork and liver or the combination of your choice. Vary the seasonings. Add a cup of chopped nuts to paté mixture. Served with David S. Stare Vintner's Selection Dry Creek Vineyard Reserve.

THREE MEAT & NUT TERRINE

(yields about 12 to 16 servings)

½ lb. chicken livers, trimmed
½ lb. ground veal
¼ lb. Italian sausage, casings removed
1-2 tsp. garlic, puréed
1 large onion, minced and sautéed in 2 tbsp. butter until golden
½ cup parsley, minced

1 cup almonds, toasted and chopped
½ cup heavy cream
2 large eggs
2 bay leaves
1 lb. bacon, sliced
4 tbsp. brandy or bourbon
6 tbsp. capers
1 tsp. salt
white pepper to taste

1. Preheat the oven to 350°.
2. Scald the cream in a small saucepan with 2 bay leaves. Remové and reserve the leaves.
3. Combine all the ingredients except for the almonds and bacon in a food processor fitted with the metal blade.
4. Mix in the almonds. Fry 1 tbsp. of the mixture. Taste and adjust the seasonings.
5. Line a 1½-qt. terrine or loaf pan with bacon and place one bay leaf on the bottom. Fill the terrine with the purée. Fold the flaps of bacon over, and

top with one bay leaf. Cover with foil and a lid or 3 layers of foil and place in pan of hot water that reaches halfway up sides of the paté pan.

6. Bake at 350° for 1 hour, 15 minutes. Let stand for 30 minutes. Remove it from the pan of water. Weight the terrine with 2 to 3 lb. weight or can, and chill overnight.

7. Drain off any accumulated juices and remove the lid.

Fast: Can prepare up to 4 days in advance and refrigerate, or freeze for up to 6 months.

Flashy: Remove and discard bacon. Serve on a large platter with sprigs of watercress, thinly sliced cucumbers, gherkins, assorted mustards, thinly sliced baguettes, and pumpernickel squares.

Fabulous: With all ground pork and liver or the combination of your choice. Vary the seasonings.

BAKED CHICKEN LIVER PATÉ

A delightful paté with a creamy texture and an interesting mix of subtle flavors.

(yields about 8 cups)

2 lb. chicken livers, trimmed
water or milk, for soaking
   the liver
sherry, for soaking the liver
2 cups mushrooms, washed and
   minced
1 oz. shiitake mushrooms,
   rehydrated, stemmed,
   and minced
1½ cups milk
2 tbsp. brandy
1 onion, minced

1¼ cups heavy cream
½ cup flour
4 eggs
2 tbsp. pickled ginger,
   minced, or to taste
zest from 1 or more
   lemons, finely grated
3 tbsp. capers, or more to taste
1 tbsp. fresh thyme,
   minced or ½ tsp. dried
1 lb. bacon, sliced
½ tsp. white pepper

¼ cup shallots, minced
½ cup parsley, minced
2 tbsp. butter

salt and freshly grated
nutmeg to taste

1. Preheat the oven to 300°.
2. Place liver in a bowl and soak in water or milk for 1 hour. Drain and add a goodly amount of sherry. Cover and refrigerate for several hours or overnight.
3. Melt 2 tbsp. of butter in a sauté pan and add the onion and shallots. Sauté until tender.
4. Add the minced mushrooms and sauté until the moisture cooks out.
5. Stir the flour into the above mixture and cover over medium-low heat for several minutes. Stir in the milk and cook until thickened.
6. Drain the livers and place them in a food processor fitted with the metal blade. Process until puréed.
7. Add the onion mixture to the food processor and combine thoroughly.
8. Add remaining ingredients (except bacon) to the food processor. Fry 1 tsp. to test the seasonings.
9. Line paté molds, terrines, or loaf pans with bacon. Use two pans, 8¼" × 4¼" × 3" or try even smaller molds.
10. Fill the molds with the paté mixture and fold the flaps of bacon over the top.
11. Place the molds in a pan of hot water that reaches halfway up the sides of the molds. Bake in a 300° oven until the paté reaches an internal temperature of 150° or about 1½-2 hours. Remove the patés from the oven and water bath and allow them to cool to room temperature. Cover and refrigerate for at least 5 hours before serving.

Fast: Can prepare up to 4 days in advance and refrigerate, or freeze for up to 3 months.
Flashy: Remove and discard bacon. Serve on a large platter with sprigs of watercress, thinly sliced cucumbers, gherkins, assorted mustards, thinly sliced baguettes, and pumpernickel squares.

HERBED PORK & LIVER TERRINE

Wonderfully hearty.

(yields about 6 cups)

1½ lb. ground pork
½ lb. chicken liver, trimmed,
   marinated for at least
   1 hour in Marsala wine
1½ lb. frozen spinach,
   thawed and with all excess
   moisture squeezed out
4 eggs
⅓ cup parsley, minced
½-1 cup green onions, minced
2-4 cloves garlic, minced

⅓ cup heavy cream
⅓ cup Marsala wine
1⅓ tbsp. dried basil, or to taste
1 tbsp. dried thyme, or to taste
1 tbsp. salt, or to taste
2 tbsp. gelatin, softened
   in 2 tbsp. Marsala wine
1 lb. bacon, sliced
1-2 bay leaves
white pepper and freshly
   grated nutmeg to taste

1. Preheat the oven to 350°.
2. Add the spinach, drained liver, pork, and eggs to a food processor fitted with the metal blade.
3. In a saucepan, add the parsley, garlic, basil, thyme, green onions, Marsala and seasonings. Bring to boil and reduce by about half. Stir in the cream and reduce by half again. Stir in the softened gelatin over low heat until it is dissolved.
4. Add the gelatin-herb mixture to the processor and combine. Fry 1 tsp. to test the seasonings.
5. Line a 6 to 8 cup terrine or use several small terrines or loaf pans, with bacon. Let the bacon flaps hang over the sides.
6. Fill the terrine with the paté mixture and top with 1-2 bay leaves. Fold the flaps of bacon over the top. Cover with foil and a lid or 3 layers of foil.
7. Put it in a pan with water that reaches halfway up the sides. Bake at 350° for 2 hours. Let the terrine stand for 15 minutes, then remove the lid, leaving foil in place. Put a 4-lb. weight on it and cool to room temperature. Chill it, weighted, overnight.

Fast: Can prepare up to 3 days in advance and refrigerate, or freeze for up to 3 months.

Flashy: Remove and discard the bacon. Serve on a large platter with sprigs of watercress, thinly sliced cucumbers, gherkins, assorted mustards, thinly sliced baguettes, and pumpernickel squares.

Fabulous: Add ½ cup or more of toasted sesame seeds.

SHRIMP & SCALLOP TERRINE

Unbelievably delicious and simple too.

(yields about 6 or more servings)

½ lb. shrimp, raw	white pepper, lemon juice,
½ lb. scallops, raw	and freshly grated nutmeg
1 large shallot, or more to taste	to taste
1 large egg white	layering ingredients:
1 cup heavy cream	zest of 2 lemons, finely grated
several drops hot pepper sauce	capers
1 tbsp. fresh dill weed	fresh dill weed, minced
or 1 tsp. dried, or more	green onions, minced
to taste	roasted red peppers, minced
1½ tsp. salt	parsley, minced

1. Preheat the oven to 350°.
2. Peel and devein shrimp. Rinse scallops and blot dry.
3. In a food processor fitted with the metal blade add the seafood, shallot, seasonings, and egg white and process well.
4. Add the cream; process until everything is blended and the mixture is thick. Fry 1 tsp. to test the seasonings.
5. Butter the inside of a 6 to 8 cup mold or terrine. Cut a piece of parchment paper to fit the bottom of the terrine. Put it in the bottom and butter it well. (This will make the terrine unmold like a dream!)
6. Fill the terrine with half of the mixture (depending on how many layers you wish to make). Place any or a combination of the layering ingredients

on top of the mixture. Top with the remaining seafood mixture.

7. Pack the mixture well and bang the mold on the counter to release any trapped air.

8. Place the mold in a pan filled with boiling water that comes halfway up the sides of the mold. Cover with a piece of well-buttered parchment.

9. Bake at 350° for 45 minutes to 1 hour. Test by inserting a knife in the center; it should come out clean.

10. Remove from the oven and take out of the water bath. Allow it to rest for 20 to 30 minutes before unmolding. If liquid has accumulated, use a paper towel to sponge it up.

Fast: Can prepare up to 2 days in advance and refrigerate, or freeze for up to 1 month.

Flashy: Serve hot or cold with COLD LEMON TARRAGON SAUCE, DILL CREAM SAUCE, COLD CUCUMBER SAUCE, or Smoked Salmon Sauce.

Fabulous: SErve as an appetizer course with a garnish of lettuce and/or watercress leaves and a cold sauce of your choice, or as a light luncheon or supper entree.

CRAB & VEGETABLE TERRINE WITH WATERCRESS MAYONNAISE

(yields about 4 cups)

1 lb. crabmeat or imitation crab

¾ lb. carrots, julienned, blanched, and refreshed under cold water

¾ lb. zucchini, julienned, blanched and refreshed under cold water

¾ lb. artichoke hearts; if using marinated, drain well

½ cup parsley, minced

zest of 2 lemons, finely grated

¼ cup ricotta cheese

¼ cup goat cheese (chevre)

¼ cup sherry

5 eggs

¼ tsp. salt

¼ tsp. dried dill weed, or more to taste

2 shallots, minced

pinch of cayenne pepper

white pepper and freshly grated nutmeg to taste

⅓ cup flour
¾ cup milk

Watercress Mayonnaise
(recipe follows)

1. Preheat the oven to 350° and butter a 1½-qt. terrine. Line the bottom with buttered parchment paper.
2. To dry the vegetables, place them in large pot over high heat for 30 seconds and stir.
3. Combine the eggs, cheeses, milk, sherry, shallots, and seasonings in a food processor with the metal blade and process well. Add the flour through the feed tube while the machine is running, and combine.
4. Place the vegetables, crabmeat and lemon zest in bowl and mix in with the batter.
5. Pour the batter into the terrine and bang it on the counter to remove any air pockets.
6. Cover with buttered foil and place in a pan filled with boiling water that comes halfway up sides of the terrine.
7. Bake 1½ hours, or until an inserted skewer comes out clean.
8. Allow the terrine to come to room temperature. Chill for about 4 hours, or until completely cold, before unmolding and serving. Serve with Watercress Mayonnaise.

Watercress Mayonnaise:
1 egg yolk
2 tbsp. Dijon-style mustard
1 cup grape seed oil
   or avocado oil

¼ cup watercress leaves
1 shallot
1 tbsp. lemon juice,
   or more to taste
salt and white pepper to taste

1. Combine the egg yolk, mustard, lemon juice, shallots, salt, white pepper, and watercress leaves in a food processor fitted with the metal blade and process well.
2. While the machine is running, slowly add the oil through the feed tube. Taste and adjust the seasonings.

Fast: Can prepare the mayonnaise up to 3 days in advance and refrigerate. Can prepare the terrine up to 2 days in advance and refrigerate.
Flashy: Serve with WATERCRESS MAYONNAISE and thinly sliced baguettes.

PATÉ OF SALMON & ARTICHOKE HEARTS

I like to serve this mousse-like paté for spring and summer *al fresco* dining.

(yields about 8 servings)

7 oz. salmon or tuna
2 6-oz. jars marinated artichoke
   hearts, drained and chopped
¼ cup parsley, minced
¼ cup watercress leaves,
   minced
2-6 tbsp. capers
6-8 green onions, minced
2 envelopes plain gelatin

⅓-½ cup dry vermouth
2 tbsp. brandy
1½ cups chicken broth,
   homemade or canned
1 stick unsalted butter
1 tbsp. dried dill weed
4 anchovy filets
juice of 1 lemon
salt and white pepper to taste

1. Purée the capers and green onions in a food processor fitted with the metal blade.
2. Combine the broth, dry vermouth, and brandy in a saucepan. Stir in the gelatin and cook over low heat until it dissolves. Set aside.
3. Add all the remaining ingredients to the food processor. Process until smooth.
4. Add the gelatin mixture and process until well-combined. Taste and adjust the seasonings.
5. Put the mixture in a large, oiled mold or several smaller oiled molds. Chill until firm, for about 4 hours.

Fast: Can prepare up to 3 days in advance and refrigerate, or freeze for up to 1 month.
Flashy: Serve with assorted crackers, melbas, and/or thinly sliced breads, and garnish with sliced cucumbers and watercress leaves.

MOUSSES

Mousses are divine, delicate, and decadent. They are especially well-suited to spring and summer entertaining and are the perfect prelude to a formal dinner. For large groups mousses are a fabulous choice, as they can be prepared quickly and easily doubled or tripled and frozen. This is another area where your food processor will be invaluable. If you plan to serve a mousse outdoors, remember not to let it sit in the direct sun. Place the mousse on a plate in a bowl of ice or on blue ice to prevent an embarrassing meltdown.

SMOKED SALMON MOUSSE

Divine decadence without blowing the budget!

(yields about 4½ cups)

1½ oz. smoked salmon (lox)
3 tbsp. dry vermouth
1 envelope unflavored gelatin
3 cups heavy cream, whipped
3 tbsp. lemon juice, or to taste
zest of 1 to 2 lemons,
   finely grated
1 tbsp. shallot, minced,
   or to taste

¼ cup red or green
   onion, minced
¼ cup fresh dill weed
   or 1 tbsp. dried
salt and white pepper
   to taste
garnishes: capers, dill weed,
   smoked salmon, and/or minced
   green or red onion

1. Oil a 5 cup mold.
2. Place the dry vermouth in a small pan. Stir in the gelatin and dissolve it over low heat. Allow it to cool slightly.
3. Purée the salmon and shallots, along with the gelatin mixture, in a food processor fitted with the metal blade.
4. Add the whipped cream and process very briefly, or it will curdle.
5. Add the lemon juice, minced onions, and seasonings and process just until combined. Taste and adjust the seasonings.

6. Place mousse in the prepared mold and chill until firm, about 1½ hours in the refrigerator or ½ to ¾ hour in the freezer.
7. Unmold and garnish.

Fast: Can prepare up to 3 days in advance and refrigerate, or freeze for up to 3 months.
Flashy: Serve with BAGEL CHIPS.
Fabulous: Substitute smoked turkey, prosciutto, or smoked trout for the salmon.

SMOKED SALMON & CHEVRE MOUSSE

This mouthful of soft, subtle luxury is the perfect prelude to an elegant meal, and a marvelous way to welcome spring.

(yields about 2 cups)

4-8 oz. smoked salmon (lox)	2 tbsp. lemon juice
4 oz. goat cheese (chevre)	zest of 1 lemon, finely
1 envelope unflavored gelatin	grated
2 tbsp. dry white wine	green onions, minced, for
1 shallot	garnishing
1½ cups heavy cream	white pepper to taste

1. Oil a 2 to 4 cup mold or small individual bowls of your choice.
2. Purée the shallot, smoked salmon, white pepper, lemon juice, and goat cheese in a food processor fitted with the metal blade.
3. Dissolve the gelatin in the wine in a bowl set into a larger bowl of hot water, or in the microwave for ½ minute on low power. Add the dissolved gelatin to the food processor and blend.
4. Transfer the mixture from the processor to a bowl and whip the cream in the food processor until it forms stiff peaks.
5. Fold the cream and lemon zest into the salmon mixture. Taste and adjust the seasonings.
6. Place the salmon mixture into the prepared mold.

7. Refrigerate until set, approximately 1½ hours. Unmold and garnish before serving.

Fast: Can prepare up to 3 days in advance and refrigerate, or freeze for up to 3 months.
Flashy: With BAGEL CHIPS, pumpernickel squares, or thinly sliced baguettes.
Fabulous: With minced green onion or watercress leaves mixed in before molding. Use fresh dill as a seasoning and a garnish.

COLD SPINACH MOUSSE

(yields about 2 cups)

1 pkg. frozen spinach, thawed, and squeezed to remove the excess moisture	1 tbsp. capers
	1 envelope unflavored gelatin
	2 tbsp. sherry
½ cup sour cream	1-2 shallots, minced
1 cup chicken broth, homemade or canned	¼ tsp. dried tarragon (optional)
	salt, white pepper, and freshly grated nutmeg to taste
½ cup mayonnaise	

1. Combine the sherry and gelatin in a small bowl set in a larger bowl of hot water or place in the microwave on low power for ½ minute to dissolve.
2. Purée all the ingredients in a food processor fitted with the metal blade. Taste and adjust the seasonings.
3. Place the mixture into a well-oiled 2 to 4 cup mold and chill until firm, about 4 hours. Unmold and serve.

Fast: Can prepare up to 3 days in advance and refrigerate, or freeze for up to 3 months.
Flashy: Serve with thinly sliced baguettes, crackers, BAGEL CHIPS, or PITA CHIPS.
Fabulous: Substitute other cooked vegetables for the spinach, and/or thyme, basil, or oregano, for the tarragon.

CAVIAR MOUSSE

Here's to the good life at an affordable price.

(yields about 1½ cups)

3 oz. black lumpfish caviar
3 tbsp. mayonnaise
¾ cup sour cream
¼ cup shallots, minced
3 hard-boiled eggs
½-1 tsp. prepared horseradish
1½ pkgs. unflavored gelatin
3 tbsp. dry vermouth

1 tsp. dried dill weed
  or 1 tbsp. fresh, or to taste
salt, white pepper, and
  lemon juice to taste
garnishes: finely minced
  hard-boiled egg, minced
  green onion, grated lemon
  zest, caviar and/or sour cream

1. Combine the mayonnaise, sour cream, shallots, and hard-boiled eggs in a food processor fitted with the metal blade.
2. Dissolve the gelatin in the dry vermouth in a bowl set into a larger bowl of hot water or in the microwave for ½ minute on low power.
3. Add the dissolved gelatin to the processor, along with the horseradish and remaining seasonings, and process well.
4. Add the caviar, being careful not to destroy its texture.
5. Oil a 2 cup mold or several smaller ones and fill with the mixture. To set, chill for about 3 hours in the refrigerator or 1½ hours in the freezer.
6. Unmold and garnish.

Fast: Can prepare up to 3 days in advance and refrigerate, or freeze for up to 3 months.
Flashy: To garnish, frost with sour cream and sprinkle the garnishes of your choice over the top. Serve with pumpernickel squares.
Fabulous: This is a wonderful formula that offers you the opportunity for limitless variations. For example, if you have some leftover cooked fish, turn it into a cold fish mousse. If your garden has a bumper crop of basil, make a cold basil mousse. If you have leftover roast beef, what about a cold roast beef mousse? Served with Gloria Ferrer Royal Cuvée Sparkling Wine.

SEAFOOD MOUSSE

(yields about 5 cups)

1½ lb. cooked shrimp, shelled
   and deveined (or crabmeat)
½ cup sherry
2 envelopes unflavored gelatin
1 cup chicken broth,
   homemade or canned
1 cup mayonnaise or sour cream

1 cup heavy cream
1 tsp. horseradish, or to taste
1 tbsp. capers, or to taste
3 tbsp. shallots, minced
salt, white pepper, lemon
   juice, and dried tarragon
   to taste

1. Oil a 6 cup mold or several smaller ones.
2. Combine the sherry, broth, and gelatin in a saucepan and heat until the gelatin dissolves.
3. Whip the cream in the food processor fitted with the metal blade until it holds peaks. Remove and set aside.
4. Combine the shrimp, mayonnaise, horseradish, capers, shallots, seasonings, and dissolved gelatin in the food processor. Process until smooth. Taste and adjust the seasonings.
5. Gently fold in the whipped cream and pour the mousse into the prepared molds. Refrigerate for about 4 hours, until firm.

Fast: Prepare up to 3 days in advance and refrigerate, or freeze for up to 3 months.
Flashy: Serve with BEATEN BISCUITS, BAGEL CHIPS, PITA CHIPS, or thinly sliced baguettes, squares of pumpernickel, and/or crackers.
Fabulous: Substitute cooked chicken, chicken liver, lobster, or salmon for the seafood. Garnish with watercress leaves or thinly sliced cucumbers.

SMOKED HAM MOUSSE

I made my debut on national *TV* with this.

(yields about 12 servings)

11 oz. smoked ham, trimmed
   and cut in 1" pieces
2-3 chicken livers, cleaned
milk or wine, for soaking
   the liver in
2 tbsp. butter
1½ envelopes unflavored gelatin
¼ cup Madeira
1¾ cup heavy cream
2-4 tbsp. shallots, minced
2 cloves garlic, minced

¼ cup butter
¼ tsp. dried thyme
1 tsp. dried dill weed
zest of 2 lemons, finely grated
1½ tsp. Dijon-style mustard,
   or to taste
¼ cup shiitake mushrooms,
   rehydrated, stemmed, and
   thinly sliced
salt and white pepper to taste

1. Soak the livers in milk or wine for at least 1 hour at room temperature, or refrigerate overnight.
2. Melt 2 tbsp. butter in a skillet. Sauté the shallots and garlic until soft.
3. Add the livers and sauté until just pink on the inside.
4. Combine the Madeira and gelatin in a bowl and place it in a larger bowl of hot water, or place it in the microwave for ½ minute on low power, to dissolve.
5. Process the liver, ham, ¼ cup butter, dissolved gelatin, and mustard in a food processor fitted with the metal blade until smooth.
6. Add the cream and process until blended, being careful not to overprocess, or the cream will curdle.
7. Add the seasonings, lemon zest and mushrooms. Process briefly, so as not to destroy texture of lemon zest or mushrooms.
8. Pour into a 6 to 8 cup oiled mold, or several smaller molds, and chill until set, about 6 hours.

Fast: Can prepare up to 3 days in advance and refrigerate, or freeze for up to 3 months.

Flashy: Serve with thinly sliced cucumbers, gherkins, mustards, watercress leaves, sliced breads, melbas, or crackers.

Fabulous: With pistachios, capers, and/or green peppercorns added.

CHICKEN LIVER MOUSSE

(yields 6 4-oz. ramekins)

½ lb. chicken liver, trimmed
milk, for soaking the liver
1 cup heavy cream
2 large eggs
½ tsp. salt
2-4 tsp. shallots, minced
2 tbsp. capers
3 tbsp. Madeira

½ tsp. dried thyme or rosemary
1 onion, minced
2 tbsp. butter
3 tbsp. parsley, minced
zest of 1 orange
white pepper and freshly
    grated nutmeg to taste

1. Clean the liver and remove any dark spots. Soak in milk for 1 hour at room temperature or refrigerate overnight.
2. Sauté the onion in butter until soft.
3. Purée all the ingredients, except the cream, in a food processor fitted with the metal blade. Fry 1 tbsp. of the mixture to test the seasoning.
4. Add the cream and process until blended.
5. Oil ramekins or a 4 cup loaf pan and fill with the mousse. Place in a larger pan of water (warm) that reaches halfway up the sides of the ramekins or loaf pan and bake for 1 hour in a 325° oven, or until firm to the touch.

Fast: Can prepare up to 3 days in advance and refrigerate, or freeze for up to 3 months.

Flashy: Serve with thinly sliced cucumbers, gherkins, mustards, watercress leaves, sliced breads, melbas, or crackers.

Fabulous: Substitute duck or pork liver for the chicken liver.

CALIFORNIA CHILE & AVOCADO MOUSSE

A mousse with a Southwestern flair!

(yields about 6 cups)

2-3 large avocados
1½ cups sour cream
½ cup mayonnaise
3 green onions, or more
  to taste
2 cloves garlic
¼ cup cilantro, or more
  (I use about 1 bunch)

¼ cup dry white wine or chicken
  broth (homemade or canned)
2 envelopes unflavored gelatin
7 oz. whole green chiles, seeded,
  and deveined (canned)
lime juice to taste
½ tsp. cumin
¼ tsp. chili powder
1 tsp. salt

1. Purée all ingredients, except the gelatin, and wine or broth in a food processor fitted with the metal blade. Taste and adjust the seasonings.
2. Combine the gelatin with the wine or broth in a bowl and set it in a larger bowl of hot water, or in the microwave for ½ minute on low power, to dissolve. Add to the processor and combine well.
3. Oil small molds or 1 large 6 to 8 cup mold. Pour the mixture in and refrigerate for about 4 hours or until firm. Unmold and serve.

Fast: Can prepare up to 3 days in advance and refrigerate, or freeze for up to 3 months.
Flashy: Serve with breads, crackers, and/or tortilla chips.
Fabulous: Garnish with any or all of these ingredients: sour cream, minced green onions, cilantro, chiles, minced black olives, sliced radishes. Served with Dry Creek Vineyard Fumé Blanc or David S. Stare Estate Bottled Chardonnay Reserve.

WATERCRESS MOUSSE

Astringent and refreshing, well-suited to accompany meats or to balance rich hors d'oeuvres.

(yields about 4 cups)

1-2 bunches of watercress
1¼ cups sour cream
¾ cup mayonnaise, homemade
   or purchased
¼ cup parsley, minced
1 shallot, minced

1 tbsp. capers
1 tsp. Dijon-style mustard
1 envelope unflavored gelatin
¼ cup sherry or chicken broth
   (homemade or canned)
salt and white pepper to taste

1. Process all the ingredients except for the gelatin and wine or broth in a food processor fitted with the metal blade, until puréed. Taste and adjust the seasonings.

2. Combine the gelatin with the wine or broth in a bowl and set it in a larger bowl of hot water, or in the microwave for ½ minute on low power, to dissolve. Add it to the processor and combine well.

3. Oil small molds or 1 large 6 to 8 cup mold. Pour the mixture in the molds and refrigerate for several hours, or until firm. Unmold and serve.

Fast: Can prepare up to 3 days in advance and refrigerate, or freeze for up to 3 months.

Flashy: Serve with roast beef, smoked salmon, or ham and BEATEN BISCUITS, or pumpernickel squares and thin slices of cucumber.

Fabulous: With 1 cup minced Black Forest ham mixed in.

MOLDS

Molds are just as luscious as mousses and are sometimes referred to more appealingly as cold soufflés or terrines. They are especially well-suited to warm weather entertaining or to precede a large meal. They are handy for large groups as they can be prepared easily in huge quantities and frozen.

MOLDED GUACAMOLE

This is perfect for outdoor summer entertaining.

(yields about 4 cups)

1 cup avocado, mashed
(2-3 avocados)
2 envelopes unflavored gelatin
¼ cup lemon juice
1 cup sour cream
1 cup sharp cheddar cheese,
grated
1 cup salsa, homemade or
purchased

6 tbsp. cilantro, or more
to taste
3 cloves garlic, minced
½-1 tsp. cumin
3-6 tbsp. green onions,
minced
salt, white pepper, and
lemon or lime juice
to taste

1. Oil 9½" porcelain quiche dish, flan tin, or glass pie pan.
2. Sprinkle the gelatin over the lemon juice in saucepan. Cook over medium heat until it dissolves.
3. Blend all the ingredients in a food processor fitted with the metal blade.
4. Pour the mixture into the prepared mold and refrigerate until firm.
5. Unmold and serve.

Fast: Can prepare up to 2 days in advance and refrigerate, or freeze for up to 6 months.
Flashy: Serve with tortilla chips.
Fabulous: Garnish with chopped tomatoes, green onions, olives, sour cream, and/or sliced radishes.

COLD SPINACH & HAM SOUFFLÉ

(yields about 3 cups)

2 10 oz. pkgs. frozen
 spinach, thawed, and squeezed
 to remove excess moisture
¼ lb. smoked ham, minced
¼ cup mayonnaise
¾ cup sour cream
¼ cup fresh parsley, minced
¼-½ cup almonds, toasted and
 finely chopped (optional)
¼-½ cup Parmesan cheese, grated

½ cup chicken broth, homemade
 or canned
1 envelope unflavored gelatin
2 tbsp. white wine
¼ cup shallots, minced
¼ tsp. dried tarragon, or
 to taste
zest of 1 lemon, finely grated
salt and white pepper to taste

1. Combine the ham, spinach, sour cream, mayonnaise, parsley, shallots, and all the seasonings in a food processor fitted with the metal blade.
2. Dissolve the gelatin in the wine in a small bowl set into a larger bowl of hot water, or in the microwave on low power for ½ minute. Add it to the food processor and process thoroughly.
3. Mix in almonds by hand.
4. Place this mixture in a well-oiled 3 to 6 cup mold, or soufflé dish and chill until firm, about 4 hours. Unmold before serving.

Fast: Can prepare up to 3 days in advance and refrigerate, or freeze up to 3 months.
Flashy: Serve with crackers or thinly sliced baguettes.
Fabulous: Substitute blanched, minced asparagus or marinated, minced artichoke hearts for the spinich.

FAST & FLASHY COLD BLEU CHEESE SOUFFLÉ

Rich and creamy, with a light, delicate flavor.

(yields about 1½ cups)

4 oz. bleu cheese	1 egg
4 oz. cream cheese	1 tsp. Dijon-style mustard,
4 tbsp. butter	or more to taste
½ cup heavy cream, whipped	1 shallot, minced
1 envelope unflavored gelatin	dash Worcestershire sauce
4 tbsp. sherry	white pepper to taste

1. Combine the gelatin with the sherry in a small bowl set in a larger bowl of hot water, or place it in the microwave for ½ minute on low power, to dissolve.
2. Combine all the ingredients, except for the cream, in a food processor fitted with the metal blade. Transfer to a mixing bowl.
3. Fold the whipped cream into the cheese mixture. Taste and adjust the seasonings.
4. Oil a 2 to 4 cup small soufflé dish and fill with the mixture.
5. Chill until firm, about 2 hours, and unmold.

Fast: Can prepare up to 4 days in advance and refrigerate, or freeze for up to 6 months.
Flashy: Serve with thinly sliced breads or assorted crackers. Garnish with sesame seeds, walnuts, fresh dill, minced green onions, and/or roasted peppers. Serve in the soufflé dish or unmold.
Fabulous: Served with David S. Stare Vintner's Selection Dry Creek Reserve, or Dry Creek Vineyard Cabernet Sauvignon.

COLD SMOKED SALMON SOUFFLÉ

When you want to splurge!

(yields about 6 cups)

1 lb. smoked salmon, (lox)
   thinly sliced, then minced
2 cups sour cream
2 cups cream cheese
zest of 4 lemons, finely grated
¼-½ cup fresh dill weed,
   plus extra for garnishing

¼-½ cup red onions,
   minced
2-4 shallots, minced
2 envelopes unflavored gelatin
4 tbsp. Madeira
salt and white pepper
   to taste

1. Combine the gelatin with the wine in a small bowl set in a larger bowl of hot water, or place it in the microwave for ½ minute on low power, to dissolve.
2. Combine all the ingredients, except for the smoked salmon, in a food processor fitted with the metal blade.
3. Add the salmon to the cheese mixture and mix well.
4. Oil a 6 cup bowl, timbale, or soufflé dish, and fill.
5. Cover and refrigerate for 4 hours or until firm.
6. To unmold, run a small knife around the inside edge of each mold. Dip in warm water if necessary.

Fast: Can prepare up to 3 days in advance and refrigerate, or freeze for up to 3 months.
Flashy: Serve with BAGEL CHIPS, PITA CHIPS, pumpernickel squares, or thinly sliced baguettes and Belgian endive leaves. Garnish with fresh dill weed, lemon zest, and thinly sliced cucumbers.
Fabulous: Served with David S. Stare Estate Bottled Chardonnay Reserve.

COLD PROSCIUTTO BASIL SOUFFLÉ

Another light and luxurious appetizer course.

(yields about 6 cups)

1 lb. prosciutto, thinly
  sliced, and minced
2 cups sour cream
2 cups cream cheese
3-4 cloves garlic
½ cup fresh basil leaves,
  plus extra for garnishing,
  or 4-6 tbsp. dried basil

¼ cup parsley, minced
2 tbsp. capers
¼ cup walnuts, minced
  (optional)
½ cup Romano cheese, grated
2 envelopes unflavored gelatin
4 tbsp. Madeira
salt and white pepper to taste

1. Combine the gelatin with the Madeira in a small bowl set in a larger bowl of hot water, or place it in the microwave for ½ minute on low power, to dissolve.
2. Combine remaining ingredients, except for the prosciutto, in a food processor fitted with the metal blade.
3. Add the prosciutto to the cheese mixture and mix well.
4. Oil a 6 cup bowl, timbale, or soufflé dish, and fill. Chill for 4 hours or until firm.
5. Unmold by running a knife around the inside edge of the mold. Dip in warm water if necessary.

Fast: Can prepare up to 3 days in advance and refrigerate, or freeze for up to 3 months.
Flashy: Serve with thinly sliced baguettes and kiwi and/or melon slices. Garnish with thin slices of cantaloupe (when available) and surround with parsley or watercress leaves.
Fabulous: Served with Dry Creek Vineyard Fumé Blanc.

COLD SUN-DRIED TOMATO & FETA SOUFFLÉ

(yields about 6½ cups)

2 cups sun-dried tomatoes,
   minced, or more
½-¾ cup feta cheese
2 cups sour cream
2 cups cream cheese
½ cup parsley, minced
2 tbsp. dried dill weed
   or rosemary

2-4 shallots
3-4 cloves garlic
¼-½ cup marinated red
   bell peppers or pimentos
2 envelopes unflavored gelatin
4 tbsp. Madiera
sesame seeds, toasted
salt and white pepper to taste

1. Combine the gelatin with 2 tbsp. of the Madeira in a small bowl set in a larger bowl of hot water, or place it in the microwave for ½ minute on low power, to dissolve.
2. Combine all the ingredients, except for half of the tomatoes, in a food processor fitted with the metal blade. Taste and adjust the seasonings.
3. Mix in the remaining tomatoes, using care not to destroy their texture.
4. Oil a 6 cup soufflé dish or several smaller soufflés, and fill with the mixture.
5. Chill for 4 hours or until firm.
6. Unmold by running a knife around the inside edge of the mold. Dip in warm water if necessary.

Fast: Can prepare up to 4 days in advance and refrigerate, or freeze for up to 3 months.
Flashy: Serve with BAGEL CHIPS, PITA CHIPS, pumpernickel squares, or thinly sliced baguettes and Belgian endive leaves. Garnish with watercress leaves.
Fabulous: Served with Gloria Ferrer Brut Sparkling Wine.

TORTAS

You could describe these recipes accurately as molded rich cheese spreads, layered with interesting ingredients. As far as I am concerned, It's enough to say that they are pure ambrosia! I first tasted a torta at my friend's home—a Pesto and a Smoked Salmon torta, and I instantly began to get ideas for exciting variations. Terrifically versatile, they offer opportunities for experimentation in any size or shape.

GORGONZOLA PISTACHIO TORTA

(yields about 3½ cups)

1½ lb. gorgonzola cheese, crumbled
½-1 cup pistachios, shelled and chopped
½ lb. cream cheese
½ lb. unsalted butter

¼ cup parsley, minced
½ cup green onion, minced
2-4 tbsp. Madeira
2 18" squares of cheesecloth
white pepper to taste

1. Combine the butter, cream cheese, ½ lb. of gorgonzola, green onions, parsley, Madeira, and white pepper in a food processor fitted with the metal blade.
2. Moisten the cheesecloth and squeeze out the excess moisture. Line a 4 to 5 cup straight-sided mold or bowl with a double layer of cheesecloth.
3. Add a layer of the remaining crumbled gorgonzola and pistachios to the mold. Top with ⅓ of the butter/cheese mixture. Repeat this until the mold is filled, ending with a layer of the cheese mixture.
4. Wrap the cheesecloth over the top and gently press the layers down. Chill for at least 1 hour, or until firm, before unmolding.
5. To serve, invert onto a serving dish and remove the cheesecloth.

Fast: Can prepare up to 5 days in advance and refrigerate, or freeze for up to 6 months.
Flashy: Serve with assorted crackers, melbas, or thinly sliced breads and sliced fruit.

CHEVRE & LOX TORTA

I created this especially for my first appearance on "Hour Magazine," and Gary Collins loved it!

(yields about 4 cups)

½ lb. smoked salmon (lox), minced (or as much as you can afford)
½ lb. cream cheese
½ lb. unsalted butter, cut into pieces
¾ lb. chevre (French goat cheese)
2-4 tbsp. dry vermouth

1 shallot, minced
zest of 2 or more lemons, finely grated
½ cup green onions, minced, or more to taste
2 18" squares of cheesecloth
white pepper, and fresh or dried dill weed to taste

1. Combine the butter, cheeses, dry vermouth, shallot, lemon zest and white pepper in a food processor fitted with the metal blade.
2. moisten the cheesecloth and squeeze out the excess moisture. Line a 4 to 5 cup straight sided mold or bowl with a double layer of cheesecloth, or use two smaller molds.
3. Add a layer of the green onions, dillweed, and lox to the bottom of the mold. Alternate with the cheese mixture, until the mold is filled, ending with a layer of the cheese mixture.
4. Wrap the cheesecloth over the top and gently press down to compact the layers.
5. Refrigerate for at least 1 hour or until firm. To unmold, remove cheesecloth and place on a serving plate.

Fast: Can prepare up to 5 days in advance and refrigerate, or freeze for up to 6 months.
Flashy: Serve with BAGEL CHIPS, pumpernickel squares, or French bread. Garnish this with scored, thinly sliced cucumbers and lemon slices.
Fabulous: Make thicker layers of lox if you feel like splurging, or substitute cooked seafood or ham for the lox. Served with Gloria Ferrer Royal Cuvée Sparkling Wine.

TOASTED ALMOND & GREEN ONION BRIE TORTA

(yields about 3½ cups)

¾ lb. brie cheese
1 cup blanched almonds, toasted
  and slivered or minced
1 cup green onions, minced
½ lb. cream cheese
½ lb. unsalted butter,
  cut into pieces

2-4 tbsp. brandy
1 shallot, minced
2 eighteen inch
  squares of cheesecloth
white pepper to taste

1. Combine the butter, cheeses, brandy, shallot and white pepper in a food processor fitted with the metal blade.

2. Moisten the cheesecloth and squeeze out the excess moisture. Line a 4 to 5 cup straight-sided mold or bowl with a double layer of cheesecloth, or use two smaller molds.

3. Add a layer of the green onions and almonds to the bottom of the mold. Alternate with the cheese mixture, until the mold is filled, ending with a layer of the cheese mixture.

4. Wrap the cheesecloth over the top and gently press down to compact the layers.

5. Refrigerate for at least 1 hour or until firm. To unmold, remove cheese-cloth and place on a serving plate.

Fast: Can prepare up to 5 days in advance and refrigerate, or freeze for up to 6 months.

Flashy: Serve with BAGEL CHIPS, thinly sliced French bread, or pumper-nickel squares.

Fabulous: Substitute walnuts or pecans for the almonds, or your favorite French cheese for the brie.

FETA & SUN-DRIED TOMATO TORTA

This could make me your hero.

(yields about 3½ cups)

¾ lb. feta cheese
½ lb. cream cheese
½ lb. unsalted butter,
  cut into pieces
¾ cup sun-dried tomatoes, minced
1 clove garlic, peeled
1 shallot, peeled
½ cup parsley, minced

4-6 green onions, minced
¼-½ cup watercress
  leaves, minced
¼ cup sesame seeds,
  toasted
2-4 tbsp. dry white wine
2 18" squares of cheesecloth
white pepper to taste

1. Combine the butter, cheeses, wine, shallot, garlic, and white pepper in a food processor fitted with the metal blade.
2. Moisten the cheesecloth and squeeze out the excess moisture. Line a 4 to 5 cup straight-sided mold or bowl with a double layer of cheesecloth, or use two smaller molds.
3. Combine the parsley, watercress, green onions, sun-dried tomatoes and sesame seeds in a bowl.
4. Add a layer of this mixture to the mold and top with the cheese mixture. Repeat until the mold is filled, ending with a layer of the cheese mixture.
5. Wrap the cheesecloth over the top and gently press down to compact the layers.
6. Refrigerate for at least 1 hour or until firm. To unmold, remove cheesecloth and place on a serving plate.

Fast: Can prepare up to 5 days in advance and refrigerate, or freeze for up to 6 months.
Flashy: Serve with BAGEL CHIPS, thinly sliced pumpernickel squares, or French bread.
Fabulous: Served with David S. Stare Estate Bottled Fumé Blanc.

FETA & ROASTED RED PEPPER TORTA

(yields about 3½ cups)

¾ lb. feta cheese
½ lb. cream cheese
½ lb. unsalted butter,
  cut into pieces
4 red peppers, roasted,
  skinned, seeded, and minced,
  or more to taste

2-4 tbsp. dry vermouth
1 shallot, peeled
1 clove garlic, peeled
sesame seeds, toasted
2 18″ squares of cheesecloth
white pepper, and oregano,
  dried or fresh to taste

1. Combine the butter, cheeses, dry vermouth, shallot, garlic, and white pepper in a food processor fitted with the metal blade.
2. Moisten the cheesecloth and squeeze out the excess moisture. Line a 4 to 5 cup, straight-sided mold or bowl with a double layer of the cheesecloth, or use two smaller molds.
3. Add a layer of the red pepper with the desired amount of oregano and sesame seeds to the mold. Top with a layer of the cheese mixture. Alternate until the mold is filled, ending with a layer of the cheese mixture.
4. Wrap the cheesecloth over the top and gently press down to compact the layers.
5. Refrigerate for at least 1 hour or until firm before unmolding. To unmold, remove the cheesecloth and place on a serving plate.

Fast: Can prepare up to 5 days in advance and refrigerate, or freeze for up to 6 months.
Flashy: Serve with BAGEL CHIPS, thinly sliced French bread, or pumpernickel squares.
Fabulous: Substitute fresh basil or fresh dill weed for the oregano, and pecans for the sesame seeds. Create a caviar torta by layering caviar with minced green onions and lemon zest instead of the roasted red peppers.

PUFFS

Hors d'oeuvre puffs need not be overly fussy, bland-tasting little cream puffs. I'm not very fond of *paté choux* (the classic cream puff batter). I find it tasteless and uninteresting, which led me to create the Gougère Puffs. For the most part, I've interpreted puffs to mean small, individual tidbits that rise when baked. You'll see a variety of recipes, ranging from well-seasoned, mayonnaise-based mixtures that top French bread or even tortilla chips to small cubes of French bread that have been drenched in cheese-based mixtures, lightened with beaten egg whites, and baked until fluffed. All puff recipes are extremely *FAST AND FLASHY* and offer you a chance to prepare individual hors d'oeuvres with the greatest of ease.

SESAME SCALLOP TOAST

A western touch to a Chinese classic.

(yields about 24)

8 oz. scallops	1 shallot, minced
¼ cup ham, minced	1 cup fresh sourdough
4 oz. cream cheese	breadcrumbs
1 egg	½ cup sesame seeds,
2 tbsp. cilantro, minced,	toasted
or more to taste	6 slices sourdough bread
2 tbsp. pickled ginger,	sesame oil
minced, or more to taste	½ tsp. salt
1 clove garlic	white pepper to taste

1. Remove the crusts from the bread, cut each slice into 6 fingers. Toast in a 350° oven until lightly brown.
2. Combine all the ingredients, except for the sesame oil, toasted bread, breadcrumbs, and sesame seeds, in a food processor fitted with the metal blade. Process until the mixture reaches the consistency of a thick paste.
3. Fry 1 tsp. of the mixture in a small skillet to check the seasonings.
4. Spread the scallop mixture on the toast fingers. Combine the breadcrumbs and sesame seeds, and dip the bread fingers in the breadcrumb mixture.

5. Place the toast on a cookie sheet; drizzle with sesame oil.

6. Bake at 375° for 15 minutes, until puffed and lightly browned.

Fast: Can prepare the scallop mixture up to 1 day in advance and refrigerate. Can assemble several hours before serving, or flash freeze for up to 1 month. The bread can be toasted up to 2 weeks in advance and stored in an airtight jar or frozen for up to 6 months.

Fabulous: Substitute shrimp or mild white fish for the scallops, or chopped almonds for the sesame seeds. Serve with any cold vinegar-based Chinese-Style Dipping Sauces from Chapter 1.

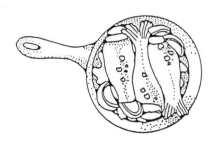

MEDITERRANEAN GOUGÈRE PUFFS

(yields about 24)

¼ cup water
¼ cup milk
¼ cup butter, cut into pieces
½ tsp. Dijon-style mustard
2 eggs, at room temperature
1 tbsp. shallot, minced
½ cup flour
½ cup fresh basil leaves, or more

¼ cup chevre or feta cheese
¼ cup Parmesan cheese, grated
4 sun-dried tomatoes, minced,
   or more to taste
⅛ tsp. salt
¼ tsp. white pepper
⅛ tsp. sugar
freshly grated nutmeg to taste

1. Combine the water, milk, shallot, butter, sugar, mustard, salt, and white pepper in a saucepan. Stir while the mixture comes to a boil and the butter melts.
2. Add the flour and stir over medium heat until the mixture leaves the sides of the saucepan and leaves a slight film on the bottom of the pan.
3. Transfer the above mixture to a food processor fitted with the metal blade. While the machine is running, add the eggs through the feed tube, one at a time. Process well.
4. Add the sun-dried tomatoes, cheeses, basil, and nutmeg, and combine.
5. Drop from a teaspoon or pipe from a pastry bag onto a greased cookie sheet.
6. Bake at 425° for 20 minutes. Turn off the heat and let the puffs remain in the oven for 3 minutes.

Fast: Can prepare through step 5 up to a day in advance, refrigerate, and bake just before serving.
Flashy: Serve hot or at room temperature.

GOUGÈRE PUFFS

This combination of ingredients and seasonings is especially suited to winter entertaining.

(yields about 24)

¼ cup dry vermouth
¼ cup milk
½ cup flour
¼ cup butter, cut up
1 tbsp. Dijon-style mustard
1 shallot, minced
2 eggs, at room temperature
1 cup Gruyère cheese, shredded

¼ cup fresh dill weed
 or 1-2 tbsp. dried
zest of 1 lemon, finely grated
⅛ tsp. salt
⅛ tsp. sugar
white pepper and freshly
 grated nutmeg to taste

1. Combine the butter, milk, dry vermouth, mustard, shallot, dill weed, lemon zest, salt, sugar, pepper, and nutmeg in a small saucepan. Stir until the butter melts and mixture boils.
2. Stir in the flour over medium heat until mixture leaves sides of the saucepan and forms a slight film on the bottom.
3. Transfer the mixture to a food processor fitted with the metal blade. While the machine is running, add the eggs through the feed tube, one at a time, and combine.
4. Add the Gruyère and process well.
5. Drop from a teaspoon or pipe from a pastry bag onto a greased cookie sheet.
6. Bake at 425° for 15 to 20 minutes, until golden. Turn off the oven and let the puffs remain inside for 3 minutes.

Fast: Can prepare through step 5 up to a day in advance, refrigerate, and bake just before serving.
Flashy: Serve hot or at room temperature.
Fabulous: For added flavor, top with extra cheese before baking.

CHINOISE GOUGÈRE

An East-West combination of flavors.

(yields about 24)

¼ cup sherry
¼ cup heavy cream
½ cup flour
3 Chinese sausages, cooked according to the directions and thinly sliced
¼ cup butter, cut into pieces
1 tsp. Dijon style mustard
2 eggs, at room temperature

1 tsp. garlic, minced
3-6 green onions, minced
2 tbsp. pickled ginger, minced, or more to taste
4 tbsp. sesame seeds, toasted
sesame oil
⅛ tsp. salt
⅛ tsp. sugar

1. Combine the sherry, cream, butter, mustard, salt, sugar, garlic, and pickled ginger in a saucepan. Bring the mixture to boil and stir until the butter melts.
2. Add the flour and stir over medium heat until the mixture leaves the sides of the saucepan and leaves a slight film on the bottom.
3. Transfer the mixture to a food processor fitted with the metal blade. While the machine is running, add the eggs through the feed tube, one at a time, and combine.
4. Add the sausages, green onions, and sesame seeds and combine, being careful not to destroy the texture.
5. Oil a baking sheet with sesame oil and drop the mixture from a teaspoon. Brush the tops with more oil.
6. Bake at 425° for 20 minutes. Turn the heat off and let the puffs remain there for 3 minutes.

Fast: Can prepare through step 5 up to a day in advance, refrigerate, and bake just before serving.
Flashy: Serve with PLUM MAYONNAISE or any vinegar-based Chinese-Style Dipping Sauce from Chapter 1.
Fabulous: Substitute barbecued pork or roast duck for the sausage. Served with Gloria Ferrer Brut Sparkling Wine.

MAYONNAISE-BASED PUFFS

Here are further *Fabulous* opportunities for timid cooks to shine and build their culinary confidence. Mayonnaise-Based Puffs are simply a mixture of mayonnaise, seasonings, and cheese. Create your own combination; the possibilities are endless!

TORTILLA CHILE PUFFS

Great for barbecues, Mexican dinners, or casual cocktail parties.

(yields about 2 cups)

7 oz. green chiles, deveined
   and seeded (canned)
½ cup green onions, minced
½ cup mayonnaise, homemade
   or purchased

1 clove garlic, minced
1 cup Jack cheese, grated
¼-½ tsp. cumin
tortilla chips

1. Combine all the ingredients, except the chips, in a food processor fitted with the metal blade. Taste and adjust the seasonings.
2. Spread the mixture over the chips and place on a cookie sheet.
3. Place under the broiler until golden, or microwave on high for 1 minute.

Fast: Can prepare the chili mayonnaise mixture up to 5 days in advance and refrigerate. Can assemble up to 2 hours before serving and leave at room temperature.
Fabulous: To fill mushrooms and TORTILLA CUPS, or to dress a pasta or rice salad.

CHUTNEY CHEESE PUFFS

(yields about 1½ cups)

½ cup mayonnaise, homemade
  or purchased
1-1½ cups Jack cheese,
  grated
¼-½ cup chutney

1-2 cloves garlic, minced
¼ cup parsley and/or
  cilantro, minced
French bread slices,
  melbas, or crackers

1. Combine all ingredients in a food processor fitted with the metal blade, except for the bread or crackers and place on a cookie sheet.
2. Spread this mixture generously on thinly sliced rounds of bread, melbas, or crackers.
3. Place under the broiler until hot and puffed.

Fast: Can prepare the cheese mixture up to 5 days in advance and refrigerate. Can assemble up to 2 hours in advance and leave at room temperature.
Fabulous: To stuff mushrooms, spread on English muffins, or on PITA CHIPS. Top cooked broccoli, cauliflower, or asparagus and broil as directed in step 3 for a delicious vegetable dish.

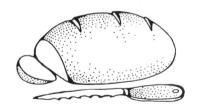

Casual Hors d'Oeuvres Buffet served with David S. Stare
Estate Bottled Chardonnay Reserve, Dry Creek Vineyard
Zinfandel, and Dry Creek Vineyard Fumé Blanc.
(1) Hummus with Pita Chips (2) Potted Pork Beans with
Tortilla Chips (3) California Chile and Avocado Mousse
(4) Roasted Garlic with Sliced Baguette (5) Dijon Sauce with
Grilled Sausages.

Christopher Saul Photography

above:
Caesar Dunk with Belgian Endive
served with Gloria Ferrer Brut
Sparkling Wine.

Prosciutto and Saint André in
Yogurt Pillows served with
Gloria Ferrer Royal Cuveé
Sparkling Wine.

CHEDDARED SOURDOUGH PUFFS

Addictive.

(yields about 60 1" cubes)

8 oz. sharp cheddar cheese,
   grated
1 8-oz. pkg. cream cheese
¼ cup butter
1 tsp. Dijon-style mustard
2 egg whites, beaten until stiff
1 tsp. garlic, minced

2 tbsp. shallots, minced
1 tbsp. dried dill weed
1 loaf sourdough bread,
   sliced, crusts removed,
   and cut into 1" cubes
white pepper to taste

1. Melt the butter in a saucepan and add the mustard, garlic, shallots, dill weed, and pepper. Place over a pan of hot water.
2. Add the cheeses and stir until they melt.
3. Cool slightly and stir in part of the egg white mixture thoroughly; then fold in the remaining egg whites.
4. Dip the bread cubes into the cheese mixture, place on a cookie sheet, and flash freeze. Bake frozen at 400° for 8 to 10 minutes, or until golden and puffed.

Fast: Can prepare and flash freeze for up to 6 months in advance.
Fabulous: Substitute Swiss, Jack, or Gruyère cheese for the cheddar. To create a Reuben Puff, add 1 tsp. of caraway seeds plus ¼ to ½ cup minced corned beef and spread on square cubes of rye bread. Other variations: add sesame seeds, nuts, minced ham, finely chopped olives, chopped chiles, or crabmeat to the cheese mixture.

Stuffed Romaine with Gloria Ferrer
Royal Cuveé Sparkling Wine.

FRIED HORS D'OEUVRES

When I was younger, I didn't think twice about filling my wok with oil and frying up a batch of hors d'oeuvres. Now, it takes a lot to motivate me to deep-fat fry, so you can be sure that the fried hors d'oeuvres I've included are worth it.

In case you are worried about this technique being greasy, it simply isn't, if done correctly. Have your oil hot and fry in small batches. Overcrowding lowers the temperature of the oil. When the temperature isn't hot enough, food absorbs the oil and becomes greasy. To determine whether the oil is at the right temperature, drop a piece of green onion in; when it fries, it's ready.

For added convenience, use the Chinese technique of twice-frying. Fry the first time until the item is only partially cooked (this can be done in advance). The final frying is done right before serving and requires only half the amount of time.

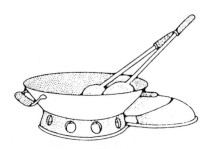

MANGO PAPER-WRAPPED CHICKEN

(yields 20)

Exotic but easy.

4 chicken breasts, boned and
  skinned
20 slices Virginia ham, cut
  in 1½" pieces
1 bunch cilantro, washed

20 pieces of green onion,
  green part only
20 pieces of pickled
  ginger, optional
20 pieces foil, cut into 5" squares

Marinade:
3 tbsp. soy sauce
3 tbsp. Madiera
3 tbsp. sesame oil
3-6 tbsp. mango chutney

1 tsp. garlic, puréed
1 tbsp. fresh ginger root, minced,
  or ¼ tsp. powdered
1 tbsp. sesame seeds,
  toasted

1. Cut chicken into 20 small, bite-sized pieces.
2. Combine all the marinade ingredients and allow the chicken to marinate for at least 1 hour.
3. On each piece of foil, place a piece of chicken, ham, green onion, cilantro, pickled ginger, and a little of the marinade.
4. Fold the foil envelope-style and seal.
5. Deep-fat fry or cook on the barbecue until just cooked. Experiment to determine the exact time needed. When deep-fat frying, packets will float to the top when they are done.

Fast: Can marinate the chicken up to 2 days in advance and refrigerate, or freeze for up to 1 month. Can prepare the marinade up to 2 months in advance and refrigerate.
Fabulous: Substitute pork, turkey, lamb, uncooked shrimp, firm textured fish, or scallops for the chicken.

DOUBLE-FRIED CHICKEN WINGS

For those who love crisp textures with bold flavors.

(serves 6 to 8)

2 lb. chicken wings	½ cup sherry
4-8 green onions, cut in ¼" lengths	½ cup soy sauce
3 cloves garlic, crushed, or more to taste	½ tsp. salt
	¼ cup brown sugar
a piece of ginger root, the size of a walnut	cornstarch
	peanut or **avocado** oil

1. Combine all ingredients except for the chicken wings, cornstarch, and oil in a bowl. Marinate the wings for 30 minutes or overnight in the refrigerator.
2. Drain the wings and dredge them in the cornstarch. Shake off the excess.
3. Fry the wings in batches in hot oil until they are pale golden. Remove the wings from the oil. Reheat the oil and fry for about 2 minutes more, until crisp and golden brown.

Fast: Can prepare up to 1 day in advance after the first frying and refrigerate, or freeze for up to 3 months.
Flashy: Serve with any assortment of Chinese-style Dipping Sauces in Chapter 1.

SESAME FRIED MUSHROOMS

Here's the perfect batter for almost anything.

(serves 6 to 8)

Mushrooms:
1 lb. mushrooms, washed and dried
oil for deep-fat frying (peanut or avocado)
Batter (recipe follows)

1. Heat the oil in a wok, deep-fat fryer, or a large pot. The oil is ready for cooking when piece of green onion or parsley cooks rapidly.
2. Remove the batter from the refrigerator and dip the mushrooms in it. Fry the mushrooms in small batches; don't crowd. Remove the fried mushrooms to a cookie sheet lined with several layers of paper towel. Keep cooked mushrooms warm in a 350° oven.

Batter:

1½ cup instant flour	½ cup peanut oil
1 tbsp. baking powder	1 cup ice water
½ tsp. salt	1 shallot, minced (optional)
¼ tsp. sugar	¼-½ cup sesame seeds, toasted

1. Combine all ingredients in a food processor fitted with the metal blade.
2. Refrigerate while preparing the mushrooms.

Fast: Can prepare the batter up to 2 days in advance and refrigerate. The mushrooms can be fried up to 1 day in advance (remove them from the oil before they are browned). Finish frying before serving, or reheat them in a 425° oven.

Fabulous: This batter is perfect for all kinds of vegetables, chicken, or seafood.

REUBEN BALLS

This is a fried meatball and well worth the effort. Let the kids help!

(yields about 75 balls)

Balls:

2 slices rye bread, crumbled	½ cup milk
¾ lb. corned beef, cooked and ground	½ cup dry vermouth
3 cups sauerkraut, drained and chopped	1 tsp. dill weed, or more to taste
1½ cups Gruyère cheese, grated	salt and white pepper to taste
1 tsp. caraway seeds	1 cup flour
1 onion, minced and browned in 2 tbsp. butter or oil	rye breadcrumbs
3 tbsp. parsley, minced	oil for deep fat frying (avocado or peanut)
1 tbsp. Dijon-style mustard	Batter (recipe follows)
	Mustard Mayonnaise Sauce (recipe follows)

1. Combine the meat, onion, parsley, mustard, sauerkraut, caraway seed, dill weed, and the rye breadcrumbs in a food processor fitted with the metal blade.

2. Transfer to a skillet and heat. Blend in the milk and vermouth. Cook until thickened.

3. Over low heat, stir in the cheese and cook until it melts. Taste and adjust the flavors.

4. Place the mixture in a bowl or container and chill for at least 1 hour, or until cold.

5. Shape into 1" balls and roll in the flour.

6. Dip the balls in the batter and then in the crumbs. Chill the balls for at least one hour.

7. Deep-fat fry and serve with Mustard Mayonnaise Sauce (recipe follows).

Batter:

2 eggs, beaten

⅔ cup water

1. Combine the eggs with the water in a small bowl.

Mustard Mayonnaise Sauce:

½ cup mayonnaise,
  homemade or purchased

½ cup yogurt

1 tbsp. Dijon-style mustard

1 tsp. shallots, minced

1 tsp. dried dill weed

zest from 1 lemon, finely grated

white pepper to taste

1. Combine all ingredients. Taste and adjust the flavors.

Fast: Can prepare through step 6 up to 1 day in advance and refrigerate, or flash freeze for up to 6 months. Can prepare the sauce up to 1 week in advance and refrigerate.

SCALLOP & SHRIMP BALLS

(serves 8 to 10)

1 lb scallops
¼ lb. shrimp, raw,
   shelled, and deveined
2 green onions, minced
10 water chestnuts, chopped
1 slice ginger root, about the size
   of a walnut, chopped

6 sprigs cilantro, chopped
1 egg white
1 tsp. cornstarch
2 tbsp. soy sauce
1 tsp. sherry
½ tsp. salt
white pepper to taste

1. Grind the scallops and shrimp together in a food processor fitted with the metal blade. Add the cilantro, green onions, ginger root, salt, white pepper, soy sauce, sherry, and water chestnuts, using care not to destroy the texture.
2. Beat the egg white stiffly with the cornstarch. Fold it into the mixture and form into walnut-sized balls.
3. Fry in batches in 350° oil until golden (2 to 3 minutes).
4. Remove the balls, drain and serve.

Fast: Can prepare through step 2 up to 4 hours in advance and refrigerate.
Flashy: Serve with any of the Chinese-Style Dipping Sauces from Chapter 1.
Fabulous: Garnish with lemon wedges and cilantro.

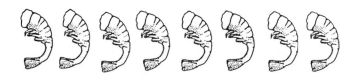

FRIED CAMEMBERT

This fabulous fried cheese makes a very satisfying first course, luncheon, or dinner entrée.

(yields about 4 to 8 servings)

1 8-oz. pkg. Camembert cheese, chilled	1 cup breadcrumbs
2 eggs	1 clove garlic
2 tbsp. water	¼ cup sesame seeds, toasted
	peanut oil, for frying

1. Process the breadcrumbs, garlic, and sesame seeds in a food processor fitted with the metal blade. Transfer to a small bowl.
2. Cut the Camembert into 12 wedges.
3. In another small bowl, whisk the eggs with the water.
4. Dip the Camembert in the egg, then in the breadcrumbs. Repeat to coat thoroughly.
5. Place on a cookie sheet and cover with plastic wrap. Freeze for at least 30 minutes, or refrigerate for 1 hour.
6. Heat 1″ of oil to 400°. Fry a few cheese wedges at time, for about 15 seconds on each side, until they are lightly browned. Drain on paper towels and serve.

Fast: Can prepare through step 4 up to 1 day in advance and refrigerate, or flash freeze for up to 3 months.
Flashy: Serve with a *FAST & FLASHY* MARINARA. FRIED CAMEMBERT isn't a finger food; serve on plates with forks or your guests will have singed fingers.
Fabulous: Substitute Swiss, mozzarella, or Gruyère for the Camembert.

FRITTATAS AND FLANS

Think of frittatas and flans as crustless quiches that can be whipped up at a moment's notice for brunches, picnics, luncheons, or light suppers, as well as for cocktail parties.

CHILE SQUARES

Mock chile rellenos.

(yields about 32 pieces)

4 oz. whole green chiles,
   seeded and deveined
   (canned)
4 tbsp. butter
5 eggs
2 cups Jack cheese, grated
¼ cup flour

½ tsp. baking powder
1 cup cottage cheese
2 cloves garlic, peeled
¼-½ cup green onions, minced
¼ cup cilantro, minced
salt, white pepper, and
   cumin to taste

1. Preheat the oven to 400°.
2. Melt butter in a small square baking pan.
3. Beat the eggs, flour, and baking powder in a food processor fitted with the metal blade.
4. Add the remaining ingredients, except for the chiles, and combine well.
5. Process in the chiles, being careful not to purée them completely. Transfer to the pan with the melted butter.
6. Bake for 15 minutes, then reduce the heat to 350° and bake for another 30 to 35 minutes. Cut into small squares and enjoy.

Fast: Can assemble up to 1 day in advance and refrigerate, or freeze for up to 3 months.
Flashy: Serve hot or at room temperature with any of the Mexican-Style Dunks and Sauces from Chapter 1.
Fabulous: Cut into larger pieces for a brunch or luncheon entrée.

CHILE CORN SQUARES

(serves 6 to 8)

Here's an assertive mouthful!

¾ cup cornmeal, yellow
  or white
1¼ cup flour
2 tsp. baking powder
2 tsp. cumin
½ tsp. salt
1 stick butter, cut into
  small pieces
2 eggs
1 cup sour cream

¼ cup dry white wine
7 oz. whole green chiles,
  seeded, deveined, and
  minced (canned)
1 clove garlic, or more
  to taste
¼ cup cilantro, minced,
  or more to taste
2-4 green onions, minced
1 cup sharp cheddar cheese,
  grated

1. Preheat the oven to 375°.
2. Combine the butter and sour cream in a food processor fitted with the metal blade.
3. Add all the dry ingredients and process until combined.
4. While the machine is running add the eggs, wine, green onions, cilantro, chiles, and garlic through the feed tube. Process until well blended.
5. Butter a jelly roll pan 10½" × 15½". Pour in the batter and tilt the pan to distribute the batter evenly. Sprinkle with cheddar cheese and bake for about 30 minutes, or until the cheese melts and the mixture is firm.
6. Cut into the desired size squares and serve warm or at room temperature.

Fast: Can assemble and refrigerate up to 1 day in advance or freeze for up to 3 months. Allow it to come to room temperature before baking. If frozen, thaw before baking.
Fabulous: Add chopped or sliced black or green olives to the batter.

ITALIAN SAUSAGE & ROASTED RED PEPPER FRITTATA

Here's a solution for all of those times when your pantry is empty. As long as you have eggs in the refrigerator you can usually find enough interesting odds and ends to prepare a frittata.

(serves 10 to 12)

5 eggs
1 lb. Italian sweet sausage,
   casings removed and fried
   until fully cooked, or cooked
   in the microwave
½-1 cup mozzarella or
   Jack cheese, grated
2-4 tbsp. Parmesan cheese, grated
1-2 cloves garlic, peeled

½ lb. mushrooms, thinly sliced
2 tbsp. olive oil
¼-½ cup parsley, minced
1 cup onion, minced
4 red peppers, roasted,
   peeled, seeded, and cut
   into thin strips
salt and white pepper to taste

1. Sauté the mushrooms, onions, and garlic in oil until the liquid from the mushrooms evaporates.
2. While the mixture is cooking, combine the eggs, cheeses, parsley, salt and white pepper in a food processor fitted with the metal blade.
3. Cool the cooked sausage and vegetables before adding them, or process quickly so that the egg does not scramble. Process until finely minced, but not puréed.
4. Pour the mixture into a heavily buttered 12″ × 7″ baking pan. Top with the red pepper strips. Bake in a 350° oven for 30 minutes or until a toothpick comes out clean.
5. Cool slightly before cutting into squares. Serve warm or at room temperature.

Fast: Can assemble or fully prepare up to 2 days in advance and refrigerate.

Fabulous: Experiment with different cheeses and vegetables. Here are several variations:

    sautéed chard and sun-dried tomatoes
    blanched asparagus and cheese
    spinach (cooked or frozen, thawed, and well drained) and
       minced smoked ham
    tomatoes (peeled, seeded, and sliced) and fresh basil
    zucchini (blanched or sautéed and chopped) and Gruyère
    artichoke hearts, chopped (cooked or marinated) and brie

HAM & CHEESE SQUARES

A magical variation of a tried-and-true combo.

(yields about 48 squares)

1½ cup cooked ham, minced
6 eggs, beaten until light
¼ cup soft butter
¼ cup cracker crumbs
1 cup sour cream
¼ cup Parmesan cheese, grated

2 tsp. caraway seeds
3-6 tbsp. green onions,
  minced
1 tsp. Dijon-style mustard,
  or more to taste
white pepper to taste

1. Combine all the ingredients in a food processor fitted with the metal blade.
2. Pour into a greased jelly roll pan and bake at 375° for about 15 minutes, until browned and set.

Fast: Can assemble up to 1 day in advance and refrigerate.
Fabulous: Try any of these variations:
    onion and cheese
    spinach and mushroom
    broccoli and olive
    ham and broccoli
    sausage and onion
    crab and spinach
    shrimp, salmon, tuna, sauerkraut, or corned beef
    bell peppers and mushrooms
    green chiles and cheese.
The options are endless, as you can see!

CHAPTER FIVE

WRAPS

*O*nce again, it sounds as if I've switched the topic from food to clothing. Wraps simply refers to hors d'oeuvres that are bases or enclosures for fillings or toppings. This chapter explores the complete range, from the sophisticated individual hors d'oeuvre pastries, to the informal potato skin.

Nothing could be more flattering to guests than to be served an array of individual items that reflect thoughtful attention to detail. Such flattery clearly shows that you think they deserve the best. You will learn how to accomplish this without joining the ranks of the kitchen martyrs.

STUFFED VEGETABLES

Stuffed vegetables from POTATO SKINS to very elegant CAVIAR MUSH-ROOMS are easy to prepare. Cooks, be they beginners or experienced, can serve these with pride.

POTATO SKINS

A thin, crisp version of the popular restaurant appetizer that is baked, not fried.

(yields about 32)

8 large baking potatoes, washed
salt
olive or peanut oil

1. Bake potatoes at 425° for about 45 minutes or until soft. When they are cool enough to handle, cut them in half. Scoop out the pulp and reserve it for another use. (Remove as much pulp as possible without tearing the skin.)
2. Cut each half in half, brush with oil and sprinkle with salt.
3. Place on a cookie sheet and bake at 350°-400° for about 20 minutes or until crisp.

Fast: Can prepare through step 2 up to 1 day in advance and refrigerate. Can also prepare fully and reheat before serving.
Flashy: Serve with GUACAMOLE or your choice of Mexican-Style Sauces and Dunks from Chapter 1.
Fabulous: Top with grated cheddar or Jack cheese, herbs, browned onions, crumbled cooked bacon, and/or minced chiles.

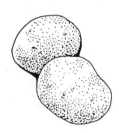

ZUCCHINI ROUNDS MENDELSON

(serves 6 to 8)

When home-grown zucchini is threatening to take over your kitchen, this recipe will rescue you.

1 lb. zucchini, cut into ¼″ thick
   rounds (fatter zucchini
   are perfect for this)
4 tbsp. green onion, minced
4 tbsp. parsley, minced

1-2 cloves garlic, peeled
Parmesan cheese, grated, to taste
½ cup mayonnaise, homemade
   or purchased
salt, white pepper, and
   Italian herbs to taste

1. Preheat the oven to 375°.
2. Combine all ingredients, except the zucchini, in a food processor fitted with the metal blade.
3. Place the zucchini rounds on a greased cookie sheet and spread some of the cheese mixture on each round.
4. Bake at 375° until hot and golden, or longer until they are dry and crisp, depending on personal preference.

Fast: Can prepare through step 2 up to 1 day in advance and refrigerate.
Fabulous: Top with toasted sesame seeds. Substitute eggplant for the zucchini or dried or fresh basil for the herbs.

STUFFED MUSHROOMS WITH BECHAMEL SAUCE

Appropriate for family-style Italian meals or more formal occasions.

(serves 4 to 6)

12 large mushrooms, washed and stemmed (reserve the stems)
4 tbsp. butter
1 tbsp. shallots, minced
3 tbsp. ham or prosciutto, chopped

3 tbsp. Parmesan cheese, grated
sourdough breadcrumbs, dry
salt, white pepper, and dried rosemary to taste
Bechamel Sauce (see recipe below)

1. Mince the mushroom stems.
2. Preheat the oven to 450°.
3. Melt 2 tbsp. of butter in a skillet and sauté the shallots just until golden. Add the mushroom stems and sauté until the released juices evaporate.
4. Add the ham and sauté briefly.

Bechamel Sauce:
2 tbsp. butter
2 tbsp. flour
¼ cup heavy cream
¼ cup dry white wine
½ cup milk

1 tsp. shallots, minced
1 tsp. Dijon-style mustard
salt, white pepper, and freshly grated nutmeg to taste

1. Melt the butter in a saucepan. Sauté the shallots until just tender, but don't brown.
2. Stir in the flour and mustard and cook for 1 minute more; do not brown.
3. Remove the pan from the burner and mix in the wine. Return to the burner and cook until thickened, stirring constantly.
4. Whisk in the cream and milk. Cook until thickened while stirring.
5. Add the seasoning and cook for 1 minute more.

Assembly:

1. Combine the sauce, sautéed mixture and all the remaining ingredients except for the remaining 2 tbsp. of butter, mushroom caps, and breadcrumbs.
2. Taste and adjust the seasonings.
3. Fill the mushrooms with the mixture and place them in a buttered baking dish and top with breadcrumbs. Dot with the remaining butter.
4. Bake for about 15 minutes at 450° and allow them to rest for 5 minutes before serving.

Fast: Can prepare the sauce up to 3 days in advance and refrigerate, or freeze for up to 3 months. Top it with a bit of butter to prevent a skin from forming. Can stuff the mushrooms up to 2 days in advance and refrigerate.
Fabulous: Add toasted, chopped walnuts; roasted, peeled, seeded, and minced red pepper; rehydrated minced Italian or Chinese mushrooms; cooked and crumbled Italian sausage; or minced artichoke hearts. As a dinner party vegetable dish.

STUFFED GRAPE LEAVES

(yields about 6 dozen)

1 lb. jar grape leaves
1 lb. ground lamb
½ cup raw rice
3 large onions, chopped
3 cloves garlic, chopped
4 tbsp. fresh dill weed
½ cup parsley, chopped
8 green onions, chopped
fresh or dried mint to taste
½ cup walnuts, toasted

1 cup lemon juice
3 cups chicken broth,
   homemade or canned,
   or water
parsley or dill stems
lemon wedges
1 tsp. salt
¼ tsp. black pepper,
   freshly ground
½ cup olive oil

1. Sauté the onions and garlic in ¼ cup of oil until they are translucent.
2. Add the dill weed, green onions, seasonings and rice. Cook for 10 minutes, slowly.
3. Add 1 cup of the broth or water. Stir and simmer until the water is absorbed, about 15 minutes. Stir in the lamb and walnuts.
4. Rinse the grape leaves and place the shiny side down. If the leaves are small, put 2 together.
5. Place a spoonful of the rice mixture on each leaf and roll up jelly roll fashion, making sure to tuck in the sides.
6. Place the remaining oil, lemon juice and 1 cup of the broth or water in a large skillet. Arrange the rolls in the skillet using parsley or dill stems to separate the layers.
7. Place a heavy plate on top and simmer for 25 minutes. Add remaining broth or water and cook for 10 minutes longer or until the rice is tender. Cook and serve with lemon wedges and COLD CUCUMBER SAUCE.

Fast: Can fully prepare up to 4 days in advance and refrigerate or flash freeze for up to 3 months, cooked or uncooked.
Fabulous: Substitute 1 additional cup of rice and the corresponding amount of additional liquid for the lamb, to create a meatless version.

FAST & FLASHY ITALIAN EGGPLANT FINGERS

(served 4 to 8)

1 large eggplant, peeled
   and cut into ¼″ thick
   finger-shaped slices
olive oil
2 cloves garlic, minced

parsley, minced, to taste
fresh or dried basil, to taste
Parmesan cheese, grated
  (optional)
salt and white pepper to taste

1. Place the eggplant on an oiled cookie sheet and sprinkle generously with olive oil. Sprinkle with the seasonings to taste and let sit at room temperature for at least 1 hour.
2. Broil until the eggplant is lightly browned and tender.
3. Serve hot or at room temperature.

Fast: Can prepare up to 3 days in advance and refrigerate.
Fabulous: Substitute different herbs and cheeses, top with slices of prosciutto, roasted bell pepper, or salami before serving. Sprinkle with balsamic vinegar, wine, or rice vinegar before serving. Serve with a variety of dipping sauces from Chapter 1. Substitute Japanese eggplant for regular eggplant, and just slice it into ovals. Spread with a filling or spread of your choice, and roll up jelly roll fashion, secure with a toothpick, and enjoy. Can also cut eggplant into squares instead of fingers for a vegetable course.

COLD MUSHROOMS STUFFED WITH SMOKED SALMON

A *FAST & FLASHY* classic—simple, special, and well-suited for summer entertaining.

(serves about 8)

6-7 oz. smoked salmon (lox), minced

12 oz. cream cheese, at room temperature

4-6 tbsp. fresh dill weed or 1-2 tbsp. dried

2 tbsp. lemon juice, or to taste

2-4 shallots, minced

1 lb. mushroom caps, washed, stems removed and reserved for another use

1. Combine the first 5 ingredients by hand or in a food processor fitted with the metal blade. Taste and adjust the seasonings.
2. Fill the mushroom caps and garnish with the parsley or dill weed. Chill and serve.

Fast: Can assemble fully up to 1 day in advance and refrigerate.
Fabulous: Substitute smoked trout, smoked clams, or sun-dried tomatoes for the smoked salmon. Substitute chevre for the cream cheese. Served with Gloria Ferrer Royal Cuvée Sparkling Wine.

CAVIAR MUSHROOMS

More instant elegance.

(serves about 6)

6 tbsp. caviar
¾ cup sour cream
2 tbsp. avocado or peanut oil
2 tbsp. shallots, minced
1 egg, hard-boiled and minced

1 tbsp. fresh dill weed,
   or 1 tsp. dried
12 large mushrooms, washed,
   stems removed and reserved
   for another use
salt, white pepper, and
   lemon juice to taste

1. Heat the oil in a large skillet and add the mushroom caps; season with salt and white pepper. Cook uncovered just until they are tender, about 3 minutes. Allow them to cool to room temperature.
2. Blend the egg, shallots, sour cream, caviar, lemon juice, and dill weed in a mixing bowl. Taste and adjust the seasonings.
3. Fill the mushroom caps with the caviar mixture.

Fast: Can assemble fully up to 1 day in advance and refrigerate.
Flashy: Garnish with cooked, minced egg white; dill weed; caviar; and/or lemon zest.
Fabulous: With the mushroom caps raw. Serve with Gloria Ferrer Brut Sparkling Wine.

MUSHROOM WRAP-UPS

This was created as a way to use up leftover rice. There are no amounts, so just have fun!

mushrooms, washed, stems
   removed and reserved
cooked rice or pilaf
bacon
burgundy or dry red wine

lemon juice
dill weed
olive oil
garlic, minced

1. Cook the bacon partially (not until crisp). Drain on paper towels.
2. Mince the stems and sauté them in a small amount of oil seasoned with garlic, just until the liquid they release cooks away.
3. Combine the rice or pilaf, dill weed, and sautéed stems and fill the mushrooms with this mixture.
4. Marinate the mushrooms in burgundy or dry red wine, and lemon juice for 30-60 minutes, at room temperature.
5. Wrap each mushroom with ½ or 1 slice of bacon. Secure with a toothpick.
6. Sprinkle with dill weed and bake at 350° until the bacon is cooked and brown, for about 35 minutes.

Fast: Can assemble fully and allow the mushrooms to marinate for up to 1 day in advance in the refrigerator.
Fabulous: Use rosemary and green onions in the pilaf. Substitute bulghur or couscous for the rice.

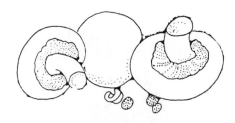

BRIE-STUFFED MUSHROOMS

Even the non-cook will shine with this!

(serves about 8)

16 pieces brie cheese, cut to
    fit into the mushrooms
16 medium to large mushrooms,
    washed, stems reserved
    for another use
3 cloves garlic, minced
6 tbsp. butter

4 tbsp. parsley, minced
4 tbsp. green onion, minced
salt and white pepper to taste
optional garnishes:
    ½ cup walnuts, chopped;
    ¼-½ cup green onions,
        minced

1. Preheat the oven to 350°.
2. Melt the butter in a skillet. Add the garlic, parsley, green onions, salt, and white pepper.
3. Briefly sauté the mushrooms, but do not cook fully. Coat the mushrooms well with butter.
4. Remove the mushrooms to an ovenproof serving platter. Place a piece of brie in each one.
5. Bake at 350° just until the cheese melts.

Fast: Can prepare through step 4 up to 1 day in advance and refrigerate.
Flashy: Sprinkle with walnuts and green onions before serving. Serve hot.
Fabulous: Substitute Camembert for the brie and pecans for the walnuts. For an unbelievable flavor, sauté the walnuts in garlic and green onions. Served with Dry Creek Vineyard Chardonnay.

MUSHROOM-STUFFED MUSHROOMS

Specially created for mushroom devotees.

(serves about 6)

12 large mushrooms, stems removed and reserved
2-4 shiitaki mushrooms, rehydrated, stemmed, and minced
5 tbsp. butter, melted
2 tbsp. butter, unmelted
2 tbsp. shallots, minced
2-4 tbsp. Madeira
½ tbsp. flour
½ cup heavy cream
3 tbsp. parsley, minced
¼ cup Gruyère cheese, grated
salt and white pepper to taste

1. Preheat the oven to 375°.
2. Brush the mushroom caps with melted butter and arrange them on a baking dish. Season with salt and pepper.
3. Mince the stems and squeeze the liquid out, using a clean kitchen towel.
4. Sauté the stems, shallots, and shiitake mushrooms in 2 tbsp. of butter for about 5 minutes.
5. Add the Madeira and cook until it is almost evaporated.
6. Lower the heat and stir in the flour. Cook for 1 minute without browning.
7. Stir in the cream and cook until it thickens.
8. Add the parsley. Taste and adjust the seasonings.
9. Fill the caps with this mixture. Top each with the cheese and drizzle the melted butter over the tops.
10. Bake at 375° for 10 to 15 minutes.

Fast: Can assemble up to 2 days in advance and refrigerate. Bake before serving.

Fabulous: Intensify the shiitaki flavor by straining the soaking liquid and adding it to the pan along with the wine. Cook until it reduces to about 1 tbsp.

CRAB & ARTICHOKE-STUFFED MUSHROOMS

A marvelous combination of flavors!

(serves about 6)

½ cup crabmeat, fresh
   or imitation
10 oz. artichoke hearts
   or bottoms, minced
12 large mushrooms, washed,
   stems removed and reserved
3 tbsp. butter, melted
2 tbsp. butter, unmelted
1-2 tsp. garlic, minced
2-6 tbsp. onion, minced
3 tbsp. parsley, minced

1 tsp. Dijon-style mustard
1 tbsp. flour
½ cup heavy cream
2 tsp. Madeira, or more to taste
¼ cup Gruyère cheese, grated
3 tbsp. lemon juice, or
   more to taste
Parmesan cheese, grated, to taste
salt, white pepper and freshly
   grated nutmeg to taste

1. Preheat the oven to 375°.
2. Brush the mushroom caps with melted butter and season with salt and white pepper.
3. Mince the stems and sauté them in 2 tbsp. of butter with the onions, parsley, and garlic. Cook until liquid from the stems evaporates.
4. Stir in the flour and cook for 1 minute, without browning.
5. Remove the pan from the burner and whisk in the cream and Madeira. Return the pan to the burner and add the crab, artichoke hearts, Gruyère, lemon juice, mustard and nutmeg. Cook over medium-low heat until the cheese melts and the flavors develop. Taste and adjust the seasonings.
6. Fill the mushroom caps with the crab mixture. Top with Parmesan cheese and melted butter. Bake at 375° until hot.

Fast: Can fully assemble up to 1 day in advance, and refrigerate. Bake before serving. Can freeze the filling for up to 3 months.
Fabulous: Substitute minced spinach, broccoli, or asparagus for the artichoke hearts, or any seafood for the crab. Use as an entree in crepes or on pasta, rice, or couscous.

CHEESE-STUFFED MUSHROOMS IN GRAPE LEAVES

Here's another playful choice for summer!

mushrooms washed, stems
   removed and reserved for
   another use
Jack cheese, cubed to
   fit the mushroom caps

green onion and parsley,
   minced
grape leaves, purchased
   in brine
olive oil

1. Preheat the oven to 375° or fire up the barbecue!
2. Brush each mushroom cap with olive oil and fill with a piece of cheese, some green onion and parsley.
3. Wrap the mushrooms in the grape leaves and place in an oiled oven-proof pan. Bake at 375° for 20 minutes or grill on the barbecue, just until the mushrooms are hot and the cheese starts to melt.

Fast: Can assemble up to 2 days in advance and refrigerate.
Fabulous: Serve hot or at room temperature. Experiment with different cheeses and herbs for the stuffing. Feta and rosemary make a good combination.

FAST & FLASHY JEWISH-STYLE SUSHI BITES WITH SMOKED SALMON SAUCE

I've used the Japanese technique to produce an eclectic variation.

(serves about 10)

½ cup smoked salmon (lox),
   minced, or more to taste
1 cup California pearl rice*,
   rinsed in cold water until
   the water runs clear
2-3 oz. cream cheese or chevre
1¼ cup cold water

zest of 2 lemons, finely grated
2 tbsp. fresh dill weed,
   minced, or 1 tsp. dried,
   or more to taste
2 tbsp. red onion, minced,
   or more to taste
salt and white pepper to taste

¾ cup dry white wine

Smoked Salmon Sauce
(recipe follows)

1. Combine the rice, water, and wine in a heavy saucepan. Bring to a boil; reduce the heat to low and cook, covered, for about 15 minutes.
2. Uncover the pot and cook over high heat for about 1 minute to evaporate the excess moisture.
3. Mix the remaining ingredients into the rice. Taste and adjust the seasonings.
4. Transfer to a bowl and refrigerate for about 30 minutes.
5. When the rice is chilled, shape it into balls or logs by hand. To make a sushi roll, place the desired amount of rice on a square of plastic wrap and roll it into a log of any thickness and length.
6. Cut the logs into slices and top with a bit of the Smoked Salmon Sauce, or serve the sauce on the side.

Smoked Salmon Sauce:

¼ cup smoked salmon (lox), minced, or more
1 cup sour cream
¼ cup cream cheese or chevre

2 tbsp. fresh dill weed, minced, or ¾ tsp. dried
2-4 tsp. red onion, minced
white pepper and lime or lemon juice to taste

Combine all ingredients in a food processor fitted with the metal blade. Taste and adjust the seasonings.

Fast: Can prepare the sushi and sauce up to 1 day in advance and refrigerate.
Fabulous: To stuff peapods, cherry tomatoes, hollowed out cucumbers, mushroom caps, or artichoke hearts. On cucumber slices, topped with SMOKED SALMON SAUCE and dill weed. Garnish with dill weed and minced red onion. Wrap each log in more smoked salmon and tie a thin strand of green onion or chive around it, for the ultimate. Use the sauce for dipping or as a dressing for pasta and rice salads.

---

*See Helpful Terms for information about California pearl rice

FAST & FLASHY ITALIAN-STYLE SUSHI BITES

Here's another variation.

When I prepared this on "Hour Magazine," I splashed extra virgin olive oil all over Gary Collins!

(serves about 10)

2 oz. prosciutto, cut
   paper thin, and minced
3 tbsp. red bell pepper,
   roasted, seeded, and minced
2-3 tbsp. Italian parsley, minced
2-3 tbsp. red onion, minced
2-3 tbsp. fresh basil leaves,
   minced
2-3 tbsp. sun-dried tomatoes,
   minced (optional)

1 cup California pearl rice,
   rinsed in cold water
   until the water runs clear
1 ¼ cups cold water
¾ cup dry white wine
1 clove garlic, peeled
freshly ground black
   pepper to taste
Roasted Red Pepper Sauce
   (recipe follows)

1. Combine the rice, water, wine and garlic in heavy saucepan. Bring to a boil; reduce heat to low and cook covered for about 15 minutes. Remove garlic and discard.
2. Uncover the pot and cook over high heat for 1 minute to evaporate the excess moisture.
3. Mix in the remaining ingredients. Taste and adjust the seasonings.
4. Transfer to a bowl, and refrigerate for about 30 minutes.
5. When the rice is chilled, shape it into balls or logs by hand. To make a sushi roll, place desired amount of rice on a square of plastic wrap and roll it into a log of any thickness and length.
6. Cut the logs into slices and serve with ROASTED RED PEPPER SAUCE.

Roasted Red Pepper Sauce:

1 large red pepper,
    roasted, peeled, and seeded
1 clove garlic, or more

½ cup extra virgin olive oil
salt, white pepper and lemon
    or lime juice to taste

Combine all the ingredients in a food processor fitted with the metal blade. Taste and adjust the seasonings.

Fast: Can prepare the sushi up to 1 day in advance and refrigerate. Can prepare the sauce up to 3 days in advance and refrigerate.
Flashy: Garnish with fresh basil and minced red onion.
Fabulous: To stuff peapods, cherry tomatoes, hollowed-out cucumbers, mushroom caps, or artichoke bottoms. A slice of the sushi log on a cucumber slice, topped with the ROASTED RED PEPPER SAUCE and a basil leaf is excellent. The sauce can be served alongside the sushi for everyone to dunk in.

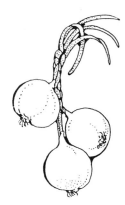

STUFFED MUSHROOMS PARMIGIANA

(serves 6 to 8)

1 lb. mushrooms, washed, stems removed and reserved
3 cloves garlic
½ cup Parmesan cheese, grated, or more to taste
1 tsp. dried oregano, or to taste
⅓-½ cup parsley, minced
½ cup sourdough breadcrumbs

2 tbsp. tomato paste
¼-½ cup imported pepperoncini, stemmed
Jack cheese, cut into small pieces, or grated
dry white wine
chicken broth, homemade or canned

1. Preheat the oven to 350°.
2. Mince the mushroom stems and squeeze the excess moisture out in a clean kitchen towel.
3. Combine the mushroom stems, parsley, garlic, oregano, pepperoncini, ¼ cup grated Parmesan cheese, tomato paste and breadcrumbs in a food processor fitted with the metal blade. Taste and adjust the seasonings.
4. Fill the mushroom caps with this mixture and place in a baking dish. Top with the Jack cheese and sprinkle with Parmesan cheese.
5. Carefully pour equal amounts of chicken broth and white wine into the dish to a depth of about ¼".
6. Bake at 350° for about 30 minutes, or until hot, and the cheese is nicely browned.

Fast: Can assemble up to 2 days in advance and refrigerate. Can freeze the filling for up to 3 months.
Fabulous: Use this filling to stuff chicken breasts, zucchini, or veal. Add minced salami, ham, or prosciutto. Substitute olive oil for the wine and broth.

STUFFED ROMAINE

Great as a summer hors d'oeuvre or for an unusual salad course. There are no amounts; just have fun and create!

brie cheese, at room temperature	smoked oysters
Saint André cheese, at room temperature	caviar
romaine lettuce, inner leaves, washed and dried	walnuts, toasted and chopped or halved
	parsley, minced
	green onions, minced

1. Spread half the leaves with brie; and half with Saint André.
2. Top the Saint André with a dollop of caviar and a sprinkle of minced green onions.
3. Top the brie with a smoked oyster and sprinkle of walnuts and parsley.

Fast: Can assemble up to 4 hours in advance and refrigerate.
Fabulous: Variations: brie with roasted red pepper or pesto; Saint André or brie topped with a slice of prosciutto, chevre, and sun-dried tomatoes. Substitute Belgian endive for the romaine. Served with Gloria Ferrer Royal Cuvée Sparkling Wine.

PROSCIUTTO & VEGETABLES

An unusual variation on the classic.

asparagus, blanched	cucumber spears
zucchini spears, raw	jicama spears
baby corn, blanched or canned	tiny red potatoes, blanched

Wrap prosciutto around vegetable(s) of your choice, and *voila!*

Fast: Can prepare up to 1 day in advance and refrigerate.
Fabulous: Substitute Westphalian ham, smoked salmon, and/or pastrami for the prosciutto.

PROSCIUTTO & FRUIT

Prosciutto is a *FAST & FLASHY* cook's best friend, symbolizing opulence and style.

melon, of your choice	papayas
kiwi	mangoes
apricots	peaches
nectarines	prosciutto, thinly sliced

1. Slice the fruit(s) of your choice.
2. Wrap prosciutto around the fruit and enjoy!

Fast: Can prepare up to 1 day in advance and refrigerate.
Fabulous: Use a large assortment of fruit. Substitute Westphalian ham, smoked salmon, and/or pastrami for the prosciutto. Served with Gloria Ferrer Brut Sparkling Wine.

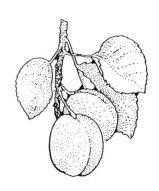

STUFFED WRAPPERS

Another curious sounding category. Stuffed wrappers deals with the use of potstickers sui mai and won ton wrappers as generic pastry dough and explores countless ways for using them, ranging from Chinese to Greek.

Substituting these wrappers for pastry not only saves time, but also allows you to prepare a tremendous variety of unique hors d'oeuvres. Have you ever considered making a tartlet shell out of a won ton and sui mai wrapper? Or, what about a mini calzone (calzette) made from a potsticker wrapper? It requires only minutes, no special skills, and results in a crisp appetizer, lower in fat than most pastries. Invest in a potsticker mold. It costs less than a dollar and makes shaping and sealing these items a breeze, plus a fun job for the kids.

GREEN CHILE WON TON CUPS

A tasty marriage between China and Mexico.

(yields about 60 cups)

1 lb. Jack cheese, grated
1 cup sour cream
½ cup pitted black olives, chopped
⅔ cup green chiles,
    seeded, deveined, and
    chopped (canned)

½ cup green onions, minced
1 tsp. cumin, or more to taste
1 tsp. dried oregano, or
    more to taste
1 pkg. won ton wrappers
peanut oil

1. Preheat the oven to 350°.
2. Combine all the ingredients, except for the won ton wrappers. Taste and adjust the seasonings.
3. To prepare Won Ton Cups, oil a mini-muffin tin and place 1 wrapper in each cup. Brush each with oil.
4. Bake at 350° until crisp, for about 10-15 minutes. Remove the cups from the muffin tin, and place them on a cookie sheet.
5. Fill the cups with a filling and bake at 375° for about 10 minutes, or until filling is hot and bubbly.

Fast: Can prepare the cups up to 1 week in advance and store in plastic bag(s) or in airtight jar(s), or freeze for up to 6 months. Can assemble up to 2 hours in advance and leave at room temperature or flash freeze for up to 3 months.

SEAFOOD WON TONS FLORENTINE

(yields about 60)

½ lb. raw shrimp, shelled, deveined, and chilled

½ lb. fresh scallops, chilled, or ¼ lb. scallops and ¼ lb. fillet of sole

4 lb. frozen spinach, chopped, thawed, and well-squeezed

½ cup ricotta cheese

2 eggs

¼ cup shallots, minced

1 cup heavy cream

sui mai or won ton wrappers

olive oil

salt, white pepper, dried thyme and freshly grated nutmeg to taste

1. Preheat the oven to 350°.
2. Combine all the ingredients, except the wrappers and cream, in a food processor fitted with the metal blade. Process until the seafood is puréed.
3. Add the cream and process only until it is combined.
4. Fry 1 tsp. of the mixture. Taste and adjust the seasonings.
5. Place 1 tsp. of the filling in the middle of each wrapper and fold in half. To seal, lightly moisten the edge of 1 half of the wrapper with water and press the edges together.
6. Place on a greased cookie sheet and brush each one with olive oil.
7. Bake at 350° for about 10-15 minutes, or until crisp and golden.

Fast: Can assemble up to 1 day in advance and refrigerate (unbaked) on a greased cookie sheet. To freeze: flash-freeze on a floured cookie sheet for up to 1 month. Do not thaw before baking!

NICOISE CUPS

(yields 8 to 10 servings)

1 pkg. won ton wrappers made into cups (see GREEN CHILE WON TON CUPS, the preceding recipe, for directions)

Filling:

1 small eggplant, chopped	2 cloves garlic, minced
1 cup onions, minced	2-4 tbsp. fresh basil, minced
1 bell pepper, seeded, and chopped	1 tsp. dried oregano
3 tomatoes, peeled, seeded, and chopped	6 tbsp. olive oil, or more to taste
½ cup parsley, minced	salt and white pepper to taste

1. Sprinkle the eggplant with salt and put it in a colander over a bowl. Let it drain for 1 hour.
2. Meanwhile, heat 2 tbsp. of olive oil in a heavy skillet. Add the onion and garlic. Sauté until soft and golden.
3. Add the tomatoes and cook until the mixture is a thick purée. Season with salt, pepper, oregano, parsley, and basil.
4. Drain the eggplant on paper towels. Toss it with the remaining 4 tbsp. of oil. Place it on a cookie sheet and bake for about 15 minutes in a 400° oven. Combine it with the tomato mixture.
5. Stir in the sauce (recipe follows).

Sauce:

3 tbsp. butter	4 tbsp. Parmesan cheese, grated, or more to taste
4 tbsp. flour	salt, white pepper, and
1¾ cups milk	freshly grated nutmeg to taste
¼ cup dry vermouth	

1. Melt the butter in a heavy saucepan. Whisk in the flour, and cook for about 1-2 minutes over medium-low heat. Do not brown the mixture.
2. Remove the saucepan from the burner and whisk in the milk. Return to the burner and bring to a boil. Cook until it is very thick, while whisking frequently.

3. Whisk in the wine and cheese, and cook for several minutes more. Taste and adjust the seasonings.

4. Season and remove it from the heat.

Assembly:

1. Preheat the oven to 350°.

2. Place the won ton cups on a cookie sheet and fill. Bake at 375° for about 10 minutes, or until the filling is hot and bubbly.

Fast: Can assemble up to 3 hours in advance and leave at room temperature, or flash freeze for up to 3 months. Can prepare the filling up to 4 days in advance and refrigerate, or freeze for up to 6 months.

Fabulous: Sprinkle crumbled feta cheese over the tops of the cups. Substitute zucchini or marinated artichoke hearts for the eggplant. Can also use the filling without the sauce. Add shrimp, lamb, or chicken to the filling, and serve it on couscous, pasta, or rice as an entree.

SHRIMP & CHEESE SUI MAI

Here's California-style sui mai.

(yields about 30)

1 lb. raw shrimp, shelled, deveined, and minced
1 egg
1 cup ricotta cheese
1 cup Jack cheese, grated
½ cup walnuts, chopped
6 green onions, minced
1-2 tbsp. cilantro, minced
1 tsp. garlic, minced
1 tsp. dry sherry
1 tsp. sesame oil
salt and white pepper to taste
sui mai wrappers
cornstarch
CHILI VINEGAR DUNK
   (see recipe)

1. Combine the shrimp, cheeses, green onions, 2 tbsp. of cornstarch, cilantro, walnuts, sherry, sesame oil, and garlic in mixing bowl. Fry 1 tsp. of this mixture to check the seasonings.
2. Dust a piece of waxed paper with cornstarch.
3. Place 2 tsp. of filling in the center of each sui mai wrapper. Draw the edges around the filling and squeeze it a bit to allow some of the filling to show on the top. Set on the cornstarch and repeat with the remaining filling. Cover with a dry kitchen towel while preparing the remainder.
4. Arrange the sui mai on a layer of foil or on a steamer tray in a skillet with about 1" of water. Cover and steam until they are no longer raw, about 8 minutes. Serve hot, with CHILI VINEGAR DUNK.

Fast: Can assemble up to 1 day in advance and refrigerate (unbaked), or flash freeze for up to 3 months through step 3.
Fabulous: Can use the filling in WON TON CUPS, CROUSTADES, as a Calzette, or in potsticker wrappers.

CHINESE CABBAGE SUI MAI WITH PORK & SHRIMP

(yields about 60)

1 head Chinese cabbage, shredded
1 lb. ground pork
½ lb. raw shrimp, shelled,
   cleaned, and chopped
½ cup almonds, toasted
   and slivered or chopped
2 tbsp. sherry
4-8 green onions
¼ cup pickled ginger, minced
2 tbsp. ginger root, minced
2-4 cloves garlic, minced

⅓-½ cup cilantro, minced
1 tbsp. Chinese barbecue sauce
1 egg
1 tsp. sugar
2 tbsp. cornstarch
2 tbsp. peanut oil
sesame oil
salt, white pepper, and
   sugar to taste
1 pkg. won ton or sui mai
   wrappers

1. Preheat the oven to 350°.

2. Heat 2 tbsp. of peanut oil in a wok or large skillet. Add the ginger root, garlic, and cabbage, and stir-fry. Season with salt, white pepper, and sugar. Cook until cabbage wilts, just for a few minutes. Remove the cabbage from the wok and place in a strainer. Allow the juices to drain out, while preparing the rest of the filling. (Save the juices and add to soups.)

3. Combine all the remaining ingredients except for the wrappers and cabbage, in a bowl.

4. Press any remaining moisture out of the cabbage; combine it with the pork and shrimp mixture. Fry 1 tsp. of the filling to test the seasonings.

5. Place 1 tsp. of the filling in the middle of each wrapper and fold in half. To seal, lightly moisten the edge of one-half of the wrapper with water and press the edges together.

6. Place sui mai on an oiled cookie sheet and brush the tops liberally with sesame oil. Bake at 350° for 10-15 minutes, or until golden and fully cooked. Serve with any Chinese-Style dunk in Chapter 1.

Fast: Can assemble through step 5 up to 1 day in advance and refrigerate (unbaked), or flash freeze for up to 3 months. Do not thaw before cooking.
Fabulous: When deep-fat fried. Substitute ground turkey for the ground pork.

ONION OLIVE POTSTICKERS

(yields about 30)

1 pkg. potsticker wrappers

Onion and Olive Filling:
2½ cups onions, thinly sliced
6 oz. can pitted black olives, drained and chopped
¼ cup parsley, minced
1 tsp. garlic, minced
¼ cup butter

1 tsp. Dijon-style mustard
1 tsp. dried thyme, crumbled
olive oil
salt and white pepper to taste
Bechamel Sauce (see recipe)

1. Preheat the oven to 400°.
2. Melt butter in a skillet, and sauté the onions and garlic until soft and golden.
3. Stir in the remaining ingredients and just enough of the Bechamel Sauce to bind the mixture. Taste and adjust the seasonings.
4. Place the mixture in the freezer until chilled, about 30 minutes.
5. Place a generous teaspoonful of the mixture in the center of each potsticker. Fold in half; slightly dampen the outer edges with cold water. Press the edges together to seal, using the tines of a fork or a potsticker mold.
6. Place on an oiled cookie sheet and brush the tops with olive oil. Bake in a 400° oven until lightly browned, about 10 minutes.

Fast: Can assemble up to 1 day in advance and refrigerate, or flash freeze for up to 3 months. Do not thaw before cooking.
Fabulous: Add Jack, Swiss, feta, or chevre cheese to the filling.

FLORENTINE SAUSAGE SUI MAI

One of my favorites!

(yields about 60)

½ lb. sweet Italian sausage
1 8-oz. pkg. frozen spinach,
   thawed and squeezed to
   remove excess moisture
1 onion, minced
1 tsp. garlic, minced
4-8 green onions, minced

½ cup Parmesan cheese, grated
1 lb. ricotta cheese
¼ cup dry vermouth
1 pkg. sui mai wrappers
olive oil
salt, white pepper, and freshly
   grated nutmeg to taste

1. Preheat the oven to 350°.
2. Remove the casings from the sausages and brown the meat in a skillet with the onions and garlic. Pour off the excess fat. Add the wine and cook until it evaporates.
3. Place all the ingredients, except for the wrappers and oil, in a food processor fitted with the metal blade and blend. Taste and adjust the seasonings.
4. Place 1 tsp. of the mixture in the middle of each wrapper and fold in half. To seal, lightly moisten the edge of one half of each wrapper with water, and press the edges together.
5. Place on a greased cookie sheet and brush with olive oil. Sprinkle with extra grated Parmesan cheese, if desired.
6. Bake at 350° for about 10-15 minutes, or until crisp and golden.

Fast: Can assemble up to 1 day in advance and refrigerate (unbaked), or flash freeze for up to 3 months.
Flashy: Serve with *FAST & FLASHY* MARINARA SAUCE.
Fabulous: Omit the sausage and sauté the onions in a few tablespoons of olive oil instead. Use potsticker wrappers instead of sui mai. Use this filling in WON TON CUPS, CROUSTADES, or PHYLLO CUPS.

BARBECUED PORK & RED CABBAGE POTSTICKERS

(yields about 60)

½ lb. Chinese-style
  barbecued pork, minced
½ head of red cabbage,
  medium sized
1 cup California pearl rice
2 eggs
¼-½ cup sesame seeds, toasted
¼-½ cup cilantro, minced
garlic, minced, to taste
1 tbsp. ginger root, minced
4-8 green onions, minced
1 tbsp. Chinese barbecue sauce

2-4 tbsp hoisin sauce
2 cups chicken broth,
  homemade or canned
peanut or avocado oil
soy sauce to taste
sesame oil as needed
Szechuan peppercorns to taste
white pepper and Chinese
  five spice powder to
  taste (optional)
green peppercorns, optional
2 pkgs. potsticker wrappers

1. Preheat the oven to 375°.

2. Cook the rice in the chicken broth as usual.

3. While the rice cooks, stir-fry the cabbage in 2 tbsp. of peanut oil. Season while cooking with soy sauce, cilantro, green onions, ginger root, white pepper, and Szechuan peppercorns. Cook until just tender.

4. Add the rice and barbecued pork to the cabbage mixture.

5. Add all the remaining ingredients, except for the potsticker wrappers, to the wok; stir well. Taste and adjust the seasonings.

6. Place a generous tsp. full of the mixture in the center of each potsticker. Fold in half, slightly dampen the outer edges with cold water. Press the edges together to seal, using the tines of a fork or a potsticker mold.

7. Grease a cookie sheet with a generous amount of peanut or avocado oil.

8. Brush the top of the potstickers with sesame oil.

9. Bake at 375° for about 15-20 minutes, until crisp and golden brown.

Fast: Can assemble up to 1 day in advance and refrigerate, or flash freeze (unbaked) for up to 3 months. Do not thaw before cooking.
Flashy: Serve with MERLOT GINGER SAUCE, any of the Chinese-Style Dipping Sauces, or Sweet and Sour-Style Sauces from Chapter 1.
Fabulous: This filling also makes an excellent rice dish, or filling for WON TON CUPS.

NORTHERN-STYLE POTSTICKERS

(yields about 60)

Dough:
2 pkgs. potsticker wrappers

Filling:

½ lb. bok choy, chopped	1 tbsp. soy sauce
1 lb. ground pork	1 tsp. salt
1 tbsp. ginger root, chopped	1 tbsp. sesame oil
	2 tbsp. peanut oil
4-8 green onions, minced	1 cup chicken broth,
1 tbsp. sherry	homemade or canned

1. Combine the bok choy, pork, green onions, ginger root, salt, soy, vinegar, garlic, and sesame oil in a bowl. Mix well and fry 1 tsp. to test the seasonings.

2. Place a generous teaspoonful of the mixture in the center of each potsticker. Fold in half, slightly dampen the outer edges with cold water. Press the edges together to seal, using the tines of a fork or a potsticker mold.

3. Place on floured cookie sheet, and cover until ready to use.

4. To fry: put 2 tbsp. of oil in a 12″ skillet. Add the potstickers and brown the bottoms for 2 minutes over medium low heat. Add the broth; cover the pan and cook until the liquid is absorbed. Serve hot with the Chinese Dipping Sauce. (Recipe follows).

Chinese Dipping Sauce:

¼ cup soy sauce

2 tbsp. Chinese rice vinegar

2-4 cloves garlic, minced

4-8 green onions, minced

Combine all of the above.

Fast: Can prepare the sauce up to 1 week in advance and refrigerate. Can assemble the potstickers up to 1 day in advance and refrigerate, or flash freeze for up to 3 months. Do not thaw before cooking.

Fabulous: If you are short on time, bake the potstickers as described in the BARBECUED PORK & RED CABBAGE POTSTICKERS.

CURRIED CARROT POTSTICKERS

A great vegetarian hors d'oeuvre with an Indian influence.

(yields about 40)

½ lb. carrots, shredded

1 cup peanuts, roasted and salted

½ cup dried apricots, minced

1 large onion, minced

½ cup parsley, minced

¼-½ cup cilantro, minced

¼ cup pickled ginger, minced, or more to taste

3-6 cloves garlic, minced

4 tbsp. butter

2 tbsp. flour

¼ tsp. fennel seeds, or more to taste

½ tsp. curry powder, or more to taste

¼ tsp. cumin, or more to taste

¼ cup plum sauce, or more to taste

¼ cup sherry or Madeira

peanut oil

1 pkg. potsticker wrappers

1. Preheat the oven to 375°.

2. Melt the butter in a skillet. Add the garlic, onion, cilantro, and parsley, and sauté until tender.

3. Add the carrots, ginger, apricots, seasonings, plum sauce, peanuts, and wine. Sauté slowly until the carrots are tender.

4. Stir in the flour and cook for several minutes.

5. Cook until the flavors develop. Cool the mixture.

6. Place a generous teaspoonful of the mixture in the center of each potsticker. Fold in half; slightly dampen the outer edges with cold water. Press the edges together to seal, using the tines of a fork or a potsticker mold.

7. Place on a peanut-oiled cookie sheet and brush the tops with more peanut oil.

8. Bake at 375° until golden, about 15 minutes.

Fast: Can assemble up to 1 day in advance and refrigerate, or flash freeze (unbaked) for up to 3 months. Do not thaw before cooking.

Flashy: Serve with MERLOT GINGER SAUCE, any of the Chinese-Style Dipping Sauces or Sweet and Sour-Style Sauces from Chapter 1.

Fabulous: Use in WON TON CUPS.

GREEK POTSTICKERS

A wonderful way to use up leftover lamb.

(yields about 60)

½ lb. leftover lamb or ground lamb, cooked	6-12 Greek or marinated green olives, pitted
½ lb. ground turkey, uncooked	2 green onions, minced
1 cup rice, cooked	¼-½ tsp. dried oregano, crumbled
½ cup feta cheese, crumbled	olive oil
2 cloves garlic, minced	salt and black pepper to taste
¼-½ cup parsley, minced	2 pkgs. of potsticker wrappers

1. Preheat the oven to 375°.

2. Combine all the ingredients, except the olive oil and wrappers, in a food processor fitted with the metal blade. If necessary, process in batches and combine the batches in a mixing bowl. Fry 1 tsp. of the mixture, to test the seasonings.

3. Place a generous teaspoonful of the mixture in the center of each potsticker. Fold in half; slightly dampen the outer edges with cold water. Press the edges together to seal, using the tines of a fork or a potsticker mold.

4. Place on an olive-oiled cookie sheet and brush the tops with more olive oil.

5. Bake at 375° until golden, about 15 minutes. Serve with ROASTED RED PEPPER SAUCE.

Fast: Can assemble up to 1 day in advance and refrigerate, or flash freeze (unbaked) for up to 3 months. Do not thaw before cooking.

Fabulous: Cook it like a traditional potsticker.

1. Place the potstickers in a large skillet with about 2-4 tbsp. of olive oil. Do not overcrowd. Cook over medium to medium-high heat until the bottoms are well-browned and just beginning to stick.

2. Throw in a handful or 2 of minced green onions, a pinch of oregano, and some minced garlic, along with enough chicken broth to reach halfway up sides of the potstickers.

3. Cover and reduce the heat to low. Simmer for 30 minutes, or until tender.

CHINESE SAUSAGE POTSTICKERS

(yields about 30)

¼-½ lb. Chinese sausage, minced or cut into thin slices
1 cup short-grain rice
4 green onions, minced
2-4 whole green chiles, seeded, and deveined (canned)
pickled ginger, minced, to taste

4 large shiitake mushrooms, rehydrated, stemmed, and minced
(reserve the soaking liquid)
1 tbsp. sweetened chile sauce or plum sauce
1 cup dry white wine
sesame oil
1 pkg. potsticker wrappers
salt and white pepper to taste

1. Preheat the oven to 400°

2. Cook the sausage in a saucepan over moderate heat until some of the fat is rendered.

3. Add the rice, pickled ginger, mushrooms, sweetened chili sauce or plum sauce, green onions, and chiles. Stir and cook over low heat for a minute or two. Do not brown the rice.

4. Strain the reserved mushroom liquid and add 1 cup of it, along with the wine, to the rice. Bring to a boil, and cover; reduce the heat to low. Cook for 20 minutes.

5. Taste and adjust the seasonings.

6. Transfer the rice mixture to a bowl and place in the freezer to chill, for about 30 minutes.

7. Place a generous teaspoonful of the mixture in the center of each potsticker. Fold in half; slightly dampen the outer edges with cold water. Press the edges together to seal, using the tines of a fork or a potsticker mold.

8. Place on an oiled cookie sheet and brush the tops with sesame oil. Bake in a 400° oven until crisp, about 15-20 minutes.

Fast: Can assemble up to 1 day in advance and refrigerate, or flash freeze for up to 3 months. Do not thaw before baking.

Flashy: Serve with MERLOT GINGER SAUCE.

Fabulous: Substitute Chinese barbecued pork for the sausage. Cook as a traditional potsticker, see NORTHERN-STYLE POTSTICKERS for directions.

ARTICHOKE HEART & GOAT CHEESE CALZETTE

Calzette, is a name I coined for a mini calzone. If you happen to be unfamiliar with calzone, it is a crescent-shaped pizza turnover. The *FAST & FLASHY* factor here is the dough; you do not have to prepare it yourself. A calzette uses potsticker wrappers, which produce a lovely, effortless crust.

(yields about 40)

2 6 oz. jars marinated
   artichoke hearts, drained
¾ cup goat cheese,
   chevre, or feta
1 cup Jack cheese, grated
½ cup ricotta cheese
1-2 cloves garlic

¼-½ cup parsley, minced
olive oil
salt, white pepper, and
   dill weed (fresh or
   dried), to taste
1 pkg. potsticker or
   sui mai wrappers

1. Preheat the oven to 400°.
2. Combine all the cheeses, garlic, and parsley in a food processor fitted with the metal blade.
3. Add artichoke hearts to the food processor. Process only until chopped, using care to preserve their texture.
4. Taste and adjust the seasonings.
5. Place a generous teaspoonful of the mixture in the center of each potsticker. Fold in half; slightly dampen the outer edges with cold water. Press the edges together to seal, using the tines of a fork or a potsticker mold.
6. Place on an oiled cookie sheet and brush the tops with olive oil. Bake in a 400° oven until crisp, about 15-20 minutes.

Fast: Can assemble and refrigerate up to 1 day in advance, or flash freeze for up to 3 months. Don't thaw before cooking.
Fabulous: Add ¾ cup cooked shrimp or crabmeat to the filling or substitute a can of hearts of palm for the artichoke hearts.

ITALIAN SAUSAGE & MUSHROOM CALZETTE

Assertive flavors!

(yields about 60)

1 lb. mild or hot Italian
   sausage, casings removed
1 lb. mushrooms, minced
1 medium to large onion,
   minced
½ cup parsley, minced,
   or more to taste
½ cup ricotta cheese
¾ cup Jack cheese, grated

¼-½ cup Parmesan cheese,
   freshly grated
¼-½ cup sun-dried
   tomatoes, minced (optional;
   they provide nice
   flavor contrast)
¼ cup Madeira or sherry
olive oil
2 pkgs. potsticker wrappers

1. Preheat the oven to 375°.
2. Cook the sausages in a skillet. When fully cooked, remove them and pour off all but 2 tbsp. of the excess fat.
3. Add the onions and mushrooms to the skillet and cook over medium heat until the mushrooms are almost completely dry.
4. Place all the ingredients except the potstickers, in a food processor fitted with the metal blade and combine. Taste and adjust the seasonings.
5. Place a generous teaspoonful of the mixture in the center of each potsticker. Fold in half; slightly dampen the outer edges with cold water. Press the edges together to seal, using the tines of a fork or a potstick mold.
6. Place on an oiled cookie sheet and brush the tops with olive oil. Bake in a 375° oven until crisp, about 15-20 minutes.

Fast: Can assemble up to 1 day in advance and refrigerate (unbaked), or flash freeze for up to 3 months.
Flashy: Serve with *FAST & FLASHY* MARINARA.

LEEK & GOAT CHEESE CALZETTE

Sinfully delicious!

(yields about 60)

1 bunch leeks, well washed,
    with all grit removed,
    and finely chopped (white and
    tender green part only)
3 tbsp. butter
1½ cup goat cheese,
    chevre, or feta
½ cup ricotta cheese
½ cup Jack cheese

1 cup (½ lb.) smoked ham, thinly
    sliced and roughly minced
¼ cup parsley, minced
¼ cup Madeira or sherry
1 clove garlic, minced
olive oil
salt, white pepper and freshly
    grated nutmeg to taste
1 pkg. potsticker or
    sui mai wrappers

1. Preheat the oven to 375°.
2. Melt the butter in a skillet. Add the leeks, parsley, and ham and sauté until tender.
3. Add the Madeira and cook until it is absorbed.
4. While the leeks are sautéeing, add all cheeses and garlic to a food processor fitted with the metal blade.
5. Add the sautéed leek mixture to the food processor and combine. Season to taste with salt, white pepper, and nutmeg.
6. Place a generous teaspoonful of the mixture in the center of each potsticker. Fold in half; slightly dampen the outer edges with cold water. Press the edges together to seal, using the tines of a fork, or use a potsticker mold.
7. Place on an oiled cookie sheet and brush the tops with olive oil. Bake in a 375° oven until crisp, about 15-20 minutes.

Fast: Can assemble up to 1 day in advance and refrigerate, or flash freeze (unbaked) for up to 3 months. Do not thaw before cooking.

Flashy: Serve with CREAMED TOMATO MADEIRA SAUCE.
Fabulous: Use the filling for CROUSTADES, Flo Braker's Magic Puff Pastry, TARTLETS, stuffed mushrooms, omelets, crepes, or cooked pasta shells. Toss the leek, ham, and cheese mixture into freshly cooked pasta. Add ½ cup minced, sun-dried tomatoes to the filling.

MELBAS

A crisped piece of bread, or how to turn a leftover piece of bread into an hors d'oeuvre that can be served for any occasion.

HERBED & CHEDDARED TOMATO CHEESE MELBAS

(serves 4 to 6)

2½ lb. tomatoes, fresh or
   canned, peeled, seeded,
   and chopped coarsely
2 cloves garlic, minced,
   or to taste
3 tbsp. olive oil
¼ cup fresh basil, minced,
   or 2 tsp. dried, or to taste

½ tsp. dried oregano,
   or to taste
½ cup fresh parsley, minced
1 cup sharp cheddar cheese,
   shredded
1 baguette, thinly sliced
   and toasted
salt and white pepper to taste

1. Preheat the oven to 375°.
2. Combine all the ingredients, except the baguette, in a food processor fitted with the metal blade.
3. Top the bread slices with the processed mixture and place on a cookie sheet. Bake at 375° for 5 to 10 minutes or until hot.

Fast: Can assemble up to 3 days in advance and refrigerate or, flash freeze for up to 3 months.
Fabulous: Vary the cheeses and herbs. Create tomato, bacon, and cheese melbas by adding crumbled, cooked bacon.

HERBED CHEVRE BAGUETTES

Another confidence-builder. You can't miss, even though no measurements are given!

extra virgin olive oil
minced seasonings: rosemary,
   green onions, shallots, parsley,

basil, dill, sun-dried tomatoes
chevre or feta cheese
thinly sliced baguettes

1. Preheat the oven to 350°.
2. Spread or sprinkle the cheese on baguette slices and top with your choice of herbs. Drizzle olive oil over the top
3. Bake on a cookie sheet until hot. Serve hot or at room temperature.

Fast: Can prepare through step 2 up to 1 day in advance and refrigerate, or freeze for up to 3 months. Do not thaw before baking.

GREEN ONION SOURDOUGH MELBAS

East meets West on sourdough.

(yields about 70 1½" squares)

½ cup peanut oil
½ cup green onions, minced
¼ cup cilantro, minced, or to taste
1 tbsp. sesame oil

¼ cup sesame seeds, toasted
salt to taste
sourdough bread, cut very thin
   into 1½ to 2" squares

1. Combine all the ingredients, except the bread, in a food processor fitted with the metal blade. Taste and adjust the seasonings.
2. Spread mixture on the bread. Place on a cookie sheet and bake at 300° until crisp, about 30 minutes.

Fast: Can prepare and store in airtight jar(s) or plastic bag(s) for up to 1 week, or freeze for up to 6 months.

HOT CHEESE FINGERS

Simple and zesty.

(yields about 30)

⅔ cup Gruyère or extra sharp
   cheddar cheese, grated
2 tbsp. Parmesan cheese, grated
1 tsp. brandy
several dashes hot pepper sauce
1 egg
¼ cup butter

1 tsp. Dijon-style mustard
   or more to taste
1 shallot, minced
6 or more slices sourdough
   bread, crusts removed, cut
   into long, narrow fingers
salt and white pepper to taste

1. Preheat the oven to 350°.
2. Place the bread fingers on a cookie sheet and toast in the oven until crisp, for about 15 minutes.
3. Combine remaining ingredients in a food processor fitted with the metal blade.
4. Test the seasonings by dipping a small piece of bread in the filling and baking it.
5. Top the bread fingers with the mixture, place on a cookie sheet, and bake at 350° for 8 minutes, or until hot and the cheese is melted. Serve hot or at room temperature.

Fast: Can assemble up to 2 days in advance and refrigerate.
Fabulous: Add finely minced ham, cooked shrimp, minced marinated artichoke hearts, capers, olives, minced green onions, frozen chopped spinach (thawed and well squeezed), or herbs to the cheese mixture. Substitute rye, pumpernickel, or egg bread for the sourdough.

FAST & FLASHY FOCACCIA

Another instance of a recipe that didn't fit neatly into any category, so here it is!

(serves 4 to 8)

frozen bread dough, thawed
   and at room temperature
garlic, minced
pesto, frozen or homemade
   (WALNUT PESTO SAUCE)

olive oil
Parmesan cheese, grated
mozzarella cheese, grated,
flour

1. Preheat the oven to 450°.
2. Roll the dough out on a lightly floured board. Sprinkle with garlic and the cheeses. Fold dough in half and roll out again. Repeat this process several times.
3. Grease a baking pan or iron skillet with olive oil.
4. Roll the dough out to a thickness of ½″ and place on the prepared pan.
5. Top with the desired amount of ingredients. Bake at 450° for about 30 minutes, or until crisp. Cut and serve.

Fast: Can assemble up to 1 day in advance and refrigerate.
Fabulous: Experiment with different cheeses and herb combos—for instance, green onions, dill weed, and feta cheese.

GARLIC CROUTON ROUNDS

A faster and flashier version of a croustade. Serve it as is or as a base for all sorts of toppings.

(yields about 39)

1 loaf sourdough bread, sliced
4 cloves garlic, peeled, or to taste

1 cup olive oil
salt to taste

1. Preheat the oven to 350°.
2. Cut the bread into 2″ rounds or squares (I use a wine glass to do this).
3. Combine the olive oil and garlic in a food processor fitted with the metal blade. Salt the garlic oil to taste.
4. Brush the bread with the garlic oil and place on a cookie sheet. Bake at 350° until crisp, about 15 minutes.

Fast: Can prepare up to 1 week in advance and store in airtight jar(s) or plastic bag(s), or freeze for up to 6 months.

CHEDDARED BAGEL CHIPS

1 dozen bagels
2 cups sharp cheddar cheese, grated
1 tbsp. shallots, minced, or to taste

1 cup butter
1 tbsp. Dijon-style mustard, or to taste
paprika and white pepper to taste

1. Slice the bagels vertically into thin chips.
2. Combine the remaining ingredients in a food processor fitted with the metal blade.
3. Spread mixture on the bagel slices, place on cookie sheet, and bake at 325° until crisp, about 20 to 30 minutes.

Fast: Can assemble up to 4 hours in advance and hold at room temperature, or flash freeze for up to 3 months.
Fabulous: Substitute different kinds of cheeses and add herbs.

BAGEL CHIPS

I created this recipe when I had more bagels than I knew what to do with. Gary Collins loved them on "Hour Magazine."

(yields about 18 dozen)

1 dozen bagels, cut into
   thin, vertical slices
2 cups olive oil

8 cloves garlic, smashed
dill weed, fresh or dried, to taste
salt to taste

1. Preheat the oven to 350°.
2. Combine all ingredients, except the bagels, in a food processor fitted with the metal blade. Taste and adjust the seasonings.
3. Place the bagel slices on a cookie sheet and brush with the flavored oil.
4. Bake at 350° about 20 to 30 minutes or until crisp. Watch carefully to prevent burning.

Fast: Can prepare and store up to 1 week in advance and store in airtight jar(s) or plastic bag(s), or freeze for up to 6 months.
Fabulous: Season with any herb, depending on what the chips are to be served with.

HERITAGE NACHOS

(serves 6 to 8)

oil
12 corn tortillas or
   prepared tortilla chips
½ lb. sharp cheddar
   cheese, grated

½ lb. Jack cheese, grated
1 bunch green onions, minced
NACHO SAUCE (recipe follows)

1. To prepare your own tortilla chips, cut the tortillas into eighths and deep-fat fry until crisp. Drain on paper towels. If you don't want to fry, brush them with oil, place on a cookie sheet, and bake at 350° for 10 to 15 minutes or until crisp.
2. Place the chips on an ovenproof platter and top with the cheeses and onions. Bake at 350° for 5 to 10 minutes or until the cheese melts.

NACHO SAUCE

2 cups tomato purée
4-8 green chiles, seeded, and
   deveined (canned)
4-6 green onions, minced
½ cup cilantro, minced

1 tsp. garlic, minced, or
   more to taste
lime juice, oregano, cumin,
   salt, and chili powder to taste
1 tbsp. olive oil

1. Place all ingredients in a blender or a food processor fitted with the metal blade and purée.
2. Taste and adjust the seasonings.

Fast: Can prepare the chips up to 1 week in advance and store in airtight jar(s) or plastic bag(s), or freeze for up to 6 months. Can assemble the nachos up to 4 hours in advance and hold at room temperature. Can prepare the NACHO SAUCE up to 1 week in advance and refrigerate, or freeze for up to 1 year.

Flashy: Serve with bowls of minced green onions, sliced olives, hot or cold refried beans, chopped avocado or GUACAMOLE, and/or sour cream for guests to top their own.

LAMB PITA TRIANGLES WITH CILANTRO

Rich Mediterranean flavors.

(yields about 32 triangles)

½ lb. lean ground lamb
6 green onions, minced
¼ cup parsley, minced
1 tbsp. tomato paste
1 tsp. garlic, minced
zest of 1 lemon, finely grated

2 tbsp. cilantro, minced,
  or more to taste
1-2 tsp. Dijon-style mustard
½ tsp. dried mint or 1 tbsp. fresh
salt and white pepper to taste
4 pitas, split open to form 8

1. Combine all the ingredients except the pitas in a bowl. Mix well.
2. Fry 1 tsp. of the mixture. Taste and adjust the seasonings.
3. Refrigerate for several hours to allow the flavors to develop.

Assembly:
1. Preheat the oven to 450° or fire up the barbecue.
2. Top each pita with the lamb mixture and cut into triangles.
3. Place the triangles on a cookie sheet and bake at 450° for 10 minutes or until the lamb is cooked to your liking, or barbecue. (In the summer I like to think of the barbecue as my oven and almost everything gets put on it. If you add some hickory chips, you'll get a marvelous, smoky flavor.)

Fast: Can prepare the meat mixture up to 2 days in advance and refrigerate, or flash freeze, assembled, for up to 1 month. Do not thaw before cooking.
Fabulous: Add feta cheese to the lamb mixture and/or rosemary, oregano, or thyme. Spread the mustard over the lamb and top with breadcrumbs and grated Parmesan cheese.

PITA CHIPS

(yields about 96)

1 pkg. pita bread, each
   bread cut into triangles
   and separated in half
1 cup olive oil

optional seasonings:
   garlic, minced
   oregano
   dill weed
   Parmesan cheese, grated
   salt

1. Preheat the oven to 350°.
2. Heat the olive oil with garlic and or herb(s) of choice until the flavors develop, or use plain olive oil.
3. Place on a cookie sheet and brush each triangle with seasoned or plain olive oil.
4. Sprinkle with salt, extra oregano, dill weed, and/or Parmesan cheese, if desired.
5. Bake at 350° for 15 to 20 minutes or until crisp.

Fast: Can prepare up to 2 weeks in advance and store in airtight jar(s) or plastic bag(s), or freeze for up to 3 months.

FAST & FLASHY BRIE & WALNUT TRIANGLES

Brie cheese
walnuts, toasted
pita bread, cut into triangles and separated in half

1. Preheat the oven to 400°.
2. Place the triangles on a cookie sheet and toast in a 400° oven for 15 minutes or until crisp.
3. Top each triangle with a piece of brie.
4. Place under a hot broiler until the cheese starts to melt.
5. Top each triangle with a walnut and serve.

Fast: Can prepare through step 3 up to 1 day in advance and refrigerate, or freeze for up to 1 month.

Fabulous: With different combinations of nuts or seeds, roasted red peppers, herbs, or ham slices as toppings.

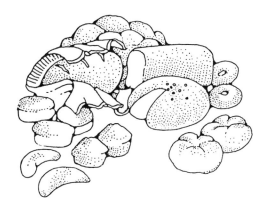

WARM GOAT CHEESE & PESTO PITA TRIANGLES

Great for any summer entertaining.

PITA TRIANGLES (see recipe)
chevre (French goat cheese)
WALNUT PESTO SAUCE (see recipe)

1. Preheat the broiler.
2. Spread each triangle with pesto and top with a piece of chevre.
3. Place on a cookie sheet and broil just until cheese starts to melt.

Fast: Can prepare through step 2 up to 2 hours in advance and hold at room temperature, or flash freeze for up to 1 month.

Fabulous: Substitute brie, Jack, Camembert, or Saint André cheese for the chevre.

ARTICHOKE ALMOND PITA TRIANGLES

Another fabulous variation

(tops about 50 triangles)

2 6-oz. jars marinated
  artichoke hearts, drained
  and chopped
½ cup blanched, slivered
  almonds

¼ cup parsley, minced
Mornay Sauce (see recipe)
PITA CHIPS (see recipe)
Parmesan cheese, grated

1. Preheat the oven to 450°.
2. Combine the Mornay Sauce, artichoke hearts, parsley, and almonds in a bowl.
3. Top the PITA CHIPS with this mixture and place on a cookie sheet. Sprinkle with Parmesan cheese and bake at 450° for about 10 minutes.

Fast: Can assemble up to 4 hours in advance and hold at room temperature, or flash freeze for up to 1 month. Can prepare the filling up to 3 days in advance and refrigerate, or freeze for up to 6 months.
Fabulous: Toss the filling into pasta or serve as a sauce for chicken breasts.

ONION & ZUCCHINI PITA PIZZAS

You'll never consider using an English muffin after trying this idea.

(yields about 32)

2 large zucchini
2 onions
¼ cup walnuts, toasted
   and minced
¼ cup extra virgin olive oil
¼ cup Parmesan cheese, grated

¼ cup mozzarella cheese, grated
1 tbsp. dried basil or
   3 tbsp. fresh basil
2 pitas, split open to form 4
salt, white pepper, and
   minced garlic to taste

1. Preheat the oven to 450°.
2. Slice the onions and zucchini in half lengthwise and then into thin slices.
3. Heat 2 tbsp. of oil in a skillet. Sauté the onions and desired amount of garlic until tender.
4. Add the zucchini and cook until tender. Season with salt, pepper, and basil.
5. Place the pitas on a cookie sheet and drizzle with the remaining olive oil.
6. Top them with cheese and then the zucchini mixture. Sprinkle the nuts over the top.
7. Bake at 450° for about 10 to 15 minutes or until golden and crisp. Cut into triangles and serve.

Fast: Can prepare the vegetable mixture up to 3 days in advance and refrigerate, or freeze for up to 3 months. Can assemble up to 2 hours in advance, leave at room temperature, or flash freeze assembled up to 1 month. Don't thaw before cooking.
Fabulous: Try these combos: ground lamb and feta cheese; roasted red peppers and feta cheese; spinach, Italian sausage and onion; Italian olives, roasted red peppers and Jack cheese; prosciutto, eggplant, and goat cheese; green tomatoes and olives; ham and tomatoes.

CROUSTADES

Here's another *FAST & FLASHY* way to create filled individual hors d'oeuvres without having to prepare your own pastry. Croustades are sourdough toast cups and can be filled with anything from lobster to peanut butter. This is a job that can be given to the non-cook and/or the children of the household. You'll love their versatility and I urge you, as always, to go beyond my recipes and create for yourself. Besides the fillings that I have specially designated as croustade fillings, refer to Chapter 3 for other choices.

CROUSTADES

(yields about 39)

1 loaf sourdough bread, sliced
1 cup butter or olive oil
garlic cloves, peeled and smashed
mini-muffin tins

1. Preheat the oven to 375°.
2. Cut the bread into 2- 2½" rounds using a cookie cutter or wine glass.
3. Melt butter or heat olive oil in a small skillet with the smashed garlic, until garlic gives off it's flavor.
4. Roll out the bread rounds with a rolling pin. Brush them and the mini-muffin cups with the garlic butter or oil and press them into the cups.
5. Bake at 375° until they are completely crisp, for about 10-15 minutes. They are now ready to be filled.

Fast: Can store in airtight jar(s) for up to 3 weeks, or freeze in plastic bag(s) for up to 6 months.

right:
Cold Sundried Tomato and Feta
Soufflé served with Gloria Ferrer
Brut Sparkling Wine.

above:
Potted Pork Degan with
Dry Creek Vineyard
Cabernet Sauvignon.

Marinated Shrimp served with
Dry Creek Vineyard Fumé Blanc.

Chile Cheese Fondue with
Dry Creek Vineyard Zinfandel.

CARROT CROUSTADES

(fills about 60 croustades)

1 lb. carrots, blanched, peeled, and puréed
3 tbsp. butter
1 tbsp. flour
1 cup heavy cream
2 tbsp. sherry
2 tbsp. brandy
1 tbsp. shallots, minced
2 tbsp. parsley, minced
2 tbsp. sesame seeds, toasted, or more to taste
Parmesan cheese, grated
salt, white pepper, dried thyme and freshly grated nutmeg to taste
CROUSTADES (see recipe)

1. Preheat the oven to 350°.
2. Melt the butter in a skillet and sauté the shallots until tender.
3. Add carrots and stir in the flour.
4. Stir in the brandy, sherry, sesame seeds, parsley and thyme.
5. Stir in the cream and cook until the mixture thickens and the flavors develop. Taste and adjust the seasonings.
6. Fill the croustades and place on a cookie sheet, sprinkle with Parmesan cheese, and bake at 350° for about 10 minutes, or until hot.

Fast: Can assemble up to 3 hours in advance, leave at room temperature, and bake just before serving. Can prepare the filling up to 3 days in advance and refrigerate, or freeze for up to 3 months.
Fabulous: Served with Gloria Ferrer Royal Cuvée Sparkling Wine.

FLORENTINE CROUSTADES

(fills about 60 croustades)

1 8-oz. pkg. frozen spinach, thawed and squeezed in tea towel to remove all the excess moisture
½ cup onion, minced
4 oz. mushrooms, minced and squeezed in tea towel to remove all the excess moisture
1-2 cloves garlic, minced

2 tbsp. butter
2 tbsp. flour
¾ cup heavy cream
½-1 Gruyère cheese, grated
¼ cup medium dry sherry
¼ tsp. dried thyme
salt, white pepper, and freshly grated nutmeg to taste
CROUSTADES (see recipe)

1. Prepeat the oven to 350°.
2. Melt the butter in a saucepan and cook the onions, garlic, and mushrooms until the onions are tender.
3. Blend in the flour and cook for 1 minute, without browning.
4. Mix in the sherry and cook for a minute more.
5. Remove the pan from the burner and stir in the cream. Return it to the burner and add the spinach and seasonings. Cook until the flavors develop and the mixture thickens. Stir frequently.
6. Fill the croustades, place them on a cookie sheet, and top with the Gruyère. Bake at 350° until hot and bubbly.

Fast: Can assemble up to 3 hours in advance, leave at room temperature, and bake just before serving. Can prepare filling up to 3 days in advance and refrigerate, or freeze up to 3 months.
Fabulous: Add ½ cup minced ham or prosciutto to the filling. Instead of spinach, substitute broccoli, chard, or asparagus.

SPINACH & HAM CROUSTADES

(fills about 60 croustades)

10 oz. frozen spinach, thawed, drained, and puréed
¼-½ cup ham, chopped
1-2 cloves garlic, minced
2 tbsp. butter
2 tbsp. flour
½ cup heavy cream
3 tbsp. brandy
¼ cup Jack cheese, grated
¼ cup Parmesan cheese, grated
1 tsp. Dijon-style mustard
4 tbsp. parsley, minced
6 tbsp. onion, minced
white pepper and freshly grated nutmeg to taste
CROUSTADES (see recipe)

1. Melt butter in a saucepan. Add the garlic and onions and sauté until tender.

2. Whisk in the flour. Cook for 1 minute without browning.

3. Whisk in the cream and brandy and cook until thickened.

4. Whisk in all the remaining ingredients, except the Parmesan cheese, and cook until the cheese melts and the flavors develop. Taste and adjust the seasonings.

5. Fill the croustades, place on a cookie sheet, and top with Parmesan cheese. Place under the hot broiler for a few minutes until the cheese melts and they are golden.

Fast: Can assemble up to 3 hours in advance, leave at room temperature, and bake at 350° for 10-15 minutes; serve immediately. Can prepare the filling up to 3 days in advance and refrigerate, or freeze for up to 3 months.

LEEK CROUSTADES

(fills about 60 croustades)

4 medium leeks, trimmed,
   halved lengthwise, rinsed,
   and cut crosswise
   into thin pieces
3 tbsp. butter
1 tbsp. flour
1 cup heavy cream

2 tbsp. sherry
2 tbsp. parsley, minced
Jack or Gruyère cheese, grated
salt, white pepper, lemon
   juice and freshly grated
   nutmeg to taste
CROUSTADES (see recipe)

1. Melt butter in a skillet and add the leeks. Sauté until tender.
2. Stir in the flour; blend well and cook for 1 minute.
3. Stir in the cream and sherry and simmer until cream is reduced by about ⅓.
4. Add seasonings; taste and adjust them.
5. Fill the croustades, place on a cookie sheet, and top with grated cheese. Place under the broiler until the cheese melts.

Fast: Can assemble up to 3 hours in advance, leave at room temperature, and bake at 350° for 10-15 minutes; serve immediately. Can prepare the filling up to 3 days in advance and refrigerate, or freeze up to 3 months.
Fabulous: Served with Gloria Ferrer Royal Cuvée Sparkling Wine.

ASPARAGUS & SHIITAKI MUSHROOM CROUSTADES

(fills about 60 croustades)

1 lb. asparagus, trimmed, minced, and blanched
1 oz. dried shiitake mushrooms, rehydrated, stemmed, and minced
¼ cup Madeira
1 cup heavy cream
2 tbsp. parsley, minced
1 tbsp. shallots, minced
3 tbsp. butter
1 tbsp. flour
Jack or Gruyère cheese, grated, to taste
salt, white pepper, lemon juice, dried thyme and freshly grated nutmeg to taste
CROUSTADES (see recipe)

1. Melt butter in a skillet and add the parsley, shallots, asparagus, and mushrooms. Stir in the flour and sauté for a minute.
2. Stir in the Madeira and cream. Simmer until the cream is reduced and the sauce is nicely thickened.
3. Stir in the asparagus and desired amount of cheese and seasonings.
4. Fill the croustades, place on cookie sheet, and top with more cheese. Place under the broiler until the cheese melts.

Fast: Can assemble up to 3 hours in advance, leave at room temperature, and bake in a 350° oven for 10 to 15 minutes; serve immediately. Can prepare the filling up to 3 days in advance and refrigerate, or freeze for up to 3 months.

TOMATO CHEESE CROUSTADES

(fills about 30 croustades)

2 tbsp. tomato paste or
  1 fresh tomato, peeled,
  seeded, and chopped
1 cup Gruyère cheese, grated,
  or more to taste
2 tbsp. Parmesan cheese, grated
¼ cup fresh basil, or 1 tsp. dried
1-2 cloves garlic, peeled

¼ cup parsley, minced,
  or more to taste
2 tbsp. capers
4 tbsp. sour cream
2 tbsp. butter, cut into small bits
salt, white pepper and freshly
  grated nutmeg to taste
CROUSTADES (see recipe)

1. Preheat the oven to 400°.
2. Combine all the ingredients, except the butter and croustades, in a food processor fitted with the metal blade. Taste and adjust the seasonings.
3. Fill the croustades, and place on a cookie sheet; top with more grated cheese and butter bits.
4. Bake at 400° for about 10 minutes or until hot and bubbly.

Fast: Can assemble up to 3 hours in advance, leave at room temperature, and bake just before serving. Can prepare the filling up to 3 days in advance and refrigerate, or freeze for up to 3 months.
Fabulous: Use the filling in omelets, on BEATEN BISCUITS or to stuff mushrooms.

PIPERADE CROUSTADES

A celebration of the fall harvest.

(fills about 60 croustades)

¼ cup olive oil
2 onions, minced
3-5 cloves garlic, minced
2 large tomatoes, peeled
   and chopped
2-4 bell peppers, seeded
   and chopped
½-1 cup parsley, minced

½ lb. ham, minced
Jack cheese, grated or
   cut into small pieces
½ bay leaf
dried thyme and basil to taste
salt and white pepper to taste
CROUSTADES (see recipe)

1. Heat the olive oil in a skillet and sauté the onions and garlic until tender, over medium-low heat.
2. Add the peppers and ham and sauté until the peppers are tender.
3. Stir in the tomatoes, parsley, and seasonings. Cook until the flavors develop and the liquid cooks away. Remove and discard the bay leaf.
4. Stir in about 1 cup of cheese and cook over low heat, until it melts.;
5. Fill the croustades, place on a cookie sheet, and top with more cheese. Place under the broiler until the cheese melts. Serve warm.

Fast: Can assemble up to 3 hours in advance, leave at room temperature, and bake in a 350° oven for 10 to 15 minutes, or until hot; serve immediately. Can prepare the filling up to 4 days in advance and refrigerate, or freeze up to 3 months.

Fabulous: Use the filling on pasta or couscous as an entrée, or as a vegetable dish.

ITALIAN SAUSAGE CROUSTADES

(fills about 60 croustades)

1 lb. Italian sausages, casings removed
2 cups ricotta cheese
2 onions, minced
4 cloves garlic, minced
½ cup parsley, minced
1 egg
¼ cup Parmesan cheese, grated, or more to taste

Jack cheese, cut into small cubes to fit in bottom of each croustade
pitted black olives, whole or halved
salt, white pepper and freshly grated nutmeg to taste
CROUSTADES (see recipe)

1. Preheat the oven to 350°.
2. Cook the sausages in a skillet until they are no longer pink. Pour off all but 2 tbsp. of the fat.
3. Add the onions and garlic to skillet and brown. Transfer them to a food processor fitted with the metal blade.
4. Add all the remaining ingredients to the food processor, except the Jack cheese and olives, and process until combined. Taste and adjust the seasonings.
5. Place the croustades on a cookie sheet and put a piece of Jack cheese in each croustade and then the filling. Top with an olive and bake at 350° until hot, about 10 minutes.

Fast: Can assemble up to 3 hours in advance, leave at room temperature, and bake just before serving. Can prepare the filling up to 3 days in advance and refrigerate, or freeze for up to 3 months.

SEAFOOD CROUSTADES

World-class!

(fills about 30 croustades)

2 oz. bay shrimp, cooked
3 oz. crabmeat, flaked,
  fresh, or imitation crab
1 cup mayonnaise, homemade
  or purchased
½ cup Parmesan cheese, grated
⅓ cup Gruyère cheese,
  grated
⅓ cup green onions, minced
½ tsp. Worcestershire
  sauce, or to taste
1 tsp. Dijon-style mustard
⅓ cup parsley, minced
½ cup water chestnuts, minced
2 tbsp. capers, drained
salt, white pepper and
  hot pepper sauce to taste
CROUSTADES (see recipe)

1. Preheat the oven to 350°.
2. Combine all the ingredients, except the croustades, in a bowl. Taste and adjust the seasonings.
3. Fill each croustade, place on a cookie sheet, and bake at 350° for 10 minutes or until hot.

Fast: Can prepare the filling up to 1 day in advance and refrigerate. Can fill the croustades up to 2 hours in advance and hold at room temperature; bake right before serving.
Fabulous: Use the filling on cooked pasta, served hot or cold. As a cold filling for cooked pasta shells, cherry tomatoes, or mushroom caps or on BEATEN BISCUITS. Use as a hot filling for Flo Braker's Magic Puff Pastry, TARTLETS, or PHYLLO CUPS. Served with Gloria Ferrer Royal Cuvée Sparkling Wine.

MUENSTERED CROUSTADES

(fills about 30 croustades)

2 cups muenster cheese,
   cut up or grated
6-12 slices bacon, cooked,
   drained on paper towels,
   and crumbled
2 cloves garlic, minced
½ cup green onions, minced
¼ cup parsley, minced
1 tbsp. butter

1 tbsp. flour
2 tbsp. stuffed green
   olives, minced
2 tbsp. dry vermouth
½ cup heavy cream
dash cayenne pepper
salt and white pepper
   to taste
CROUSTADES (see recipe)

1. Preheat the oven to 350°.
2. Sauté the onions and garlic in butter over medium-low heat, until tender.
3. Stir in the flour and cook for a minute. Remove the saucepan from the burner and stir in the wine, cream, and seasonings.
4. Return to the burner and cook until thickened.
5. Stir in the cheese, parsley, olives, and bacon. Taste and adjust the seasonings.
6. Fill the croustades, place on a cookie sheet, and bake at 350° for about 10 minutes, until they are hot.

Fast: Can assemble up to 3 hours in advance, leave at room temperature, and bake just before serving. Can prepare the filling up to 3 days in advance and refrigerate, or freeze for up to 3 months.
Fabulous: Toss the filling into freshly cooked pasta as an entrée or as a filling for crepes, to top BEATEN BISCUITS, or in mushrooms. Season with fresh basil.

PHYLLO

Phyllo is paper-thin sheets of pastry from which you can produce light, flaky, and delicate results. Purchase it in Greek or Middle-Eastern delis, or in the freezer section of your supermarket.

Phyllo items convey a special feeling to your guests and let them know you value their presence. Be sure to take the time to read all the instructions on the package. Using phyllo takes a bit of patience, but is well worth it.

PHYLLO PIZZA

Designed for picnics and relaxed summer entertaining

(serves 4 to 6)

8 tomatoes, peeled, seeded, and chopped
2 tsp. tomato paste
6 yellow or white onions, sliced thinly
3 cloves garlic, minced
½ cup parsley, minced

1½-2 cups Gruyère cheese, grated
½ cup olive oil
½ cup dry vermouth
3 tsp. sugar
8 sheets of phyllo
salt, white pepper, fresh or dried oregano, and basil to taste

1. Preheat the oven to 375°.
2. Sauté the onions in ¼ cup of olive oil for 15 minutes over low heat. Add 2 tsp. of sugar, the garlic, parsley, and vermouth and continue to cook for 30 minutes more, until golden and glazed. Stir frequently.
3. At same time, sauté the tomatoes in 2 tbsp. of olive oil in another skillet. Add the seasonings, remaining sugar, and tomato paste. Taste and adjust the seasonings. Cook until the liquid is evaporated.
4. Combine the 2 mixtures.
5. Oil a 10″ × 16″ cookie sheet and top with the phyllo, brushing each sheet with oil before topping with the next. Tuck the edges under neatly.
6. Top with the tomato-onion mixture, the cheese, olives and more fresh or dried herbs.

7. Bake at 375° for 20 to 25 minutes.

Fast: Can assemble up to 1 day in advance and refrigerate, or freeze for up to 3 months.

Fabulous: For an Italian variation, brush the phyllo with garlic butter and top with ricotta cheese, a combination of grated whole milk mozzarella, Parmesan and chevre cheeses, roasted red peppers, and sautéed eggplant.

GREEK CHEESE TRIANGLES

(yields about 48)

½ lb. phyllo pastry sheets
½ lb. ricotta cheese
½ lb. Jack cheese, grated
½ lb. feta cheese, crumbled
1 egg

2 tbsp. fresh dill weed, chopped, or to taste
3 tbsp. shallots, minced, or to taste
6 tbsp. sesame seeds, toasted
1 cup butter, melted
white pepper to taste

1. Preheat the oven to 425°.
2. Combine everything in a food processor fitted with the metal blade, except the phyllo, sesame seeds, and melted butter. Taste and adjust the seasonings.
3. Cut phyllo into long strips 2" wide. Brush 1 strip at a time with melted butter. Cover the remaining phyllo with waxed paper and a slightly dampened towel until used.
4. Place 1 tsp. of the filling at one end of each strip and fold over and over into a small triangle. While folding, make sure that bottom edge is parallel with the alternate edge. Repeat until all the filling is used. Place triangles on a buttered cookie sheet.
5. Brush each triangle with melted butter, sprinkle with sesame seeds, and bake at 425° for 10 to 15 minutes, or until golden.

Fast: Can prepare up to 1 day in advance and refrigerate, or freeze for up to 3 months.

Fabulous: Add seafood, ham, artichoke hearts, cooked chicken, spinach, bok choy, or prosciutto to the cheese mixture. Substitute chevre for the feta cheese.

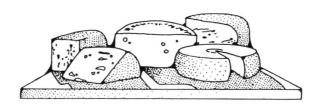

PHYLLO CUPS

Here's a faster method for using phyllo, rather than making the traditional triangles.

(yields about 48)

1 lb. phyllo
½ lb melted butter

1. Preheat the oven to 425°.
2. Brush mini-muffin cups with butter. Cut phyllo into 3"-4" squares.
3. Layer the squares in the muffin cups, brushing each with melted butter, until you have 4 layers in each cup.
4. Bake at 425° for 5 to 10 minutes or until barely golden. Watch carefully.

Fast: Can prepare up to 1 week in advance and store in airtight jar(s) or plastic bag(s), or freeze for up to 3 months.
Fabulous: Fill with ONION & HAM TARTLET FILLING, GREEK CHEESE TRIANGLES filling, CRAB & ARTICHOKE STUFFED MUSHROOMS filling, SPRING MORNAY FILLING, or the filling of your choice.

CHICKEN & PROSCIUTTO PHYLLO CUPS

(yields about 48 cups)

2 chicken breasts, skinned,
  boned, and cut up
8 slices prosciutto, chopped
4 tbsp. unsalted butter, melted
2 tbsp. olive oil
½ cup parsley, minced
2-4 cloves garlic, minced
1 onion, minced
10 oz. frozen chopped spinach,
  thawed and squeezed in
  a tea towel to remove
  all the excess moisture

4 tbsp. Romano cheese,
  grated
2 cups ricotta cheese
2 eggs
½-1 cup Jack or
  mozzarella cheese,
  grated or cubed
salt, white pepper,
  and freshly grated
  nutmeg to taste
PHYLLO CUPS (see recipe)

1. Preheat the oven to 425°.
2. Combine the cheeses and eggs in a food processor fitted with metal blade. Season with salt, white pepper, and nutmeg to taste.
3. Sauté chicken breasts and garlic in 2 tbsp. butter plus olive oil until just cooked. Transfer to the food processor.
4. Sauté the onion in 2 tbsp. butter until golden and transfer it to the food processor.
5. Add the parsley, spinach, and prosciutto to the food processor. Process briefly, taking care not to destroy the texture.
6. Fill the Phyllo Cups with the mixture and bake at 425° for 10 minutes or until hot.

Fast: Can prepare the filling up to 2 days in advance, and refrigerate, or freeze for up to 3 months. Can assemble the PHYLLO CUPS up to 1 day in advance and refrigerate, or freeze for up to 3 months. To cook frozen, add 5 minutes to the cooking time.

HORS D'OEUVRE PASTRIES

This is the most sophisticated and refined area of hors d'oeuvres. Individual pastries instantly set the stage for a memorable evening. As with phyllo, they may require a bit more effort but you will find it well worth it. When time plays a critical factor, you can always substitute frozen puff pastry. This will prove to be a *FAST & FLASHY* lifesaver. Let me stress that all of the pastry recipes I've included are *FAST & FLASHY*—designed to help you become a fearless pastry cook. Another important thing to remember is that they can be prepared in a food processor, at your leisure, and frozen, enabling you to pull out an array of delicate pastries for last-minute guests, or prepare well in advance for that special party.

CAVIAR PASTRIES

So elegant and so easy!

(yields 60 to 80)

1 pkg. frozen puff pastry, thawed	16 oz. Saint André cheese,
green onions, minced	at room temperature
lemon zest, finely grated	caviar

1. Preheat the oven to 400°.
2. Roll out each sheet of pastry 1½ times its original size.
3. Cut into 2" circles with a cookie cutter or wine glass.
4. Place the circles on cookie sheet and pierce with a fork. Bake at 400° for 15 to 20 minutes, or until crisp and golden.
5. Top each cooled pastry circle with a generous amount of Saint André, a dollop of caviar and a sprinkling of green onions and lemon zest. Serve at room temperature.

Fast: Can prepare through step 4 up to 2 days in advance and store in plastic bag(s) or airtight glass jar(s), or freeze for up to 3 months.

CHEESE TWISTS

A touch of understated elegance.

(yields about 70)

1 pkg. frozen puff pastry, thawed
½ cup Gruyère cheese,
    grated finely
½ cup sharp cheddar cheese,
    grated finely

¼ tsp sweet Hungarian
    paprika
1 egg white, lightly beaten
salt and white pepper
    to taste

1. Preheat the oven to 400°.
2. Roll the pastry dough out into 2 rectangles ¼" thick.
3. Brush with the egg white and sprinkle with salt, pepper, paprika, and the cheeses. Press this lightly into the pastry.
4. Cut into 1" strips, twist, and place on greased cookie sheets. Bake at 400° for 15 minutes, or until golden. Serve warm or at room temperature.

Fast: Can prepare up to 1 week in advance and refrigerate, or flash freeze for up to 1 month. Reheat in a 400° oven before serving.
Fabulous: Top pastry with sesame seeds and/or minced green onions, along with the cheeses. Use your favorite cheese combos. Cut pastry into thinner strips for thinner twists. Brush with melted butter and roll in chopped walnuts before baking.

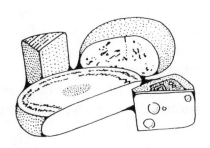

BEATEN BISCUITS

Flaky baby biscuits that make a wonderful base for countless mixtures.

(yields about 70)

2 cups flour, unbleached
1 tsp. salt
½ cup unsalted butter, frozen
   and cut into small pieces

½ cup ice water
1-2 tbsp. shallots, minced
white pepper to taste

1. Preheat the oven to 350° and place the rack in the middle of the oven.
2. Combine the flour, salt, shallots, and pepper in a food processor fitted with the metal blade. Turn the machine on and off twice.
3. Add the butter and process until the mixture is the consistency of cornmeal.
4. While the machine is running, pour in the ice water through the feed tube in a slow, steady stream. Process until the mixture forms a ball and continue for an extra 2 minutes.
5. Remove the dough and roll it into 1 ⅛" thick rectangle on a lightly floured surface.
6. Fold the dough in half to make 2 layers. Cut through both layers with a 1½" round cutter or a wine glass.
7. Bake the biscuits on an ungreased cookie sheet at 350° for 25 to 30 minutes, or until golden. Remove from the oven and split in half immediately. If the centers are soft, return them to the oven for 3 to 4 minutes to crisp.

Fast: Can prepare up to 1 week in advance and store in airtight jar(s) or palstic bag(s), or freeze for up to 6 months.
Fabulous: Add 6 tbsp. of crisp crumbled bacon, parsley, dill weed, basil, poppy seeds, sesame seeds, fried minced onions, or minced green onions added to the dough.

POLISH SAUSAGE IN PUFF PASTRY

When you want some gusto!

(yields 12 ½" pieces)

2 green onions, minced

12 small pieces caraway
   cheese, the diameter of
   the sausage and about
   ¼" thick

1-2 tbsp. coarse-grained mustard

1 sheet frozen puff pastry,
   thawed

1 long, fully cooked Polish
   sausage

1. Preheat the oven to 425°.
2. Roll a sheet of puff pastry out to a thickness of ¼". Brush the inside of the pastry sheet with mustard.
3. Sprinkle the green onions on top and then put the sausage at the edge. Roll the pastry around the sausage and seal the edge, using a fork.
4. Cut it into ½" slices and place on an ungreased cookie sheet. If the sausage is loose, crimp the pastry securely around it. Top with more mustard and a piece of cheese.
5. Bake at 425° for 5 to 10 minutes, or until the pastry is golden and puffed.

Fast: Can prepare through step 4 up to 1 day in advance and refrigerate, or flash freeze for up to 1 month. Don't thaw before baking.

Fabulous: Experiment with different kinds of sausages, mustards, and cheeses.

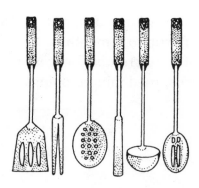

HAM & CHEESE PASTRIES

An elegant way to start a meal; keep a supply in your freezer.

(yields about 70)

Pastry:
1 recipe Cream Cheese Pastry (see recipe), or use 2 sheets frozen puff pastry, thawed.

Filling:
ham or prosciutto slices
cheese slices, (muenster, Jack, cheddar, Gouda, Edam, Port Salut or Gruyère)
green onions, minced
Dijon-style mustard

1. Preheat the oven to 400°.
2. Roll out the pastry to a thickness of ¼" on a lightly floured board.
3. Cut it into small squares about 1½" to 2".
4. Brush the pastry squares with mustard, sprinkle with some green onions, top with a piece of ham and cheese. Place pastries on a greased cookie sheet.
5. Bake at 400° for 10 to 20 minutes, or until the pastry is golden.

Fast: Can assemble up to 1 day in advance, refrigerate, and bake before serving, or flash freeze for up to 3 months.
Fabulous: Substitute cooked eggplant or sausage for the ham.

SOUTHWESTERN TARTLETS

Made of meat, not pastry, but this seemed like the most logical place to put it.

(yields about 30)

Filling:
¾ cup refried beans
¼ cup sour cream
1 cup sharp cheddar cheese, grated
2-4 cloves garlic, minced
⅓ cup black olives, chopped

¾ cup tortilla chips, crushed
¼ cup green onions, minced
½-1 tsp. cumin
4 tbsp. cilantro, chopped
salt and chili powder to taste

Mix together all the ingredients. Taste and adjust the seasonings.

Tartlet:
1 lb. lean ground beef
1 tsp. cumin
2 cloves garlic, minced

¼ cup green onion, minced
cheddar cheese, grated (optional)
salt and chili powder to taste

1. Preheat the oven to 425°.
2. Combine all the ingredients. Fry 1 tsp. to test the seasonings.
3. Press the meat mixture with your fingers or with spoons into mini-muffin tin cups, forming tartlets.
4. Place a spoonful of the filling in each and top with more cheese, if desired.
5. Bake at 425° for 7 to 8 minutes. Remove the tartlets from the muffin cups and serve.

Fast: Can prepare the filling or assembled tartlets up to 2 days in advance and refrigerate, or flash freeze the assembled tartlets for up to 3 months.
Fabulous: Use the filling in CROUSTADES, TORTILLA CUPS, or in WON TON CUPS.

TORTILLA CUPS

Little tartlets made out of masa*, adapted from a Yucatan recipe.

(yields about 70)

6 cups dehydrated masa flour
1 tsp. salt
⅔ cup butter, cut into small pieces

3 cups cold water
olive oil

1. Preheat the oven to 375°.
2. Combine the masa, salt, and butter in a food processor fitted with the metal blade, until fine crumbs form.
3. While the machine is running, add the water through the feed tube and process until the dough is evenly moistened. (If necessary, prepare in 2 batches in your food processor.)
4. Shape the dough into about 1" balls, and cover with plastic wrap to prevent them from drying out.
5. Press the dough into oiled mini-muffin tin cups, using your fingers or spoons.
6. Brush liberally with oil and bake at 375°, for about 20 minutes or until crisp. Remove them from the muffin tin.
7. To reheat before serving, bake on a cookie sheet at 350° about 10 minutes, until hot.

Fast: Can prepare up to 1 day in advance and refrigerate, or freeze for up to 6 months.

Flashy: Serve unfilled and offer selections including, but not limited to: PUMPKIN SEED CHILE SAUCE, browned and seasoned ground pork with MEXICAN TOMATO SAUCE, GUACAMOLE, YUCATAN SAUCE with grated Jack cheese, FRIJOLES CALIENTE, AVOCADO DIPPING SAUCE, COLD CAPER SAUCE with cold cooked seafood, COLD PAPAYA CREAM SAUCE with cold cooked pork or seafood and CHILE CHEESE FONDUE.

Fabulous: Fill them with the SOUTHWESTERN TARTLETS filling.

*See Helpful Terms section for information about masa.

PIROZHKI

A delicate but satisfying meat-filled crescent-shaped pastry, perfect for winter parties.

(yields about 40)

Cream Cheese Pastry:

1 cup unsalted butter, frozen and cut into small pieces	¼ cup heavy cream
	1 shallot, peeled and cut in half
8 oz. cream cheese, cut into quarters	zest of 1 lemon, finely grated
	1 tsp. salt
2½ cups flour	dash of white pepper

1. Combine the cream cheese, butter, lemon zest, salt, white pepper, and shallot in a food processor fitted with the metal blade.
2. While the machine is running, add the cream through the feed tube.
3. Add the flour and process until a smooth dough forms.
4. Remove and wrap in plastic wrap and chill in the freezer for 30 minutes before using.

Filling:

1 lb. ground pork	1 tbsp. capers, or more to taste
½ cup cooked bulghur	
2 onions, minced	3 tbsp. butter
2 hard-boiled eggs, chopped	2 tbsp. sour cream
½ cup parsley, minced	1 tsp. Worcestershire sauce
2 cloves garlic, minced	½ tsp. salt, or to taste
1 tbsp. dried dill weed, or to taste	white or black pepper to taste

1. While the pastry chills sauté the onions and garlic in butter until they are golden. Add the pork and brown it.
2. Drain off any excess fat and mix in the remaining ingredients. Taste and adjust the seasonings.

Egg Wash:
1 egg
1 tsp. water

1. Lightly beat the egg with the water.

Assembly:
1. Preheat the oven to 400°.
2. Roll out the dough between sheets of plastic wrap to a thickness of ⅛″. Cut into 2″-3″ rounds. Place 1 tsp. of the filling in each round.
3. Paint the edges with the egg wash. Fold the dough over the filling, forming a crescent. Seal the edges with the tines of a fork or a potsticker mold.
4. Place on a greased cookie sheet and brush with the remaining egg wash. Prck the top of each pastry with a fork to allow the steam to escape.
5. Bake at 400° for 15 to 20 minutes, or until lightly browned.

Fast: Can assemble and refrigerate up to 1 day in advance, or flash freeze for up to 3 months. Paint on the egg wash right before baking.

FETA & SESAME CRESCENTS

A light and delicate pastry with a Middle-Eastern-style filling.

(yields about 36)

Cream Cheese Sesame Pastry:

6 oz. cream cheese, cut into quarters

½ lb. unsalted butter, frozen and cut into small pieces

2 cups flour

4 tbsp. apple cider vinegar

½ cup sesame seeds, toasted

1 shallot, peeled and cut in half

1. Combine the cream cheese, butter, flour, sesame seeds, and shallot in a food processor fitted with the metal blade.
2. While the machine is running, add the vinegar through the food tube.
3. Process until it forms a ball.
4. Divide the pastry in half, wrap in plastic wrap, and chill in the freezer for about 30 minutes.

Filling:

8 oz. feta cheese, crumbled

½ cup cilantro, minced

4-8 green onions, minced

1-2 cloves garlic, minced

¼ tsp. hot pepper sauce

⅛ tsp. salt, or to taste

¼-½ cup sesame seeds, toasted

1. Combine all the ingredients, except for the sesame seeds. Taste and adjust the seasonings.

Egg Wash:

1 egg

1 tsp. water

1. Lightly beat the egg with the water.

Assembly:

1. Preheat the oven to 400°.

2. Roll the dough out on a lightly floured board. Cut it into 2½" circles with a wine glass or cookie cutter.

3. Place a tsp. of the filling on each circle of dough. Fold in half and press the edges together. Seal with the tines of a fork or a potsticker mold.

4. Brush the egg wash on top of each crescent and coat with sesame seeds.

5. Bake on an ungreased cookie sheet at 400° for 20 to 25 minutes, or until lightly browned.

Fast: Can assemble up to 1 day in advance and refrigerate, or flash freeze for up to 3 months.

Fabulous: Season the filling with cumin or add minced, sun-dried tomatoes and fresh basil. Use the filling for CROUSTADES, Flo Braker's Magic Puff Pastry, TARTLETS, or WON TON CUPS.

CELERY ROOT & SHIITAKI MUSHROOMS IN DILLED SHALLOT PASTRY PILLOWS

Pastry pillows? This is what I have named these hors d'oeuvre ravioli pastries.

(yields about 48)

Celery Root and Shiitake Mushroom Filling:

4 tbsp. butter
2 tbsp. flour
2 cloves garlic, minced
2 shallots, minced
½ cup parsley, minced
1 medium-sized celery root,
   peeled and finely shredded
1 oz. shiitake mushrooms,
   rehydrated, stemmed, and
   minced

½ cup blanched almonds, slivered
4 oz. cream cheese
¼ cup Parmesan cheese, grated
½ cup chicken broth, homemade
   or canned
½ cup Madeira
1 tsp. Dijon-style mustard,
   or more to taste
½-1 tsp. dried dill weed
salt and white pepper to taste

1. Melt butter in a large skillet and sauté the garlic, shallots, and almonds until tender.
2. Add the mushrooms and celery root and sauté for a few minutes.
3. Stir in the flour and cook for a minute more.
4. Stir in the liquid, cheeses, mustard, parsley, and seasonings. Cook gently while stirring until thickened and the cheese melts. Taste and adjust the seasonings.

Dilled Shallot Pastry:

½ lb. unsalted butter, frozen and
   cut into small pieces
2 cups flour
½ cup sour cream or plain yogurt
1 egg yolk

1 large shallot, peeled
   and cut in half
2 tbsp. dried dill weed,
   or more to taste
white pepper to taste

1. Process the butter, shallot, dill weed, flour, and white pepper in a food processor fitted with the metal blade, until the mixture resembles coarse cornmeal.
2. Combine the sour cream or yogurt with the egg yolk in a small bowl. Add it to the food processor through the feed tube while the machine is running, and process until a ball forms.
3. Remove the dough and divide it into 2 balls. Wrap each in plastic wrap and place in the freezer to chill for about 30 minutes.

Assembly:
1. Preheat the oven to 400°.
2. Roll the dough out to a thickness of ⅛" on a lightly floured board.
3. Place the dough in a ravioli mold and put about ½ tsp. of the filling in the center of each square. Top with another sheet of pastry and roll the rolling pin over the top to separate each pastry pillow.
4. Remove the pillows from the ravioli mold. Place them on a greased cookie sheet and bake at 400° for 25 to 30 minutes, or until golden.

Fast: Can assemble up to 1 day in advance and refrigerate, or flash freeze for up to 3 months.
Fabulous: To be *FASTER & FLASHIER,* create pastry squares by cutting the pastry with a pastry cutter and topping each square with a tsp. of the filling. Bake as directed. Use the filling in CROUSTADES, on BEATEN BISCUITS, in mushroom caps, or in potsticker or won ton wrappers.

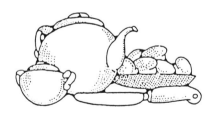

PROSCIUTTO & SAINT ANDRÉ IN YOGURT PASTRY PILLOWS

(yields about 60)

Prosciutto Saint André Filling:

¼ lb. prosciutto, thinly
   sliced and minced
1 8 oz. can of hearts of
   palm, cut up (optional)
½ cup parsley, minced

2 shallots, cut up, or more to taste
8 oz. cream cheese, at
   room temperature
½ lb. Saint André cheese,
   at room temperature

1. Combine the cheeses and shallots in a food processor fitted with the metal blade. (I guarantee that you will not need to adjust flavors.)
2. Process in the remaining ingredients, using care not to destroy the texture.

Yogurt Sesame Pastry:

2 sticks unsalted butter,
   frozen and cut into
   small pieces
2½ cups flour
1 cup yogurt, unflavored
zest of 1 lemon, finely grated

2 cloves garlic, peeled
¼-½ cup sesame seeds,
   toasted
1 tsp. salt
1 tsp. Dijon-style mustard
white pepper to taste

1. Combine the butter, yogurt, garlic, lemon zest, mustard, salt, and white pepper in a food processor fitted with the metal blade.
2. Add the flour and sesame seeds. Process until a ball forms. Add more flour if the dough is sticky.
3. Divide the dough into 2 balls, wrap in plastic wrap, and place in the freezer for about 30 minutes to chill.

Assembly:
1. Preheat the oven to 400°.
2. Roll the dough out to a thickness of ⅛" on a lightly floured board.

3. Place the dough in a ravioli mold and place about ½ tsp. of the filling in the center of each square. Top with another sheet of pastry and roll the rolling pin over the top to separate each pastry pillow.

4. Remove the pillows from the ravioli mold. Place them on a greased cookie sheet and bake at 400° for 25 to 30 minutes, or until golden.

Fast: Can assemble up to 1 day in advance and refrigerate, or flash freeze for up to 3 months.

Fabulous: To be *FASTER & FLASHIER,* create pastry squares by cutting the pastry with pastry cutter and topping each square with a teaspoon of the filling. Bake as directed. Use the filling in CROUSTADES, on BEATEN BISCUITS, in mushroom caps, or to fill potsticker or won ton wrappers. Served with Gloria Ferrer Royal Cuvée Sparkling Wine.

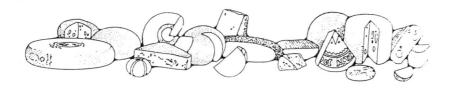

SAINT ANDRÉ & SHIITAKE TARTLETS

(yields about 24)

1 pkg. frozen puff pastry, thawed
2 tbsp. butter
2 tbsp. flour
¾ cup milk
¼ cup dry white wine
½ cup Saint André cheese, rind
   removed and cut into chunks
1 tbsp. lemon zest, finely grated
   and minced, or more to taste

1 tbsp. shallots, minced, or
   more to taste
1 tsp. Dijon-style mustard
1 oz. dried shiitake mushrooms,
   rehydrated, stemmed, and
   minced
green onions, minced, to taste
1 egg yolk combined with
   2 tbsp. heavy cream
salt, white pepper, and freshly
   grated nutmeg to taste

Tartlets:

1. Preheat the oven to 425°.
2. Cut the pastry into circles using a wine glass. Place each circle in a mini-muffin tin. Top each tartlet with a piece of foil and fill with uncooked dried beans or pastry weights, to weigh the pastry down. Bake at 425° for 5 minutes.
3. When cool remove the foil and beans or weights, and place the tartlets on a cookie sheet.

Filling:

1. Reduce the oven temperature to 350°.
2. Melt butter in a saucepan and sauté the mushrooms and shallots until tender. Do not brown.
3. Blend in the flour and mustard and cook for 1 minute over low heat.
4. Stir in the milk and wine and cook, stirring continuously, until thickened.
5. Stir in the cheese, lemon zest, green onions and seasonings. Continue stirring over low heat until the cheese melts and flavors develop.
6. Stir 2 tbsp. of the sauce into the yolk mixture, then mix this back into the sauce. Cook, stirring, over low heat for about 1 minute. Do not boil or the yolk will curdle.

7. Fill the tartlets with the filling. Bake at 350° for 10 to 15 minutes and serve hot.

Fast: Can assemble up to 1 day in advance and refrigerate, or flash freeze for up to 1 month. Do not thaw before baking.
Fabulous: Substitute minced ham or shrimp, hearts of palm, artichoke hearts, or crabmeat for the shiitake mushrooms.

ITALIAN SAUSAGE TARTLETS

(yields about 12)

1 cup ricotta cheese
¼ cup Parmesan cheese, grated or to taste
1 sheet frozen puff pastry, thawed

1 large or 2 small Italian sweet sausages
Jack or mozzarella cheese

1. Preheat the oven to 425°.
2. Cut pastry into circles using a wine glass. Place each circle in mini-muffin tins cups.
3. Prick the sausages with a fork, wrap in a paper towel, place on a plate and microwave them for 2 minutes on high. To prepare in a regular oven, place in a baking dish and cook fully in a 350° oven. Slice the sausages into ¼"-½" thick slices.
4. Combine the ricotta cheese with the desired amount of Parmesan cheese. Place some in each pastry cup, top with a Parmesan cheese. Place some in each pastry cup, top with a sausage slice, then a piece of the Jack or mozzarella cheese.
5. Bake at 425° for about 8 minutes.

Fast: Can assemble up to 1 day in advance and refrigerate, or flash freeze for up to 1 month. Do not thaw before baking.

MUSHROOM & CANADIAN BACON TARTLETS

(yields about 9 dozen)

Flo Braker is my hero, and she'll be yours after you try her pastry!

Flo Braker's Magic Puff Pastry:*

½ lb. unsalted butter, frozen and cut into small pieces

2 cups flour
½ cup sour cream or yogurt
1 egg yolk

1. Process the flour and butter in a food processor fitted with the metal blade until the mixture resembles coarse cornmeal.
2. Combine the sour cream or yogurt with the egg yolk in a small bowl and add it to the processor. Process until blended and the dough begins to form a ball.
3. Remove the dough and divide it into 2 balls. Wrap it in plastic wrap and place it in the freezer to chill for about 30 minutes.

Mushroom & Canadian Bacon Filling:

1 lb. mushrooms, washed and minced in the food processor
2 oz. shiitake mushrooms, rehydrated, stemmed, and minced
¼ lb. Canadian bacon, minced
4 tbsp. butter
2 tbsp. flour
4-6 shallots, minced

¼ cup parsley, minced
½ cup pumpkin seeds, toasted and chopped
½ cup heavy cream
¼ cup sherry
6 oz. Saint André or brie cheese
2 cloves garlic, minced
salt, white pepper and dried thyme to taste

1. Melt the butter in a skillet and sauté the shallots, Canadian bacon, shiitake mushrooms, and garlic until tender.
2. Add the mushrooms, season, and cook until the liquid released by them cooks away.
3. Mix in the flour and cook for minute; do not brown.
4. Stir in the cream and cook until thickened, while stirring.

5. Add all remaining ingredients. Cook, stirring continuously until the cheese melts. Taste and adjust the seasonings.

Assembly:
1. Preheat the oven to 400°.
2. Roll pastry out to a thickness of ⅛″ on a lightly floured board.
3. Cut into 2½″ squares or circles and place each one into mini-muffin tin cup.
4. Place the desired amount of filling in each tartlet.
5. Bake at 400° for 25 to 30 minutes, or until fully cooked and golden. To reheat, place in a 350° oven for about 10 minutes.

Fast: Can assemble up to 1 day in advance and refrigerate, or flash freeze, unbaked, for up to 3 months.
Fabulous: Use this technique for tartlets with any filling in this book. There is no end to what you can fill these tartlets with! Create Wellington Tartlets by sautéing small cubes of beef filet in butter with shallots. Cool and place 1 cube along with the mushroom filling in each tartlet and bake as directed. Served with Gloria Ferrer Royal Cuvée Sparkling Wine.

*Flo Braker, author of The Simple Art of Perfect Baking, William Morrow

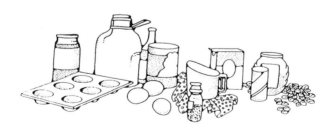

SPRING TARTLETS

A perfect way to celebrate the rites of spring.

(yields about 36)

1 recipe of Flo Braker's
  Magic Puff Pastry (see
  recipe), or 1 pkg. frozen
  puff pastry, thawed
½ cup Romano cheese, grated
1 cup sharp cheddar cheese,
  grated
1 cup smoked ham, chopped
1 cup asparagus, blanched
  and minced
1 onion, minced

4 tbsp. dry sherry
1 clove garlic, minced
2 tbsp. Dijon-style mustard
1 tbsp. dried dill weed
¼ cup sesame seeds, toasted
3 tbsp. flour
2 tbsp. butter
½ cup heavy cream
salt, white pepper, and
  freshly grated nutmeg
  to taste

1. Preheat the oven to 400°.
2. Sauté the onion and garlic in butter until softened. Whisk in the flour and cook over low heat for 1 minute. Do not brown.
3. Remove from the burner and whisk in the sherry, cream, mustard, and other seasonings. Return the pan to the burner and whisk until thickened.
4. Add the remaining ingredients, except the asparagus, and cook over medium heat until the cheese is melted. Taste and adjust the seasonings.

Assembly:
1. Roll out the pastry into a thin rectangle about ⅛″ thick on a lightly floured board and cut into 2½″ squares or circles.
2. Place each square in a mini-muffin tin cup.
3. Place a tsp. of the filling into center of each square and fold opposite ends of pastry up to meet in the center, or leave opened.
4. Bake at 400° for 25 to 30 minutes, or until golden.

Fast: Can assemble up to 1 day in advance and refrigerate, or flash freeze for up to 3 months. Do not thaw before baking. When baking frozen tartlets, bake at 350° for 10 minutes to thaw, then raise the temperature to 400° and bake until golden.

Fabulous: Substitute spinach, chard, or broccoli for the asparagus.

SUN-DRIED TOMATO & GOAT CHEESE TARTLETS

(yields about 24)

1 pkg. frozen puff pastry, thawed
¼ lb. feta cheese, crumbled,
  or more to taste
1-2 cloves garlic, minced
4-6 green onions, minced
2 oz. sun-dried tomatoes, minced
2-4 tbsp. fresh basil, chopped,
  or 1 tsp. dried

½ cup mayonnaise, homemade
  or purchased
1 tbsp. flour
3 eggs
¾ cup milk
¼ cup Madeira
white pepper to taste

Tartlets:

1. Preheat the oven to 425°.
2. Cut the pastry into circles using a wine glass. Place each circle in a mini-muffin tin. Top each tartlet with a piece of foil and fill with uncooked dried beans or pastry weights, to weigh the pastry down. Bake at 425° for 5 minutes.
3. When cool remove the foil and beans or weights and place the tartlets on a cookie sheet.

Filling:

1. Reduce the oven temperature to 350°.
2. Meanwhile, combine the garlic, pepper, basil, mayonnaise, milk, and Madeira in a food processor fitted with the metal blade.
3. Add the eggs and flour and process until just blended.
4. To each tartlet add sun-dried tomatoes, green onions, and crumbled feta cheese.
5. Fill each tartlet ⅔ full with the egg and milk mixture.
6. Bake at 350° for about 30 minutes, or until set.

Fast: Can prepare through step 5 up to 1 day in advance and refrigerate, or flash freeze, for up to 1 month. Do not thaw before baking.
Fabulous: Substitute Gruyère, gorgonzola, or Jack cheese for the feta or roasted red or green peppers for the sun-dried tomatoes.

CHAPTER SIX

THE COMPLETE PARTY

*I*f being a good cook is all it takes to be a *FAST & FLASHY* entertainer, every good cook would be a great party giver. While good food is important, successful parties require more; drama is the key.

When planning a party, think of it as a theatrical event. The set is wherever the party is staged. The guests are the cast. The host and hostess are the producer and director. Curtain up and Act I is the greeting and mixing of the guests. Act II is food and festivities. Act III is the good-byes. Each act must be orchestrated carefully.

Set design is vital. Atmosphere and function need to be considered. For instance, seating should be arranged to facilitate the free flow of conversation. If dinner tables are too close together or too many chairs are squeezed at a table, the atmospheric setting can be ruined. Comfort and pleasure, the primary ingredients of a successful party, require thoughtful planning.

Lighting is a key ingredient of the set design; it can transform a cold, stark space into a dramatic and opulent one. Candles are marvelous props, creating instant magic. It's amazing to see just how social interaction is sparked by candlelight.

Flowers and arrangements of fresh greens are also wonderful props. They symbolize the celebration of nature and provide a festive aura. Be sure to include the entrance when decorating, this instantly welcomes your guests and establishes the tone of your party. I also give equal attention to my kitchen and bathrooms.

If budget is a concern, relax—the set design need not be costly. Most of us have greens or flowers in the garden or on the patio that we can pick. In the fall and winter it's fun to take walks and collect interesting dried weeds for arrangements. As for flowers, if your garden is not in bloom ask a friend. Sharing flowers is something most gardeners take delight in. Purchasing exotic flowers and using them individually to create stark and dramatic arrangements is another approach.

Keep in mind that the rooms in which you stage a party play an important role in establishing the desired mood. For example, the family room has a relaxed warmth, whereas a living room projects more formality and elegance. If you need to use a certain room, but don't want the party to take on the feeling of that particular room, work with your props to create the mood you want. Dress up family rooms with candles and flowers, and try using tinted bulbs in the lights. Living rooms can be given a more casual feel by using pillows on the floor and arranging the furniture in a more intimate manner. Formal pieces can also be removed. Don't forget your yard— outdoor parties can be either casual or elegant, and offer the opportunity to turn an open space into a wonderful party set.

A fabulous party depends on a well-planned guest list, the cast. Don't fall in the trap of simply reciprocating, as this is a sure way to kill the feeling of celebration by turning it into an obligation. Your list needs to be well-composed, balancing character types and professions. Can you imagine a party of all introverts? It would be just as deadly as one with people of all the same profession, unless you want an evening of shop talk. One of the most successful parties I ever gave was when I invited a scientist, land developer, newsman, winery owner, golf pro, and astrologist. It turned out to be as fascinating as it was diverse.

The remaining element of our theatrical event is the star's performance. It includes everything from the invitations (verbal or written) to the good-byes (the closing act).

Dare to express yourself! Careful planning and preparation make it possible. A party is about pleasure and celebration, the opportunity to pamper people you care about, as well as yourself.

During the planning stages look for ways to please all of the senses (sight, smell, hearing, taste, and touch). Consider the limitations posed by your house and kitchen. In a small condo with one oven, don't try to squeeze in a hundred guests and serve a menu of all hot hors d'oeuvres. Make lists of what you'll be serving and what you need to purchase, and a schedule of what needs to be done when. After your menu is created, break it down and prepare as much in advance as possible. Try to leave very little to do on the day of the party. It's amazing how much time last-minute details take. Tables should be set, flowers and seating arranged, and serving pieces set out the day before.

On the party day, schedule time for rest and relaxation. A tired and haggard kitchen martyr cannot be a vivacious host. The *FAST & FLASHY* entertainer makes everything appear easy, no matter how hard you may have worked in advance.

WINES

Fast and Flashy Hors d'Oeuvres deserve good wines. Just as you would not serve caviar with potato chips, you should not serve everyday wines with special hors d'oeuvres. Not to say that you need to spend a fortune or be a certified wine connoisseur, but understanding a bit about food and wine pairing will demystify this often intimidating subject.

Wine and food are age-old companions. This long standing relationship is partly based on the natural chemical balance of wine. This allows the wines to enhance food flavors. Put simply, wines cleanse the palate.

They possess the unique ability to make each bite of food just as exciting as the first one. The hors d'oeuvre/wine marriage is further strengthened by the very essence of their character. Neither one exists to sustain man. Wine is not designed to quench a thirst, but rather to be savoured; just as hors d'oeuvres are not meant to fill a stomach, but to be relished. I classify both as palette pleasers and teasers. They are unmistakably social and entertaining in nature. Their role is to enhance, embellish and to celebrate life. Both hors d'oeuvres and wines are dedicated to pleasure and meant to be enjoyed in moderation.

The following tables consist of general information and loose guidelines to assist you in matching hors d'oeuvres with wines.

Food and Wine Pairings

Foods	Wines

1. Delicate dishes with light subleties.
   COLD SUN-DRIED TOMATO & FETA SOUFFLÉ
   SHRIMP & SCALLOP TERRINE
   ARTICHOKE HEART & GOAT CHEESE CALZETTE
	Sauvignon Blanc, Fumé Blanc, Semillon, Dry Chenin Blanc, Dry Johannisberg Riesling

2. Light, creamy dishes with fuller flavor and more complexity.
   CRAB & BRIE FONDUE
   COLD SMOKED SALMON SOUFFLÉ
   CAULIFLOWER MORNAY
	Chardonnay, Pinot Blanc, Gamay Beaujolais

3. Light, Spicy dishes or dishes with a hint of sweetness.
   CHINESE CABBAGE SUI MAI WITH PORK & SHRIMP
   ONION & HAM TARTLET
   CHINESE SAUSAGE POTSTICKERS
   GREEN CHILE WON TON CUPS

Gewurztraminer, Johannisberg Riesling, Fuller Chenin Blanc, Gamay Beaujolais, Sparkling Wines

4. Delicate dishes using pork, fowl and beef.
   POTTED PORK DEGAN
   PROSCUITTO BUTTER
   PORK & MUSHROOMS
   MERLOT

Chardonnay, Gamay Beaujolais, Pinot Noir, Merlot

5. Spicy dishes using lamb, pork, beef or fowl.
   CHINESE SKEWERED BITES
   ITALIAN SAUSAGE CROUSTADES
   LAMB PITA TRIANGLES WITH CILANTRO

Cabernet Sauvignon, Zinfandel

6. Robustly flavored dishes.
   BAKED SAUSAGE & NUT TERRINE
   BLEU CHEESE WITH MADEIRA
   GORGONZOLA WITH WALNUTS

Pinot Noir, Cabernet Sauvignon, Merlot, Cabernet Franc, Zinfandel

Basic Varietal Characteristics

SPARKLING WINES AND/OR CHAMPAGNES	These are all purpose wines that seem to instantly say "celebration." They are lively, refreshing, and diverse, with excellent palate cleansing abilities. Look for wines in this category to be produced by method champenoise. This will denote quality.
SAUVIGNON BLANC & FUMÉ BLANC	Contrary to popular opinion, these white wines should not taste like alfalfa. They can range from dry to sweet. Fumé usually indicates that the wine will be dry, with an herbaceous, smokey quality. Sauvignon Blanc tends to be sweeter with more fruit, unless labeled "dry."
CHARDONNAY	It is considered to be the Rolls Royce of whites; full-bodied, with distinctive fruit and medium acidity. At last count there were six or seven different styles of California Chardonnay. As a rule, the more expensive the Chardonnay, the richer the body and the oakier the flavor, due to the oak barrel aging.
PINOT BLANC & CHENIN BLANC	Here are two great white "middle of the roaders." Pinot Blanc is similar to Chardonnay in that it has a fuller body with pleasant acid, but more apparent fruit. Chenin Blanc is a light, flowery wine with a touch of sweetness. If you buy Dry Chenin Blanc, it was harvested earlier than usual and has a higher acid level.
GEWURZTRAMINER & JOHANNISBERG RIESLING	Here are two white wines available in three different styles. Each can be found in a dry, fruity or late harvest, sweet style. The most widely available style Johannisberg Riesling is lush and floral, with honey and apricot undertones. Early-harvest (JR's) are dry, fresh and crisp. Late harvest (JR's) are sweet with luscious undertones of peaches and apricots. Gewurztraminer has spicy and floral qualities with good acidity. It also has a similar range as Johannisberg Rieslings, from late to early harvest.
GAMAY BEAUJOLAIS, PINOT NOIR, NAPA GAMAY	These wines have the color of red wine, but the fruit and acid levels of white wine. They are light and fruity in character, designed to be enjoyed very young, at their freshest.
CABERNET FRANC, MERLOT & SOME ZINFANDELS	This group of reds have more intensity and are fuller in body than the Beaujolais group, but are not as intense as Cabernets. They are aromatic and spicy in flavor.
CABERNET SAUVIGNON	This is the biggest, boldest, and most prestigious red wine. It is dry, lush and intense. Aging brings out its complexities.

Now, the fun begins! It is time for you to experiment with different hors d'oeuvre and wine combinations. There is only one rule to keep in mind. A match must work for you, not for some authority. You'll notice that I've made many wine recommendations throughout the book. They are just suggestions. You may come up with something entirely different! I've chosen Dry Creek Vineyard wines and Gloria Ferrer Sparkling Wines for both the recipe recommendations, and for the photographs. Not only are they among my favorites, but they seem to have a consistency that spans from bottle to bottle and from year to year.

Table Decor

FLOWERS:	Think about the containers—and don't limit yourself to the standard vases! Perfume bottles, wine and beer bottles, pitchers (old and new), coffee creamers, wine carafes, and teapots are just a few possibilities.
RIBBONS AND BOWS:	Martha Stewart uses ribbons extensively to decorate tables. They are a great way to create an instant air of celebration.
CANDLES:	Instead of using the standard arrangement of two candlesticks, try using one large, bold candle or a composition of many.
CLOTHS:	Using different colored cloths to reflect the season and the mood of the event is very effective. An alternative to buying cloths is to use colored sheets or buy fabric and make your own. Don't forget about using old quilts, shawls, and interesting pieces of fabric to create unique tables. There will be times when you will find that the bare wood of your table helps to create the desired mood or sense of contrast.

GARNISHES

Garnishing is an art unto itself, with many different schools of thought concerning it. As you can see by some of my ideas, I approach it from a free-form, organic standpoint. I don't get involved in doing intricate, contrived work such as carving dancing girls out of parsnips or making palm trees out of rutabagas. My main focus is to make everything appear lush and dramatic. The garnishes must never detract from or overpower the food. This is another chance to have fun and express yourself! Here are a few ideas for garnishes:

- Parsley: The most commonly used garnish. It can be used effectively with wild abandon, or sparingly. It can also be used minced to scatter over the tops of items. Basically, you can garnish everything except brownies with it!

- Alfalfa sprouts: These can be used as a bed to place hors d'oeuvres on, or in clumps as you would use parsley.

- Green onions: They can be minced and used like minced parsley, or made into fans in the Oriental fashion.

- Fresh herbs: Mint, rosemary, dill weed, cilantro, watercress, and so forth also can be used in the same manner as parsley.

- Shredded, raw vegetables: Purple cabbage or carrots provide color, and can be used with abandon.

- Other ideas include scored cucumber slices, citrus slices, citrus zest, black olives, stuffed olives, carrot curls, celery leaves, radish and tomato roses, cherry tomatoes, and tomato slices.

Sample Menus

A *FAST & FLASHY* entertainer must carefully design her menu to fit the spirit of the season, as well as the occasion. I hope that the following menus will provide you with ideas for creating your own. Feel free to use the menus as is, expand upon them, or scale them down.

Hors d'oeuvres offer us the rare opportunity to experience a wide variety of diverse tastes. There's no reason why an hors d'oeuvre menu cannot consist of an international array of palate pleasers and teasers.

SUMMER PICNICS AND CASUAL OUTDOOR PARTIES:

Rolled Veal Loaf with Roasted Red Pepper Sauce
Chicken & Pistachio Paté with Dijon Sauce
Mushrooms à la Greque
Tapenade Sauce with Cold Vegetables and Pita Chips

Heritage Nachos
Feta Salsa and Hummus with Pita Chips
Barbecued, Marinated Skewered Pork with
    Japanese-Style Dipping Sauce
FAST & FLASHY Baked Cheese/Tortilla Chips

Avocado Dipping Sauce
Indian-Style Ground Lamb Sausages with Curry Sauce
    & Chinese Papaya Sauce
Walnut Pesto Sauce with Pita Chips
Pickled Vegetables (Mushrooms, Onions, Cauliflower)
Potted Ham & Cheese

SUMMER COCKTAIL PARTIES:

Toasted Almond & Green Onion Brie Torta
Onion & Zucchini Pita Pizzas
Chicken & Veal Paté with Shiitaki Mushrooms
Cherry Tomatoes Bon Appetit

Cold Bleu Cheese Soufflé
Smoked Ham Mousse
Warm Goat Cheese & Pesto Pita Triangles
Tortilla Cups filled with Mexican Almond Pork
Cold Mushrooms Stuffed with Smoked Salmon

Scallops Remoulade
Capanota
Barbecued Skewered Pieces of Pork and Chicken with
    Chinese Papaya Sauce (cold) and Sesame-Flavored Sauce
Molded Guacamole
Feta & Roasted Red Pepper Torta

FALL COCKTAIL PARTIES:

Stuffed Grape Leaves
Nicoise Cups
Herbed Pork and Liver Terrine
Stuffed Mushrooms with Bechamel Sauce

Zucchini Rounds Mendelson
Cheese Stuffed Mushrooms in Grape Leaves
Chinese Cabbage Sui Mai with Pork & Shrimp and
    assorted dipping sauces
Sausage & White Bean Paté with Cold Tomato Sauce

Paté Spread with Figs & Walnuts
Piperade Croustades
Mushroom & Canadian Bacon Tartlets
Country Herb Paté
Roasted, Marinated Red Peppers with Beaten Biscuits

Feta Salsa with Pita Chips
Tomato Cheese Croustades
Green Chile Won Ton Cups
Albondigas
Molded Carnitas

WINTER AND HOLIDAY COCKTAIL PARTIES:

Reuben Balls with Mustard Mayonnaise Sauce
Pickled Cauliflower with Lime Mayonnaise Sauce,
    Curry Sauce, and Dijon Sauce
Potted Pork Degan
Carrot Croustades
Caviar Torta

Mexican Tartlets
Baked Chicken Liver Paté
Ham and Cheese Pastries or Squares
Caviar Mousse
Italian Veal, Mozzarella & Anchovy Balls

Onion & Ham Tartlets
Mushroom Escargot
Crispy Cocktail Ribs with Merlot Ginger Sauce and
    Chinese Black Bean Dunk
Chicken Liver Mousse
Florentine Croustades

SPRING COCKTAIL PARTIES:

Leek & Goat Cheese Calzette
Greek Potstickers
Paté of Salmon & Artichoke Hearts
Cold Spinach Mousse
Cold Blanched Asparagus with Cold Lemon Tarragon
    Sauce, Cold Caper Sauce, and Dill Cream Sauce

Smoked Salmon Mousse
Sesame Scallop Toast
Asparagus & Shiitaki Mushroom Croustades
Greek Tartlets

California Chile & Avocado Mousse
Spring Tartlets
Artichoke Almond Pita Triangles
Leek Croustades
Roasted Garlic Decadence
Lamb Pita Triangles with Cilantro

SOME SUGGESTIONS FOR HORS D'OEUVRES TO PRECEDE AN ELEGANT
FALL OR WINTER DINNER PARTY:

Brie-Stuffed Mushrooms
Crab & Artichoke Stuffed Mushrooms
Chevre and Lox Torta
Gorgonzola Pistachio Torta
Seafood Croustades
Saint André & Shiitake Tartlets
Toasted Almond & Green Onion Brie Torta
Celery Root & Shiitake Mushrooms in
   Dilled Shallot Pastry Pillows
Cheese Twists
Leek Croustades

SOME SUGGESTIONS FOR HORS D'OEUVRES TO PRECEDE AN ELEGANT
SPRING OR SUMMER DINNER:

Jewish-Style Sushi Bites with Smoked Salmon Sauce
Italian-Style Sushi Bites with Roasted Red Pepper Sauce
Caviar Mushrooms
Shrimp & Scallop Terrine
Feta Sun-dried Tomato Torta
Smoked Salmon Mousse
Prosciutto Wrap-Ups
Assorted Stuffed Romaine

I sincerely hope this book will not only provide you with a multitude of recipes, but also fill you with wonderful ideas for hors d'oeuvres of your own. I've attempted to show you how to make a positive personal statement through your cookery and entertaining. The feeling of satisfaction that you get from being involved with the recipe and interpreting it, rather than blindly following a recipe, is vastly different. Very little pride results from being a kitchen robot. It is my hope that this book will encourage you to escape from the ranks of the Culinary Clones to become a FAST & FLASHY cook and entertainer!

ENJOY AND EXPLORE!

HELPFUL TERMS

*T*he following are food items and techniques that will help you become a *FAST & FLASHY* cook and entertainer.

CHINESE INGREDIENTS

BARBECUE SAUCE:
This sauce is much like hoisin sauce and can be used and stored in the same way.

BOK CHOY:
A variety of Chinese cabbage with large dark green leaves and nearly white, smooth stalks. The flavor is refreshing and there is almost no aroma.

CALIFORNIA PEARL RICE:
A short grained pearl-shaped rice that can be used instead of Japanese rice. It is found in the rice section of most supermarkets.

CHINESE-STYLE BARBECUED PORK:
Purchase this delicacy at Oriental meat markets.

CHINESE-STYLE SAUSAGES:
These are an absolute treat! They have a unique flavor that is sweet and salty. Use them in dishes or by themselves. In the summer, grill and slice them and serve with mustards and or any Chinese vinegar-type sauces from Chapter 1, as an hors d'oeuvre.

CHINESE FIVE SPICE:
A ground mixture typically consisting of star anise, fennel, clove, cinnamon, and Szechuan peppercorns. When purchasing it look for a finely ground mixture with a light, earthy color. The darker version is usually an inferior product.

CILANTRO:
An herb also referred to as Chinese parsley or coriander. Cilantro is used in Chinese, Mexican, and Middle-Eastern cooking.

FERMENTED BLACK BEANS:	Also referred to as salted black beans or Chinese black beans and usually purchased in plastic bags. Transfer them to a glass or plastic container and store in the refrigerator for an eternity. They have an intense, salty flavor and impart an earthy richness to dishes.
GINGER ROOT:	A pungent root that is indigenous to India and China. It can be refrigerated for about a week before it begins to mold. Store it in a jar of sherry or freeze it, whole or minced, for up to 6 months.
HOISIN SAUCE:	A prepared Chinese sauce with a jam-like consistency. It can be brushed directly on poultry, pork, or beef for barbecuing or broiling. Hoisin sauce also can be used as a seasoning ingredient in sauces or marinades. When it is purchased in a can, transfer the contents to a glass or plastic container and store it in the refrigerator for an eternity.
PICKLED GINGER:	Also called sushi ginger. I search for the undyed variety; who needs pink ginger? It is pickled in a brine of vinegar, salt, and sugar, which mellows the ginger. Feel free to substitute it for fresh ginger root in any recipe in this book.
PICKLED MANGO:	An Indian condiment with a pungent flavor. Purchase it in Middle-Eastern or Oriental markets.
PLUM SAUCE:	This prepared sauce is like gingered plum jam with chiles. It has an incredibly seductive flavor. For further information on use and storage, refer to Hoisin sauce.
POTSTICKER WRAPPER:	This resembles a Sui Mai wrapper, but it is thicker.
RICE VINEGAR:	A vinegar with a delightfully mellow and refreshing quality and a slightly sweet flavor. Once you get familiar with it, you will find many interesting ways to use it beyond Chinese cooking. It's excellent in vinaigrettes.
SESAME OIL:	This is used sparingly as a seasoning, not as a cooking oil. It has a rich, intense, nutty flavor and aroma, which not only imparts its own flavor but brings out the flavors of the food as well.

SHIITAKE MUSHROOMS:	Also referred to as Black Forest mushrooms or Chinese mushrooms. Their flavor and aroma are rich and earthy and they impart a touch of instant exotica to any dish. Most commonly, they are purchased dried and must be rinsed, then rehydrated in warm water. When softened, remove and discard the stems and squeeze out the excess liquid. The precious soaking liquid should never be discarded; strained and stored, it will make a flavorful addition or base for soups and sauces. It can be kept in the refrigerator for a week or frozen indefinitely. To speed up the rehydrating process, place the mushrooms in a bowl of water and microwave them for several minutes, until softened.
SUI MAI WRAPPER:	A round won ton wrapper. If you can't find them, substitute won ton wrappers and cut them into circles with a wine glass or biscuit cutter.
SWEET RICE:	Also referred to as glutinous or sticky rice. This type of rice is opaque and white, rather than translucent. It must be rinsed well, then soaked in warm water for at least 2 hours or overnight. This removes the coating of starch remaining from the milling process and helps to soften it.
SWEETENED CHILI SAUCE:	This sauce has a wonderful, sweet-hot flavor with a catsup-like consistency. For further information on use and storage, see Hoisin sauce.
SZECHUAN PEPPERCORNS:	Peppercorns with a unique flavor that is a combination of menthol and heat. They add an interesting flavor to Oriental and non-Oriental recipes alike. Use them whole or ground.
WON TON WRAPPER:	A square, thin Chinese pastry-type wrapper.

All the above-mentioned items can be purchased in the Oriental section or Oriental produce section of your supermarket. Occasionally some items will require a trip to a bona fide Oriental market. This will be an enjoyable experience and will provide you with a wide range of culinary discoveries.

ITALIAN INGREDIENTS

BALSAMIC VINEGAR: An Italian vinegar that can be purchased in specialty shops or markets that carry gourmet items. This vinegar is similar to rice vinegar in that it is mild and mellow, with a slightly sweet flavor and is delicious used both as a seasoning and in salad dressings.

PROSCIUTTO: A specially-cured Italian-style ham that is a delicacy. It can be used as a cold cut, or to flavor almost anything except fudge cake. Purchase it at any good deli.

SUN-DRIED TOMATOES: Italian pear-shaped tomatoes that have been salted and dried. The variety that comes packed in olive oil is astronomically expensive so buy plain dried tomatoes, let them soften in a small amount of wine vinegar, and store them in jars covered with your own olive oil. This saves quite a few dollars a pound. If you happen to be in an inspired mood, add cloves of garlic and/or the fresh herbs of your choice to the jars. The oil becomes a delicacy, infused with the pungent tomato-herb essence. Use sun-dried tomatoes as a seasoning or as a lovely addition to an antipasto plate.

MISCELLANEOUS INGREDIENTS AND ITEMS

BAMBOO SKEWERS: Must be soaked in warm water for at least 30 minutes to prevent them from burning.

BULGHUR: Toasted cracked wheat that is available in health food stores or the health food or grain section of supermarkets. It can be cooked like rice or just soaked in water until softened and used for salads.

CAPERS: Unopened flower buds of a prickly plant called the caperbush. This bush grows on the mountain slopes bordering the Mediterranean Sea in Italy, Spain, and southern Greece. Capers come packed in brine and can be found in the pickle or gourmet sections of most supermarkets.

CARDAMOM/ CARDAMON:	Two spellings for the same Indian spice, a member of the ginger family.
CHEESECLOTH:	Can be found in either the utensil or automotive section of supermarkets. Wash it out with soap and water before using to prevent it from giving off a chemical taste.
CHEVRE:	A cream-style French goat cheese with a rich herbaceous flavor.
DEHYDRATED MASA:	Dried ground corn that can be purchased in supermarkets carrying Mexican items.
EXTRA VIRGIN OLIVE OIL: (COLD PRESSED)	This is the highest quality olive oil. It has the lowest level of acidity and is the most flavorful.
FENUGREEK:	A seasoning used frequently in Greek and Eastern-style dishes.
FINES HERBES:	A pre-mixed herb combination of French origin, consisting of oregano, sage, rosemary, marjoram, and basil. Fines herbs are commonly used in soups, sauces, and marinades.
GREEN PEPPERCORNS:	They are the fresh, immature pepper berries, and can be purchased in the herb or gourmet section of supermarkets. Green peppercorns come freeze-dried, or packed in water or in brine.
INSTANTIZED FLOUR:	White flour that has been processed in such away as to make it dissolve instantly. It can be purchased in shaker cans or in bags. When preparing crepes instantized flour eliminates the necessity for having the batter sit for 1 hour before using it. In sauce making there is never the fear of lumps. As a matter of fact, you can whisk this directly into the sauce. Wondra is one brand of instantized flour.
PARCHMENT:	Can be found in gourmet and cooks' shops as well as where baking supplies are sold. It frequently is used to line molds, cake pans, and terrines to prevent food from sticking. It makes unmolding a breeze.

PUMPERNICKEL SQUARES:	This refers to thin, firm, European-style pumpernickel bread, that you cut into small squares.
SHALLOTS:	They resemble tiny brown onions and have a mild onion flavor. To save money, or when you run out of shallots, substitute the whites of green onions.
TAHINI:	A Middle-Eastern sesame seed paste, purchased in the gourmet section of many supermarkets or in health food stores.
TOMATILLOS:	These are also referred to as green Mexican tomatoes. They have a refreshing and slightly tart flavor. Fresh tomatillos are encased in a greenish-brown wrapper, which must be removed before using. Most supermarkets carry fresh and/or canned.
ZEST:	The flavorful colored part of citrus rind. It is not the bitter-tasting inner white flesh of the fruit. To remove only the zest, use a vegetable peeler or zester, which can be purchased at any store that carries gourmet gadgets.

COOKING TECHNIQUES & HINTS

Here are a few necessary techniques.

BLANCH:	The cooking of vegetables in a large pot of boiling, salted water until they reach the desired degree of tenderness. Then the vegetables are removed from the pot and immediately placed under cold, running water to stop the cooking process and lock in the color. This technique allows you to prepare the **vegetables** in advance.
FLASH FREEZE:	A technique for safely storing delicate items in the freezer and for economizing on freezer space. Place the items, unwrapped, on cookie sheets and freeze until firm. Remove them from the cookie sheet, place in plastic bags and return to the freezer.

TO PURÉE GARLIC: Most of you have seen this item in the produce section of your market, but you can make it yourself. Just peel several heads of garlic and puree them in a food processor fitted with the metal blade, or in a blender with some olive or vegetable oil. Place in small jars, keeping 1 in the refrigerator and the rest in the freezer, for future use. For a *FAST & FLASHY* way to peel garlic, hit each clove with the side of a knife or a meat pounder. For an easier way, just separate the head into cloves and place in a pot of boiling water for about 5 to 10 seconds, then drain and place under cold running water. Now you should be able to squirt the garlic out of its wrapper with your hands.

TO ROAST PEPPERS: Cut the peppers in half; remove the seeds and veins. Place them cut side down on a cookie sheet and bake in a 350° to 400° oven. Cook until charred, about 40-60 minutes. Remove them from the oven, and when cool enough to handle remove and discard the skins.

TO ROAST CHILES: Place them on a cookie sheet in a 350° oven until the skin is charred. Put under cold running water and remove their skins. Split in half, remove the seeds, veins, and stem. To freeze, cool and place in plastic bags. (They can be frozen after they are roasted, and skinned, deveined and seeded after thawing.)

HANDLING CHILES: Wear plastic gloves when working with chiles to prevent them from burning your skin, and never touch yourself after working with chiles until you have washed your hands.

TO TOAST SEEDS OR NUTS: Place on cookie sheet in a 350° oven until toasted. Be careful not to burn them.

STORING NUTS & SEEDS: To prevent these items from turning rancid, store in the freezer or refrigerator.

TO UNMOLD GELATIN-BASED DISHES AND OTHER CHILLED ITEMS: First run a knife that has been dipped in hot water around the perimeter of the mold. Place the mold in a basin of warm water for few seconds (just until the formed mixture begins to pull away from the sides of the mold). Place a plate on top of the mold and invert. Sometimes it is necessary to tap the top of the mold.

SUBSTITUTING FRESH HERBS FOR DRIED:	Dried herbs are more potent and concentrated in flavor. Therefore, you use less than when seasoning with fresh herbs. As a rule of thumb, use three times more fresh herbs than dried. Remember dried herbs don't last forever, only about a year. If they have lost their aroma or if it is unpleasant, throw them away.
GRATING JACK CHEESE:	To grate Jack cheese, partially freeze it first.
PREVENTING AVOCADO FROM DISCOLORING:	Sprinkle it with lemon juice. When preparing an avocado mixture in advance, place the pit in the bowl and leave it there until serving. This may be an old wives' tale, but it seems to work.
REDUCE/ REDUCTION:	Cooking terms referring to the process of boiling down cooking liquids to concentrate the flavors.
WATER CHESTNUT SUBSTITUTES:	Chopped fennel bulb or jicama can be used in place of water chestnuts.
CHILLING TIME:	To reduce required chilling time by half, place the food in the freezer.
PEELING TOMATOES:	Place tomatoes in a lettuce basket or strainer set in a deep bowl. Pour boiling water over the tomatoes and let stand for about 30 seconds or until the skin can easily be removed. Immediately plunge tomatoes into cold water; drain. Remove and discard the skins.
REMOVING BITTERNESS FROM EGGPLANT:	As a rule of thumb, the more seeds the eggplant has, the more bitter it is. To remove this bitterness, sprinkle with salt and let sit in a colander to drain for about 1 hour, then rinse.

HARD BOILING EGGS:

Julia Child recommends that you start with your eggs at room temperature. If the eggs are extremely fresh, first put them in a bowl of warm soapy water. This will remove the mineral oil coating that is often on eggs to keep them fresh. Then leave them at room temperature uncovered overnight. In hot weather, leave the eggs uncovered in the refrigerator for up to two days.

To cook, place eggs in a saucepan and cover with at least 1″ of water, adding about 2 tsp. of salt per quart of water. Bring the water to a boil, cover, remove from the burner, and let sit for 17 minutes. To peel, drain the water out and shake the eggs in the saucepan so the shells crack. Cover with cold water and peel when cool enough to handle.

STORING AND MINCING PARSLEY:

Mince large quantities of fresh parsley in a food processor fitted with the metal blade. To store it for up to 4 days in the refrigerator, place it in a clean kitchen towel and twist out the excess moisture. Transfer it to a container and refrigerate.

INDEX OF RECIPES

*Indicates low-fat recipes.

*Indicates low-fat recipes.

*Indicates low-fat recipes.

_____

*Indicates low-fat recipes.

*Indicates low-fat recipes.

T

U-Z

*Indicates low-fat recipes.